A GUIDE TO THE DIPLOMA IN TEACHING AND RELATED QUALIFICATIONS

LEVEL 5 AND BEYOND

Acknowledgements

Thank you to Dr Michele Fuller, Head of School of Social Sciences and PGCE FE and Skills Centre Manager at the University Centre Colchester, for her major contributions to writing and editing Chapter 9 of this book. Without her help it would not have been possible.

Neil Barnes

I sincerely thank my co-authors, colleagues, mentors and family for their unwavering support and guidance. Special gratitude to my learners and trainee teachers who inspire continuous growth. This book is a testament to collective learning.

Joyce I-Hui Chen

Thank you to my family who have supported my academic and professional journey. My contributions to this book have been motivated by my son, Albie, who serves as a daily inspiration.

Scott Clarke

A huge thank you to my co-authors, who have been so generous with their time in bringing this book to life. Also to my long-suffering colleague, Gwyneth, who has been a delight to work with and my centre manager colleagues who have been so supportive – you know who you are!

Lynn Senior

To all the teachers I have had the privilege of training. Your dedication and commitment are inspiring.

Heather Sherman

A massive thank you to Lynn Senior for her ability to control, endure and otherwise ensure the required deadlines were adhered to, as well as her patience to receive and edit our chapters to make this book a reality, without which we may well still be floundering with the first drafts.

A heartfelt thank you from all the contributors.

A GUIDE TO THE DIPLOMA IN TEACHING AND RELATED QUALIFICATIONS

LEVEL 5 AND BEYOND

Lynn Senior, Neil Barnes, Joyce I-Hui Chen, Scott Clarke and Heather Sherman

Routledge
Taylor & Francis Group
LONDON AND NEW YORK

First published in 2025 by Critical Publishing Ltd

Published 2025 by Routledge
4 Park Square, Milton Park, Abingdon, Oxon OX14 4RN
605 Third Avenue, New York, NY 10017

Routledge is an imprint of the Taylor & Francis Group, an informa business

British Library Cataloguing in Publication Data
A CIP record for this book is available from the British Library

ISBN: 9781916925588 (hbk)
ISBN: 9781916925557 (pbk)
ISBN: 9781041053941 (ebk)

Text design by Greensplash
Cover design by Out of House Limited

DOI: 10.4324/9781041053941

Contents

Meet the authors

Lynn Senior

Lynn Senior has held a variety of teaching and management roles in further and higher education. She was the Director of the Education and Training Consortium, University of Huddersfield, for four years and has a total of over 30 years' experience within the sectors. She has a background in vocational education and further education ITE, and she has taught in secondary education. She was Chair of the UCET Post-16 Committee and has worked closely with the ETF and the Department for Education on developing teacher education programmes. Lynn's research interests include vocational education and teacher development.

Neil Barnes

Neil Barnes is the Head of Professional Accreditation and Quality in the Faculty for Education, Health and Human Sciences at the University of Greenwich. Neil has been involved in curriculum design and the further education and skills sector for over 25 years, working in a variety of roles including as a centre manager/affiliate lecturer for the University of Huddersfield on their further education ITE pathways and as a Head of School/Director of Teaching and Learning in a mixed economy college. Neil's research interests include further education and student success.

Joyce I-Hui Chen

Joyce I-Hui Chen has worked in a range of educational sectors for more than 20 years, abroad and in the UK. She is a quality enhancement manager at the College of West Anglia, managing initial teacher education programmes, a LSRN co-convenor for East Anglia and one of the co-founders of CWARIF (the College of West Anglia Research and Innovation Forum). She is a member of the Chartered College of Teaching (CCT), a Fellow of SET, a member of IPDA, and a member and a co-convenor of the Practitioner Research SIG of BERA. She is passionate about creating and nurturing communities with equity and equality by using an intersectional lens.

Scott Clarke

Scott Clarke is the centre manager and programme leader for teacher education at the City of Liverpool College where he leads and teaches on both the pre-service and in-service Cert Ed and PGCE. He has over 10 years' experience of working across secondary school, sixth form college and further education settings. He began by teaching social sciences but has since moved into teacher education. Scott has completed a PhD in education, exploring the promises and limitations of research-informed education, which broadly aligns with his research interests.

Heather Sherman

Heather Sherman has over a decade of experience working in the secondary and further education and skills sectors, starting her career as a secondary history teacher. In 2015 she moved into further education, specialising in A level history teaching, also mentoring PGCE students. Heather was the centre manager and programme leader for initial teacher education at York College between 2021 and 2024 where she led and taught on both the pre-service and in-service Cert Ed and PGCE. Heather holds Advanced Teacher Status with the Society of Education and Training (SET) and has returned to full time A level history teaching.

Part 1 Introduction

1 The further education and skills sector

Professional links

This chapter contributes to the following professional links:

The Diploma in Teaching mandatory content (DfE, 2024)

- 4.13 The Occupational Standards.
- 4.18 Professional status.
- 4.19 Overview of FE and Skills sector.

Learning and Skills Teacher Occupational Standards (IfATE, 2024)

- K14 The requirements and implications of organisational policies and procedures, such as internal and external regulatory bodies and frameworks.
- S24 Act within the statutory frameworks which set out their professional duties and responsibilities.

Chapter objectives

At the end of this chapter you will be able to:

- provide a brief history and overview of the sector;
- identify routes into teaching post-14 (level 5 and above);
- describe the Professional Standards;
- describe the Learning and Skills Teacher Occupational Standards;
- define Advanced Teacher Status (ATS) and Qualified Teacher Learning and Skills (QTLS) status;
- discuss the Ofsted inspection process for further education and skills.

Introduction

The further education and skills (FES) sector is the term used to refer to education after compulsory schooling up to the age of 16. Over the last few years, various terminology has been used interchangeably, dependent upon the government policy and political landscape of the time. You may have come across terms such as post-compulsory, lifelong learning sector (LLL), further education and training and, occasionally, post-14 education. However, following recent policy guidelines and initiatives the sector is now referred to as the FES sector.

As a general rule the sector covers three distinct areas, although it is worth noting here that it is not entirely this clearcut and you may find other areas that do not fit into one of these three:

> - *vocational courses including plumbing, manufacturing and health care;*
> - *academic classroom-based learning of subjects including English and maths, including A levels in a sixth form college;*
> - *basic skills courses on literacy, numeracy, English for speakers of other languages, and special needs.*
>
> (Get Into Teaching, nd)

As a sector, it is diverse in the range of organisations within it. The following list highlights some of the organisations that you may find yourself working in or on placement at:

- further education and skills (FES) colleges;
- sixth form colleges;
- specialist and/or land-based colleges;
- independent training providers;
- community learning;
- adult education;
- offender learning;
- work-based learning;
- pupil referral units (PRUs) post-14;
- university technical colleges (UTCs).

Within these organisations you will find a range of subjects and levels, from pre-entry level up to higher education level 7, although traditionally most trainee teachers will teach subjects from pre-entry to level 5. For more information on qualification levels, go to www.gov.uk/what-different-qualification-levels-mean/list-of-qualification-levels.

Here is a sample list of professions, trades and academic subjects that are taught in the FES sector and which you may be teaching:

> - *agriculture, environment and animal care;*
> - *business, administration and office management;*

- *catering and hospitality;*
- *childcare and education;*
- *construction;*
- *creative and design;*
- *digital and IT;*
- *emergency and armed services;*
- *engineering and manufacturing;*
- *hair and beauty;*
- *health and life sciences;*
- *legal, finance and accounting;*
- *sales, marketing and procurement;*
- *social care;*
- *transport and logistics;*
- *English;*
- *mathematics;*
- *science;*
- *social sciences;*
- *humanities;*
- *modern foreign languages;*
- *art and design;*
- *performing arts.*

(DfE, 2022)

Similarly, the range of teaching qualifications for the sector are diverse in terms of their titles, and you may encounter titles that include the terms lifelong learning, education and training, FES, post-16 and post-compulsory, to name but a few. In addition, there are a range of levels that you can access for a full teaching qualification, depending upon your starting point and qualifications. These range from a level 5 Diploma in Teaching or Certificate in Education to a level 7 Postgraduate Certificate in Education. Some centres also offer a postgraduate Diploma in Education. All are equally relevant and acceptable in the sector. The qualification you are studying will be dependent upon your existing qualifications. However, regardless of the level, the recent guidance from the Department for Education states that a full award needs to be aligned with the Occupational Standards for the Learning and Skills Teacher (2023) and mapped to the mandatory content of the new Diploma in Teaching (2023). These standards are provided in the appendices and are a list of areas and competences that you need to cover and demonstrate by the end of your course. It is worth noting that there are several lower-level awards that you can access for working in the sector, but these are not classified as full teaching qualifications and there may be limitations on what you are able to do within a setting.

- The level 3 Award in Education and Training is an introductory teaching qualification. It is a short programme that provides a foundation base for anyone wishing to enter or is considering entry into the sector.
- The level 4 Certificate in Education and Training (CET) is a first-stage teaching qualification that covers some of the basic responsibilities and topics for someone who is entering the sector and is not yet ready to move on to the full award.

A brief history of the sector

There are a plethora of reports, government initiatives and documents related to the FES sector, from the 1944 McNair report which looked at deficiencies in recruiting and training teachers for the post-compulsory sector to the more recent FES White Paper 'Skills for Jobs: Lifelong Learning for Opportunity and Growth' (DfE, 2021).

Table 1.1 highlights some of the key reports and initiatives that have shaped the FES sector to date.

Table 1.1 *Key documents, government initiatives and reports*

Date of publication	Title of report/initiative	Brief overview
1944	McNair report	Report on the system of recruiting and training teachers across all three sectors (primary, secondary, post-compulsory).
1957	Jackson report	Report on the supply and training of teachers for technical colleges.
1966	Russell report	Further report on the supply and training of teachers in FES.
1972	James report	Introduced the concept of teacher training being accredited and offered by universities.
1998	FENTO standards	Standards for FES teachers in England and Wales were launched in January 1999 by the newly established Further Education National Training Organisation.
2002	Success for All (DfES, 2002)	Report on remodelling of teacher training for the sector to improve the UK workforce and economic standing.

Table 1.1 (*Cont.*)

Date of publication	Title of report/initiative	Brief overview
2002	Institute for Learning (IfL) established	Voluntary professional body for teachers in the post-compulsory sector.
2004	Equipping Our Teachers for the Future (DfES, 2004)	Implementation of Lifelong Learning UK (LLUK) and a new suite of qualifications for the sector. First report to note CPD was crucial following initial training.
2006	Prosperity for All in a Global Economy: World Class Skills (Leitch, 2006)	Recommendation of training and education up to the age of 18.
2007	Further Education Teachers' Qualifications (England, No. 2264)	Regulations specifying that all teachers in the sector should be registered with the Institute for Learning (IfL). Anyone joining the profession post 2001 needed to hold a teaching qualification. New LLUK standards introduced.
2009	Skills for Growth (BIS, 2009)	Proposed phasing out of the IfL.
2009	Workforce Strategy Report (LLUK, 2009)	Set out priorities for training teachers from a diverse range of backgrounds.
2012	Lingfield review	Recommended deregulation of the sector.
2013	Qualifications Guidance for Awarding Organisations: Level 5 Diploma in Education and Training (LSIS, 2013)	New framework for initial teacher education introduced.
2014	Education and Training Foundation (ETF)	Introduced a new set of standards to replace LLUK (2007) standards.
2015	Society for Education and Training (SET)	The new professional body for teachers in the sector, confers QTLS status.
2022	Learning and Skills Teacher Occupational Standards (IfATE)	New apprenticeship standards for the role introduced.
2023	New framework for DiT (ETF)	New qualification introduced based on the Occupational Standards.
2023	DfE changes to qualifications and funding	Removal of funding for qualifications not linked to a university or higher education provider.

CASE STUDY

Marta has just applied for a post working in an FES college. She has done some research in preparation for the interview and has identified the following areas that she feels may be asked about. To ensure that she is able to discuss them confidently, she made some notes to help her.

- **Types of learners:**
  - FES caters for a wide range of learners, including school leavers, adults and those seeking vocational qualifications.
  - The learners have diverse needs, backgrounds and aspirations.
- **Vocational focus:**
  - Much of the FES sector has an emphasis on practical skills and vocational training.
  - Courses prepare students for specific careers or further study.
- **Qualifications:**
  - FES offers various qualifications, such as BTECs, NVQs and apprenticeships.
  - FES offers qualifications from pre-entry to level 5 and sometimes level 6.
- **Challenges:**
  - Funding constraints.
  - Class sizes.
  - Student motivation.
- **Professional development:**
  - Attend workshops, conferences and training sessions.
  - Work towards QTLS.

Critical question

» Are there other areas that you feel she needs to research to ensure she is fully prepared?

Routes into teaching in the FES sector

As seen in the previous section, the FES sector has been subject to many changes in relation to routes into teaching and required qualifications. However, what has remained constant in the profession is that a teacher in the FES sector is a dual professional. First, they achieve competence in their vocational or subject specialism and then they undergo training to become a teacher. As a professional you will have dual expertise, drawing on both your technical/vocational experience and academic qualifications and skills to provide a high-quality learning experience. You will prepare students for progression to employment or further study using a solid understanding of pedagogy and evidence-based teaching methods relevant to your subject area.

Currently, two main qualifications routes exist: an apprenticeship and an academic qualification.

Apprenticeship

The apprenticeship 'Learning and Skills Teacher' relates to an occupation that, according to the Institute for Apprenticeships and Technical Education (IfATE, 2024): '*is found in all parts of the Further Education and Skills Sector (FES), usually in settings where students are aged 16 and above (a small number of teachers may teach 14–16 year-olds in alternative provision)*'. They go on to state that:

> *An employee in this occupation is responsible for helping to prepare each of their students for progression to/or within employment or to further study. To deliver this to a diverse group of students, including those with special educational needs, a Learning and Skills Teacher needs to be flexible, innovative, and adaptable, changing their behaviour and teaching style to suit the environment and level of their students. A Learning and Skills Teacher needs to have a sound understanding of pedagogy and regularly engage with robust evidence of effective teaching and learning methods and practice relevant to their subject area(s).*

As a route the apprenticeship typically takes 18 months to complete and is assessed via an end point assessment, which includes a viva against the Occupational Standards aligned to the apprenticeship. The occupational duties comprise a set of knowledge, skills and behaviours that the apprentice should demonstrate to meet the minimum expectations of the role. The full set of standards can be found in Appendix 2. To be eligible for this route a trainee requires English and maths at level 2 prior to taking the end point assessment.

Academic qualifications

The other qualification route is an academic qualification. These qualifications can be undertaken part time (in-service) or full time (pre-service).

For the part-time route you would normally work in the sector and undertake the qualification over two years, either with an awarding body or a university. For the full-time route you would normally be based in a university or college with higher education provision (the latter usually working in partnership with a university) and complete a placement to gain the teaching hours and experience required. Both routes require a minimum level 3 subject qualification or extensive experience in the sector and level 2 maths and English. Level 3 is A level or equivalent and level 2 is GCSE or equivalent.

Table 1.2 provides an overview of the qualifications available. Please note that all qualifications have to be mapped to the Diploma in Training although universities may have slightly different names as can be seen in the table.

***Table 1.2** Qualifications available for teaching in FES*

Qualification	Level	Part time	Full time	Minimum entry requirements
Diploma in Teaching	5	Two years	One year	Level 3 subject qualification or experience working in the industry. Level 2 maths and English.
Certificate in Education	5	Two years	One year	Level 3 subject qualification or experience working in the industry. Level 2 maths and English.
Professional Graduate Certificate in Education	6	Two years	One year	Degree (usually 2:2 or above). Level 2 maths and English.
Postgraduate Certificate in Education	7 (usually has some level 6 credits)	Two years	One year	Degree (usually 2:2 or above). Level 2 maths and English.
Professional Graduate Diploma in Education	7 (all M level)	Two years	One year	Degree (usually 2:2 or above). Level 2 maths and English.

A caveat to Table 1.2 is that many organisations will include the wording '(FES)' within the qualification title to avoid confusion with the compulsory sector and not all organisations will offer all levels both full and part time.

If the Diploma in Teaching route, or alternative named qualification, is the route you choose to take, you will undertake taught sessions within your organisation and produce various assessments throughout the duration of the qualification. In addition, you will be required to log a minimum of 250 hours of practice of which 150 is teaching, and the remaining 100 can be assessing, observing, continuing professional development (CPD) or other activities associated with the sector. You will also be observed teaching a minimum of ten times throughout your programme – which must also be logged.

All qualifications within the sector must now be mapped to the Occupational Standards of the apprenticeship route, the new qualification framework introduced in 2023 and the ETF Professional Standards. The qualification framework is provided in Appendix 1 and the ETF Professional Standards in Appendix 3.

The Society for Education and Training (SET)

The SET is part of the Education and Training Foundation, and its primary role is to raise the status of the profession and champion quality teaching. They are the professional membership body for the sector and they advocate three career stages following qualification:

1. early career teacher;
2. experienced teacher;
3. advanced teacher.

With regards to moving through the career stages, SET offers a series of awards that can be achieved following on from initial teacher education.

Critical question ⑦

» What do you feel are the advantages and disadvantages of having a professional membership body for the sector?

Discussion

You may have considered some of the following.

- **Networking opportunities:** The opportunity to connect with peers, mentors and industry leaders, which can lead to new job opportunities, collaborations and professional growth plus support in your subject area. In addition, many professional bodies offer discounts on conferences that may be of relevance to you, either subject wise or pedagogy wise.
- **Professional development:** Most professional bodies provide access to workshops, seminars and courses that help you stay up to date with the latest trends and skills in your field. If you look at the ETF website, you will find a range of development opportunities and courses.

→

- **Certification and accreditation:** Enhance your credibility and career prospects with recognised certifications and accreditations, such as the Qualified Teacher Learning and Skills (QTLS) status and Advanced Teacher Status (ATS).
- **Resources and publications:** Access to research, publications and industry reports in your subject area and in teaching that can keep you informed and current in your practice.
- **Career support:** Guidance on career progression, job searches and professional challenges through mentoring programmes and career services.

Qualified Teacher Learning and Skills status

The induction phase, or the phase following completion of the apprenticeship or teaching qualification, is currently non-regulated in FES. However, SET offers a professional formation process to enable you to achieve Qualified Teacher Learning and Skills (QTLS) status, which has parity with Qualified Teacher Status (QTS) for the school sector. This process takes on average 12 months and involves the completion of a portfolio. QTLS as a status has been in existence since 2007 but has changed significantly over the years.

Activity ⑦

» Go to the SET website www.set.et-foundation.co.uk/your-career/qtls and work through the interactive guide provided on QTLS to better familiarise yourself with the requirements post qualification.

Advanced Teacher Status

Advanced Teacher Status (ATS) can be conferred by SET on staff who have held their teaching qualification and QTLS for four years or more or who have held their qualification for five years. ATS is gained after successfully completing a 14-month period of professional development.

Those who achieve ATS also receive the Chartered College of Teaching's Chartered Teacher designation.

Quality assurance in the FES sector

As with any teaching organisation, your workplace or setting will be subject to regulatory quality assurance mechanisms that verify the quality of provision offered to students. The two main organisations are the Quality Assurance Agency (QAA) and Ofsted.

The Quality Assurance Agency

The QAA is an independent charity that reviews standards and quality in the higher education sector. If your work placement or setting offers higher-level qualifications you may be subject to the UK Quality Code for Higher Education (May 2023), which sets out a number of areas that can be used to monitor quality in an organisation: expectations, practices, and advice and guidance. This guidance is often translated into individual quality assurance policies for an organisation.

Critical question ?

» Considering the quality assurance policy in your setting, is there anything that you feel could be improved to provide a better experience for your learners? Explain your answer in full.

Ofsted

Ofsted is the Office for Standards in Education, the government body responsible for inspecting organisations that provide education and skills for all learners. Its aim is to:

> *Improve lives by raising standards in education and children's social care. We inspect and regulate thousands of organisations and individuals providing education, training and care – from childminders to training providers, schools to local authorities.*
>
> (Ofsted, nd)

The organisation that is in existence today came into being in 2007 when the former Office for Standards merged with the Adult Learning Inspectorate to provide inspections that included all publicly funded organisations, including post-16 organisations.

During an Ofsted inspection, inspectors make an overall effectiveness judgement as well as key judgements on:

- the quality of education;
- behaviour and attitudes;
- personal development;
- leadership and management.

They also make judgements on each major type of provision offered, as set out in Table 1.3.

Table 1.3 *Ofsted inspected provision*

Type of provision	Description of provision
Education programmes for young people	Provision funded through the Education and Skills Funding Agency (ESFA) classroom-based funding stream for study programmes and traineeships for those aged 16 to 18 and for ESFA-funded full-time provision for 14- to 16 year-olds enrolled in colleges. This may include provision funded through the 16 to 19 tuition fund. From 1 September 2023, T-level technical education programmes (and T-level transition programmes) have been included in the scope of regular inspections covered in this handbook. This includes provision funded through the Dance and Drama Awards. It does not include provision funded through the National Tutoring Fund.
Adult learning programmes	Provision funded through the adult education budget (AEB) and/or advanced learning loans, including community learning and employability training for learners aged 19 and over referred for training by Jobcentre Plus. This may include adult education provision funded by the GLA (Greater London Authority) and/or MCAs (Mayoral or Combined Authorities) through their AEB (including Skills Bootcamps funded through the AEB). It includes Skills Bootcamps funded through the Skills for Life/National Skills Fund programme with effect from 1 April 2023, whether funded directly by the DfE or through an MCA, local authority or local enterprise partnership (LEP). It also includes free courses for jobs provision. It does not cover the Diploma for Education and Training (DET) or the Multiply programme.
Apprenticeships (at all levels)	Apprenticeship training at all levels: that is, levels 2 to 7 funded by the ESFA and/or through the apprenticeship levy in whatever type of provider they are delivered. This includes, from 1 April 2021, apprenticeships at levels 6 and 7 (whether degree or non-degree). The whole of a provider's apprenticeship provision is inspected, graded and reported on collectively, irrespective of the level(s) of provision delivered. The inspection of the level 5 Learning and Skills Teacher apprenticeship standard and level 6 teacher apprenticeship fall under the initial teacher education inspection framework and handbook and not the education inspection framework and so not on inspections covered by this handbook.
Provision for learners with high needs	Provision for learners for which providers receive high-needs funding in addition to 16 to 18 ESFA funding for study programmes and/or 16 to 18 apprenticeships. Learners up to the age of 24 may be eligible for this funding.

(Ofsted, 2024)

The following activity is designed to provide you with a deeper understanding of Ofsted and your own setting. Every organisation subject to inspection produces a self-evaluation report, in which they reflect on and evaluate their provision in line with the Ofsted criteria. From this they then produce a quality improvement plan.

Activity

- Locate these documents and identify three areas that may affect you and your subject area.
- How could you personally make changes to improve?
- In what ways are these broadly in line with the quality improvement plan?

Log onto the Ofsted website (www.reports.ofsted.gov.uk) and review the last inspection report for your setting.

- What measures can you take to either maintain the standards or improve for the next inspection?

Ofsted produces a blog (https://educationinspection.blog.gov.uk) designed to update you on current developments in the sector.

- What are the current issues that you may need to consider in your teaching and subject area?

Summary

This chapter has provided an overview of the FES sector, the organisations within it and the range of qualifications and subjects that it offers. You should now be able to discuss the Professional and Occupational Standards that align with the two main routes into teaching in the sector. You should also be aware of the quality assurance mechanisms that currently exist and be able to articulate how these are impacting upon you as a teacher and your subject area.

Check your understanding (level 5)

1. What are the two main routes into a career in the FES sector?
2. What are the three domains of Occupational Standards that align with the sector?
3. What are the main qualifications that you could take to enter the profession?
4. What is SET and what does it do?
5. How can you gain QTLS following your initial route into teaching?
6. How is the FES sector inspected?

Developmental questions L6+7

1. Evaluate the pros and cons of each route into the sector.
2. Consider the list of initiatives provided and analyse how these have impacted upon the sector in today's society. What do you feel have been the most significant initiatives?
3. Using evidence-informed research, what other major government Acts or initiatives have been influential in shaping the sector?
4. Analyse how the Ofsted framework can impact upon your classroom practice.

Editor's note

At the time of going to press the Government introduced a Bill into the House of Lords (12 October 2024) to transfer all the IfATE's powers to the Department for Education, paving the way for Skills England, a new body within the DfE. This Bill, if passed, while suggesting a simple transfer of authority, may give stronger powers to the Secretary of State, streamline some of the existing higher apprenticeships, and potentially speed up amendments to or completely new standards. While we don't currently envisage any major changes to the Level 5 LST standards and qualifications, it would be remiss not to draw your attention to this change. For more information on the potential changes please look at: www.feweek.co.uk/from-ifate-to-skills-england-via-dfe-what-you-need-to-know/

References

Department for Business, Innovation and Skills (BIS) (2009) Skills for Growth, the National Skills Strategy. [online] Available at: www.gov.uk/government/publications/skills-for-growth-the-national-skills-strategy (accessed 8 October 2024).

Department for Education (DfE) (2021) *Skills for Jobs: Lifelong Learning for Opportunity and Growth*. [online] Available at: www.gov.uk/government/publications/skills-for-jobs-lifelong-learning-for-opportunity-and-growth (accessed 19 September 2024).

Department for Education (DfE) (2022) Teach in Further Education. [online] Available at: www.gov.uk/guidance/teach-in-further-education (accessed 19 September 2024).

Department for Education (DfE) (2024) The Diploma in Teaching Mandatory Content. [online] Available at: www.gov.uk/government/publications/further-education-initial-teacher-education/diploma-in-teaching-further-education-and-skills-qualification-framework (accessed 15 November 2024).

Department for Education and Skills (DfES) (2002) *Success for All: Reforming Further Education and Training*. London: DfES.

Department for Education and Skills (DfES) (2004) *Equipping our Teachers for the Future*. London: DfES.

Education and Training Foundation (ETF) (2022) *Professional Standards for Teachers and Trainers*. [online] Available at: www.et-foundation.co.uk/professional-standards/teachers (accessed 29 September 2024).

Get Into Teaching (nd) Teach in Further Education. [online] Available at: https://getintoteaching.education.gov.uk/life-as-a-teacher/age-groups-and-specialisms/further-education-teachers (accessed 28 September 2024).

Gov.UK (2006) *Prosperity for All in the Global Economy – World Class Skills: Final Report*. [online] Available at: www.gov.uk/government/publications/prosperity-for-all-in-the-global-economy-world-class-skills-final-report (accessed 28 September 2024).

Gov.UK (2024) Recognised Further Education Teacher Training Courses Eligible for Student Support: 2024 to 2025. [online] Available at: www.gov.uk/government/publications/further-education-initial-teacher-education/recognised-further-education-teacher-training-courses-eligible-for-student-support-2024-to-2025 (accessed 28 September 2024).

Gov.UK (nd) What Qualification Levels Mean. [online] Available at: www.gov.uk/what-different-qualification-levels-mean/list-of-qualification-levels (accessed 28 September 2024).

Institute for Apprenticeships and Technical Education (IfATE) (2024) *Learning and Skills Teacher*. [online] Available at: www.instituteforapprenticeships.org/apprenticeship-standards/learning-and-skills-teacher (accessed 28 September 2024).

James Report (1972) [online] Available at: www.education-uk.org/documents/james/james1972.html (accessed 28 September 2024).

Learning and Skills Improvement Service (LSIS) (2013) *Qualifications Guidance for Awarding Organisations: Level 5 Diploma in Education and Training*. Coventry: Learning Skills Improvement Services.

Leitch, S (2006) Leitch Review, Prosperity for All in the Global Economy: World Class Skills. [online] Available at: https://assets.publishing.service.gov.uk/media/5a7c9607ed915d12ab4bbc4e/0118404865.pdf (accessed 8 October 2024).

Lifelong Learning UK (LLUK) (2009) The workforce strategy Report for the Further Education Sector in England 2007–2012. [online] Available at: https://dera.ioe.ac.uk/id/eprint/2310/ (accessed 8 October 2024).

Ministry of Education (1956) *The Supply and Training of Teachers for Technical Colleges: Report of a Special Committee Appointed by the Minister of Education in September,* 1956. London: Ministry of Education. [online] Available at: https://openlibrary.org/authors/OL1816623A/Great_Britain._Ministry_of_Education (accessed 28 September 2024).

Ofsted (2024) *Further Education and Skills Inspection Handbook*. [online] Available at: www.gov.uk/government/publications/further-education-and-skills-inspection-handbook-eif/further-education-and-skills-handbook-for-september-2023 (accessed 28 September 2024).

Ofsted (nd) [online] Available at: www.gov.uk/government/organisations/ofsted (accessed 28 September 2024).

Ofsted Blog (nd) Ofsted: Schools and Further Education & Skills (FES). [online] Available at: https://educationinspection.blog.gov.uk (accessed 28 September 2024).

Parry, J P (1966) The Russell Report: The Supply and Training of Teachers for Further Education. *The Vocational Aspect of Education*, 18(41): 157–63.

Society for Education and Training (SET) (nd) Your Career. [online] Available at: https://set.et-foundation.co.uk/your-career (accessed 28 September 2024).

Part 2 Learners and learning

2 The learner in the further education and skills sector

Professional links

This chapter contributes to the following professional links:

The Diploma in Teaching mandatory content (DfE, 2024)

- 2.1 Getting to know your learners in FES.
- 2.2 Their journeys to FES.
- 2.3 Range of support needs.
- 2.4 Safeguarding or EDI.
- 2.5 English and maths abilities.
- 2.6 Their wider expectations.

Learning and Skills Teacher Occupational Standards (IfATE, 2024)

- K2 How to support contextualised opportunities to develop English and maths.
- K8 Techniques to involve learners in taking ownership of their own progress.
- K12 The range of support available for learners related to health, well-being and safeguarding.
- K13 Sources of current information, advice and guidance to support progression opportunities for learners.
- S4 Use a variety of teaching and assessment methods depending on the learning environment and learners' needs.
- S5 Encourage learners to set challenging goals.
- S10 Identify and set outcomes to enable each learner to achieve or exceed targets.

→

Professional Standards (ETF, 2022a)

- 1 Critically reflect on and evaluate your practices, values, and beliefs to improve learner outcomes.
- 3 Inspire, motivate, and raise aspirations of learners by communicating high expectations and a passion for learning.
- 4 Support and develop learners' confidence, autonomy and thinking skills, taking account of their needs and starting points.
- 5 Value and champion diversity, equality of opportunity, inclusion and social equity.
- 6 Develop collaborative and respectful relationships with learners, colleagues and external stakeholders.

Chapter objectives

At the end of this chapter you will be able to:

- describe the characteristics of the FES learner;
- identify the routes that an FES learner may take into and through the sector;
- discuss potential support needs of the FES learner;
- explain the importance of safeguarding and discuss the safeguarding protocol and practice with a setting;
- consider some of the wider needs and expectations of the FES learner.

Introduction

As you have read in the previous chapter, the FES sector is a very broad and complex sector, comprising many different types of organisation. So, can we define the type of learner that you may encounter within your setting? In short, the answer is no as the FES learner, like the sector, can be varied in terms of age, characteristics and ability. However, generally, the term refers to someone aged 16 or over studying for a range of subjects that are not degree level, including work-related courses, apprenticeships, basic skills, GCSE, A level and vocational subjects. As a teacher in the FES sector, you could be working in any of the following:

- colleges, including general colleges, sixth form colleges, land-based colleges and national specialist colleges;
- independent training providers (ITPs) in the private or charity sectors;
- adult community learning, organised by local authorities and their partners;
- workplaces;
- prisons.

Therefore, depending upon where you are teaching, you could be teaching young people or adults with a wide range of experience, ability and backgrounds.

Let us look at some of these settings in more detail.

Further education and skills settings

Further education colleges

The FES college tends to be the first type of organisation that someone thinks of when considering working in the FES sector. An FES college is an education and/or training organisation that offers a range of courses across a variety of levels, from entry level to level 5. Students at an FES college are typically between the age of 16 and 18, although some FES colleges offer courses to 14–16 year-olds, and most colleges offer programmes of learning for any age up to 90+. Indeed, in 2022, a 92 year-old man was documented to be the oldest person to sit, and pass, his GCSE maths at a college in Cambridgeshire (BBC News, 2022). According to the Association of Colleges (AoC, nd), '*there are currently 158 further education colleges in England, educating hundreds of thousands of students a year*'.

Sixth form colleges

Sixth form colleges are represented by the Sixth Form Colleges Association in England. As an organisation a sixth form college is different from a school sixth form and is set up in a similar way to a university but teaching A level or equivalent qualifications only; they are standalone and not attached to a school. The Success at School website defines sixth form colleges as follows:

> *Sixth form college can be thought of as a bit of a middle ground between a school sixth form and a further education college. Apart from sometimes also offering vocational courses, one of the main differences between the two is that sixth form college is a lot more informal.*
>
> (Success at School, nd)

The AoC currently lists 44 sixth form colleges on its website.

Specialist land-based colleges

There are currently only 11 land-based colleges in England. These colleges specialise in agriculture, land and animal sciences.

Specialist colleges

According to the AoC, a specialist college:

> *provides post-16 education to young people with learning difficulties and/or disabilities. Most students at specialist colleges have an Education Health and Care Plan (EHCP), with their needs unable to be met at a general further education college.*
>
> (AoC, nd)

There are currently around 99 specialist colleges within the UK.

Prison education

Prison education in the UK is provided by private providers, who tender for a contract. In 2022 the statistics for prisoners showed that 47 per cent of prisoners had no formal qualifications, 42 per cent had been permanently excluded from mainstream schools, 57 per cent had literacy levels comparable to an 11 year-old and 30 per cent had a SEND need (PeoplePlus, 2022).

In terms of the curriculum on offer in prisons, it very much depends on the category of prison. Table 2.1 gives an overview of the categories of prisons and the type of prisoner normally found there.

Table 2.1 *Prison categories*

Prison category	Prisoner characteristics
A High security	Dangerous prisoners. Average stay 10 years +
B Local prison	Remand prisoners and those with short sentences. Average stay 28 days
C Trainer prison	Resettlement where prisoners work towards gaining skills for entry back into a community. Average stay 12 months to four years
D Open prison	Low risk; prisoners can go out to work and have home leave

Source: PeoplePlus (2022)

In terms of the actual provision, prison education has a core curriculum of functional skills, maths and ICT plus ESOL. They also have accredited provision that offers employment skills and vocational training which is tailored to the prison needs and requirements of the local area. Most of this accredited provision is at level 1 and level 2, although there is some entry level offer. Finally, prisons also offer unaccredited qualifications that are often in conjunction with local businesses. As an example, the Glass House is an organisation that works with women prisoners to offer horticultural training (www.theglasshouse.co.uk).

The final decision on what the prison curriculum looks like is decided by the prison governor based on a needs analysis of local labour market needs, feedback from prisoners and any recommendations from Ofsted.

Adult community education

Adult community education is council run or commissioned education that offers a range of informal and formal courses from entry level upwards.

Independent training providers

Independent training providers (ITPs) are sometimes referred to as private training providers. In terms of curriculum, they provide vocational education and training to young people and adults. As organisations, ITPs are distinct from other types of FES provider such as colleges in that they are 'independent'. However, much of their work is funded and regulated by government agencies such as the Education and Skills Funding Agency and Ofsted in the same way as the rest of the FES sector. Most ITPs are companies or charities (not for profit and for profit) and some are in the third sector. As organisations in the FES sector, ITPs make up over half of the educational offer post-16; in particular, they are the largest provider of apprenticeships.

Critical questions ?

The AoC produces an annual key fact leaflet which details the number of students studying at colleges in England, together with information on demographics, types of courses and programmes which they are studying. The key facts document 23/24 identifies that the average age of a student studying in a college is 28. Go to the AoC website and have a look at some of the other statistics.

» Are they surprising to you?

» Are there any other statistics that you feel would be useful to know as a teacher in the sector?

» How does your organisation compare to these statistics?

The next section explores some of the programmes and levels of learning within the FES sector.

Programmes of learning within the FES sector

As discussed above, the curriculum on offer across the FES sector is very broad and encompasses a variety of different types of qualification. The following list provides an indication of the types of qualifications you may be teaching. However, it is worth noting that the qualification landscape is currently shifting as the government is seeking to defund certain level 3 qualifications and offer T levels and apprenticeships alongside the A level offer.

- A levels;
- GCSEs;
- BTECs;
- T levels;
- apprenticeships;
- entry level qualifications;
- HNCs.

The next section gives you an overview of some of the main qualifications you could be involved with

GCSEs

GCSEs (General Certificate of Secondary Education) are exams that students traditionally take at the end of secondary school in Year 11. However, under government policy students have to continue to take GCSEs in English and maths if they do not achieve a grade 4 or above at the end of Year 11. Hence, it is likely that your organisation will be offering at least GCSEs in mathematics and English.

GCSEs are both a level 1 and level 2 qualification, depending on the grade achieved. GCSEs are currently graded on a numerical system, which was introduced in 2017, with 9 being the highest pass and 1 being the lowest. Previous to this they were graded A*–G.

GCSE grades at 1, 2 and 3 (or grades D, E, F, G in the old grading system) are level 1 qualifications, while GCSE grades at 4, 5, 6, 7, 8 and 9 (or grades A*, A, B, C in the old grading system) are level 2 qualifications.

A levels

A levels are a level 3 qualification studied over two years. They are graded A*–E and are usually an entry requirement to go on to university.

BTECs

A BTEC (Business and Technology Education Council) – the name of the body which originally oversaw it – is a practical-based, vocational qualification which, while normally studied at college, is now also offered in schools. They can be studied at a range of levels, although in the FES sector it is normally level 2 or 3.

T levels

T levels were launched in 2020 as a level 3 post-GCSE qualification. They are two-year courses that combine both theory and work-related learning. Students undertake a work placement as part of the qualification, which for the majority of subjects equates to approximately 45 days. A T level is intended to be roughly equivalent to three A levels.

In addition, your learners could be on a range of different levels of qualification, as indicated in Table 2.2. Education qualifications are split into levels 1–8 in England. For ease, we have included all levels so that you can articulate the differences when discussing FES and higher education (HE).

Table 2.2 *Levels of qualification in the UK (adapted from Gov.UK, nd-a)*

Level	Description	Where taught
Entry level	Each entry level qualification is available at three sub-levels – 1, 2 and 3. Entry level 3 is the most difficult. Entry level qualifications are: entry level award; entry level certificate (ELC); entry level diploma; entry level English for speakers of other languages (ESOL); entry level essential skills; entry level functional skills; Skills for Life.	FES sector
Level 1	First certificates GCSE grades 1–3 (D–G) level 1 award level 1 certificate level 1 diploma level 1 ESOL level 1 essential skills level 1 functional skills music grades 1, 2 and 3	FES sector
Level 2	level 2 award level 2 certificate level 2 diploma level 2 ESOL level 2 essential skills level 2 functional skills level 2 national certificate level 2 national diploma GCSE 4–9 (C–A*)	FES sector

→

Table 2.2 *(Cont.)*

Level	Description	Where taught
Level 3	A level access to higher education diploma advanced apprenticeship applied general AS level international Baccalaureate diploma level 3 award level 3 certificate level 3 diploma level 3 ESOL level 3 national certificate level 3 national diploma level 3 NVQ music grades 6, 7 and 8 T Level tech level	FES sector
Level 4	Certificate of Higher Education (CertHE) higher apprenticeship higher national certificate (HNC) level 4 award level 4 certificate level 4 diploma	FES and HE
Level 5	Diploma of Higher Education (DipHE) foundation degree higher national diploma (HND) level 5 award level 5 certificate level 5 diploma	FES and HE

Table 2.2 *(Cont.)*

Level	Description	Where taught
Level 6	degree apprenticeship degree with honours – for example, Bachelor of the Arts (BA) hons, Bachelor of Science (BSc) hons graduate certificate graduate diploma level 6 award level 6 certificate level 6 diploma level 6 NVQ ordinary degree without honours	HE
Level 7	master's level	HE
Level 8	doctoral-level PhD or EdD	HE

Policy drivers

Government policies play a crucial role in shaping education systems and outcomes with the FES sector, its learners being no stranger to qualification reforms and changes to the educational landscape. The current drivers fall into six main categories, although arguably the first three are the ones that have the biggest impact on FES:

- economic growth and skills pipeline;
- levelling up;
- curriculum and assessment;
- parental/carer involvement;
- efficiency and effectiveness;
- leadership and professionalism.

If we consider economic skills and pipeline, it can be argued that education is the driving force for economic recovery and growth. By ensuring that education and training align with labour market needs, the FES sector not only prepares young people for work but also improves the pipeline of potential workers for that industry. Recent examples of this are the introduction of T levels, in particular, construction and engineering, and the increase in apprenticeship programmes 16 plus. Similarly, curriculum and assessment dictate the types of subject on offer, with the aim of ensuring that learners acquire essential knowledge and skills to support economic growth. An example here would be the mandatory requirement for mathematics and English for all learners who have not achieved the level 2 qualification at school. Indeed, in 2023, plans were revealed by the Conservative government to introduce mathematics to 18 for all learners in England. The basis for this was:

> *Right now, just half of all 16–19 year-olds study any maths at all. Yet in a world where data is everywhere and statistics underpin every job, our children's jobs will require more analytical skills than ever before.*
>
> *And letting our children out into the world without those skills, is letting our children down.*
>
> *Maths to 18 will equip young people with the quantitative and statistical skills that they will need for the jobs of today and the future.*
>
> (Gov.UK, 2023)

Further to this announcement, other recent updates to the sector curricula include an overview of the post-16 qualifications landscape from 2025, detailing approved qualifications, based on the following government remit:

> *The government is clear that the purpose of post-16 education is to support people to move into high-skilled jobs, either directly or through progression into good quality higher education courses.*
>
> (DfE, 2024, p 5)

However, education drivers are not the only drivers that impact on the sector and our learners. Many current societal issues also play a part in shaping the landscape in the sector. Examples include recent guidance from the Department for Education on how to support learners questioning their gender or requesting social transitioning (DfE, 2023); legislation on safeguarding and Prevent, which is looked at in more detail in the next section; plus a plethora of other guidelines, initiatives and drivers, including de-colonisation of the curriculum and other EDI areas to name but a few (please see Chapter 8 for more information).

Activity ⑦

» Go to the following website, www.education-uk.org, which is a website dedicated to information and source material, from various governments, that have shaped the FES and school sector into what it is today.

Safeguarding

Safeguarding, while perceived as relatively recent legislation, can be traced back to 1889 with the introduction of the Prevention of Cruelty to, and Protection of, Children Act. This was updated in 1999 in the Working Together to Safeguard Children guidance. The Protection of Children Act gave rise to what was commonly called the List 99 – a database held by the Department of Education of people who have been barred from working with children.

Safeguarding can be defined as:

- protecting children from maltreatment;
- preventing the impairment of children's mental and physical health or development;
- ensuring that children grow up in circumstances consistent with the provision of safe and effective care;
- taking action to enable all children to have the best outcomes.

Children include everyone under the age of 18.

For you as a teacher working in education, the key documentation and background to safeguarding is the following legislation:

1. Children's Act 1989;
2. Safeguarding Vulnerable Adults 2006;
3. Care Act 2014;
4. Children and Social Care Act 2017;
5. Working Together 2018/2019.

These five Acts resulted in the Keeping Children Safe in Education Act 2019 (KCSIE), which is updated annually on 1 September. As a teacher, you are required to ensure that you have read Part 1 of the Act, which incorporates the updates. In addition, you will be required to undertake safeguarding training within your organisation.

The key elements to be aware of is that safeguarding is everyone's business and that all workers within statutory services, which includes education, have a legal responsibility to refer child protection concerns to children's social care.

While it may sometimes be apparent which of your learners could be classed as vulnerable under KCSIE, there are some categories of vulnerability that may not be visible or apparent. The following list provides some examples of the characteristics that a vulnerable child may have:

- disabled;
- minority ethnic;
- in the public care system;
- asylum seekers;
- young carers;
- privately fostered children;
- children of parents where mental ill health, substance misuse, domestic abuse, learning disability and social exclusion are present.

In addition, safeguarding is also a legal requirement for anyone over the age of 18 who may be classed as vulnerable, or at risk of abuse or neglect. Examples could include learners in community care, learners with a mental health or other disability issue, or learners who are unable to take care of themselves or avoid harm or exploitation.

Critical question ⑦

» Consider your class. A key aspect of your role is to ensure that you protect your learners from harm. What types of harm could befall one of your learners?

Discussion

You may have come up with examples such as bullying, self-harm, radicalisation, sexual exploitation or grooming. The following list provides categories of abuse, under which there are many different aspects that you may wish to investigate. We would like to draw your attention to FGM, which has been a criminal offence in the UK since 1985, and if suspected is automatically referred to the police.

- Physical abuse.
- Sexual abuse.
- Psychological abuse.
- Modern slavery.
- Financial or material abuse.
- Neglect and self-neglect.
- Discriminatory abuse.
- Organisational abuse.
- FGM.
- Human trafficking.
- Domestic violence.
- Child criminal exploitation (CCE).
- Child-on-child abuse.

So, what is your role in safeguarding? As discussed previously, safeguarding is everyone's responsibility. However, you do have support in this. Every educational setting is required by law to have a safeguarding policy and safeguarding processes. Additionally, there should be a named safeguarding lead, often called the designated safeguarding officer or lead (DSO/ DSL). This person is responsible for taking the appropriate action should an incident be flagged or suspected. For you as an individual, it is important to listen, not judge and most importantly not make promises, such as you will keep it a secret or you will sort it for them, whatever 'it' might be. We would advise that you take notes and report the concerns to the DSO/DSL, following the organisation's guidance.

The ETF, discussed in Chapter 1, has several courses and resources to support teachers in the FES sector. These can be found at:

> www.et-foundation.co.uk/professional-development/safeguarding-prevent/safeguarding-and-prevent-training

Please take some time to have a look at these as they also include information on teaching online and safe space.

Activity

» Download your setting's safeguarding policy and familiarise yourself with the procedures should you have any safeguarding concerns, including identifying who the safeguarding lead is for the organisation.

CASE STUDY

Online bullying and cyberbullying

Sophie is a 16 year-old student who has just started a course in health and social care at an FES college. Her teacher is concerned that she appears to be quite withdrawn in class and arranges for a pastoral tutorial with her. During the tutorial, Sophie reveals to her tutor that she has been experiencing online bullying through social media platforms, and that the bullies create fake profiles, post hurtful comments and share embarrassing photos of her.

During the tutorial, her tutor listens attentively to Sophie's concerns without interruption and validates Sophie's feelings, reassuring her that she is not alone.

She also takes notes on the specifics of the bullying incidents and records dates, times and any evidence Sophie can provide (screenshots, usernames, etc).

Following this initial tutorial the tutor involves the college designated safeguarding lead (DSL), who then guides any further action, including notifying parents and any external agencies. Both the tutor and the DSL then work with Sophie on coping strategies and encourage her to block the bullies, report the incidents, and seek emotional support from friends and family.

→

The college then sets up several online safety workshop for students, addressing cyberbullying, privacy settings and responsible online behaviour.

- How would you have dealt with this?
- Could the tutor or the college have done anything different to support Sophie?

To conclude this section, safeguarding is an essential aspect of any educational setting. It is a legal and moral responsibility of the sector to ensure that learners, staff and visitors are safe and protected from harm, and by implementing robust safeguarding policies and procedures, they support all to remain safe.

Prevent

The Prevent duty is the duty in the Counter-Terrorism and Security Act 2015 that requires specified authorities to have due regard for the need to prevent people from being groomed by extremists. This guidance was updated in 2023 and is statutory for educational organisations in England and Wales. All individuals and organisations who are involved in the FES sector need to be aware of the Prevent duty and their responsibilities with respect to this. This duty requires the sector to show due regard to the need to prevent people from being drawn into terrorism. It sits alongside safeguarding with the aim to protect young and vulnerable people, and it is one element of the government's overall counter-terrorism strategy. As a duty the main aim of Prevent is to:

- *tackle the ideological causes of terrorism;*
- *intervene early to support people susceptible to radicalization;*
- *enable people who have already engaged in terrorism to disengage and rehabilitate.*

(Gov.UK, nd-b)

It is important to note that Prevent operates in a 'non-criminal' space, with the aim of preventing people from entering the criminal justice system, and any referral does not automatically get entered onto a criminal record. Let us explore some important definitions within the Prevent legislation.

- Extremism – '*The vocal or active opposition to British values, including democracy, the rule of law, individual liberty and mutual respect and tolerance of different faiths and beliefs. We also include in our definition of extremism calls for the death of members of our armed forces, whether in this country or overseas*' (Report of Government Task Force on Extremism).
- Radicalisation – '*This refers to the process by which a person comes to support terrorism and forms of extremism leading to terrorism. A radicaliser is an individual who encourages others to develop or adopt beliefs and views supportive of terrorism and forms of extremism leading to terrorism*' (Prevent Strategy).

Critical question ?

» What factors may increase someone's vulnerability to radicalisation? What might some of these signs be?

Discussion

Factors that may increase an individual's vulnerability can fall into two main categories, internal and external. Table 2.3, while not exhaustive, may provide some potential risk factors.

Table 2.3 *Possible environmental risk factors for radicalisation*

Internal	**External**
Family issues Struggling with identity Feeling angry about events like conflict Mental health issues Traumatic life event Racism, bullying, discrimination	Community tensions Events or incidents affecting specific groups Being in groups that have extreme views

Some of the individual signs you may see in your students could include those mentioned in Table 2.4.

Table 2.4 *Possible signs of radicalisation in your students*

Emotional signs	Angry Short-tempered Withdrawn Upset

→

Table 2.4 *(Cont.)*

Verbal signs	Change in language Inappropriate questions Change in use of word
Physical signs	Tattoos Change of routine Absenteeism Health

Issues surrounding radicalisation and extremism

A report by Taylor et al (2021) identified the following as being major issues surrounding radicalisation and extremism in the classroom:

- racism, misogynistic views and homophobia are widespread in classrooms across the country;
- rise in the number of children being radicalised by neo-Nazi and other extremist groups;
- young people under 24 have accounted for nearly 60 per cent of extreme rightwing terror arrests;
- more than half the teachers had heard pupils express far-right extremist views in their classroom;
- around three-quarters had heard '*extremist views about women*' or Islamophobia;
- almost 90 per cent had heard conspiracy theories;
- many teachers do not talk about extreme views in the classroom out of fear that they will '*get it "wrong"*';
- teaching about extremism is '*highly variable*', and in some cases '*superficial*' and '*tokenistic*';
- a desire to perform policy for Ofsted and a mandate to detect and report vulnerability to radicalisation rather than necessarily stamp out its root causes.

So as a teacher, what does it mean for you in the classroom? The Prevent duty comes under the auspices of safeguarding and while again you have responsibilities, should you suspect one of your learners is at risk you should contact the DSO/DSL immediately. In addition, the Prevent duty also requires the active promotion of British values within the classroom. The British values are based on the core values of British society and are as follows.

- Democracy: Young people should know that their own views count and value each other's opinions.
- The rule of law: Young people should learn about consequences of their own or other people's behaviour and learn to distinguish right from wrong.
- Individual liberty: Young people should be allowed to develop a sense of themselves, the right to privacy and personal boundaries, and a sense of self-worth.
- Mutual respect and tolerance: Young people should not only respect their own culture but also other cultures.

Critical question

» How can you ensure that you incorporate and embed British values into your lessons?

Discussion

The ETF has a range of resources to help you integrate British values into your curriculum. Have a look at the following for some ideas for your subject area: www.et-foundation.co.uk/safeguarding-and-prevent/integrating-british-values-into-adult-learning

Equality, diversity and inclusion

While equality, diversity and inclusion (EDI) is covered more fully in Chapter 8, it would be remiss not to acknowledge that the learner in your classroom may come from a multitude of backgrounds and that the FES sector is the most diverse in terms of the make-up of its student population. Therefore, as a teacher you need to be aware of making the learning inclusive for all. Please go to Chapter 8 for more information on the FES learner and EDI.

Summary

This chapter has considered the types of learner and settings within the FES sector, and the qualifications and subjects that they may be studying. As a teacher studying for a post-16 qualification, you need to be aware of the breadth and depth of the sector, and as part of your programme you will be required to undertake an alternative placement to your main setting. This may be a completely different organisation, or in some cases a different subject or level. However, regardless of your primary teaching and your alternative placement, the policy drivers and the safeguarding and Prevent legislation are crucial in your development.

Check your understanding (level 5)

1. Describe some of the settings that an FES learner may be studying in.
2. What is your role in safeguarding?
3. How should you deal with a potential safeguarding concern in your setting?
4. Name three possible signs of abuse.
5. Which one of the safeguarding concerns requires immediate referral to the police following the 1985 legislation?
6. How does the government impact the sector and the FES learner?
7. How does EDI affect the FES sector and curriculum?

Developmental questions (L6+7)

1. What are the potential criticisms of the Prevent duty in the UK?
2. What do you believe to be the most important considerations for a UK government when considering education policy for the FES sector?
3. Evaluate your organisation's safeguarding policy. How might this be developed in today's society to better protect learners?

Further reading

- Alibhai, Z (2021) Racism, Islamophobia and Conspiracy Theories among Extremist Views Witnesses in Classrooms, Study Finds. *The Independent*, 7 September. [online] Available at: www.independent.co.uk/news/education/extremist-views-school-england-racism-b1915191.html (accessed 19 September 2024).
- Busher, J, Choudhury, T and Thomas, P (2023) Surveillance and Preventing Violent Extremism: The Evidence from Schools and Further Education Colleges in England. In Kwet, M (ed) *The Cambridge Handbook of Race and Surveillance* (pp 267–87). Cambridge: Cambridge University Press.
- Cole, M (ed) (2022) *Education, Equality and Human Rights: Issues of Gender, 'Race', Sexuality, Disability and Social Class*. Abingdon: Routledge.

- Commission on Race and Ethnic Disparities (CRED) (2021) *Commission on Race and Ethnic Disparities: The Report*. [online] Available at: https://assets.publishing.service.gov.uk/media/6062ddb1d3bf7f5ce1060aa4/20210331_-_CRED_Report_-_FINAL_-_Web_Accessible.pdf (accessed 19 September 2024).
- Greenfields, M and Rogers, C (2020) *Hate: 'As Regular as Rain'. A Pilot Research Project into the Psychological Effects of Hate Crime on Gypsy, Traveller and Roma (GTR) Communities*. [online] Available at: https://gateherts.org.uk/wp-content/uploads/2020/12/Rain-Report-201211.pdf (accessed 19 September 2024).
- Home Office (2020) Individuals Referred to and Supported Through the Prevent Programme, April 2019 to March 2020. [online] Available at: www.gov.uk/government/statistics/individuals-referred-to-and-supported-through-the-prevent-programme-april-2019-to-march-2020 (accessed 19 September 2024).
- Home Office (2024) Prevent Duty Guidance: England and Wales. [online] Available at: www.gov.uk/government/publications/prevent-duty-guidance/prevent-duty-guidance-for-further-education-institutions-in-england-and-wales (accessed 19 September 2024).
- Runnymede Trust (2021) *England Civil Society Submission to the United Nations Committee on the Elimination of Racial Discrimination*. [online] Available at: www.equallyours.org.uk/runnymede-trust-report-england-civil-society-submission-to-the-united-nations-committee-on-the-elimination-of-racial-discrimination (accessed 28 September 2024).

References

Association of Colleges (AoC) (nd) [online] Available at: www.aoc.co.uk (accessed 13 September 2024).

BBC News (2022) Cambridgeshire Man, 92, Passes GCSE Maths Exam with Top Mark. 25 August. [online] Available at: www.bbc.co.uk/news/uk-england-cambridgeshire-62671962 (accessed 28 September 2024).

Department for Education (DfE) (2023) Parent First Approach at the Core of New Guidance on Gender Questioning Children. [online] Available at: www.gov.uk/government/news/parent-first-approach-at-the-core-of-new-guidance-on-gender-questioning-children (accessed 28 September 2024).

Department for Education (DfE) (2024) *Guide to Post-16 Qualifications at Level 3 and Below in England*. [online] Available at: www.gov.uk/government/publications/review-of-post-16-qualifications-at-level-3-in-england--2 (accessed 28 September 2024).

Education and Training Foundation (ETF) (2022a) *Professional Standards for Teachers and Trainers*. [online] Available at: www.et-foundation.co.uk/professional-standards/teachers (accessed 29 September 2024).

Education and Training Foundation (ETF) (2022b) Integrating British Values into Adult Learning. [online] Available at: www.et-foundation.co.uk/safeguarding-and-prevent/integrating-british-values-into-adult-learning (accessed 13 September 2024).

Extremism Taskforce (2013) Tackling Extremism in the UK: Report by the Extremism Taskforce. [online] Available at: www.gov.uk/government/publications/tackling-extremism-in-the-uk-report-by-the-extremism-taskforce (accessed 8 October 2024).

Gov.UK (2015) *Prevent Duty Guidance: England and Wales*. [online] Available at: www.gov.uk/government/publications/prevent-duty-guidance/prevent-duty-guidance-for-further-education-institutions-in-england-and-wales (accessed 13 September 2024).

Gov.UK (2023) Prime Minister Sets Ambition of Maths to 18 in Speech. [online] Available at: www.gov.uk/government/news/prime-minister-sets-ambition-of-maths-to-18-in-speech (accessed 28 September 2024).

Gov.UK (nd-a) What Qualification Levels Mean. [online] Available at: www.gov.uk/what-different-qualification-levels-mean/list-of-qualification-levels (accessed 19 September 2024).

Gov.UK (nd-b) Prevent Duty Training: Learn How to Support People Susceptible to Radicalisation. [online] Available at: www.support-people-susceptible-to-radicalisation.service.gov.uk (accessed 19 September 2024).

Institute for Apprenticeships and Technical Education (IfATE) (2024) *Learning and Skills Teacher*. [online] Available at: www.instituteforapprenticeships.org/apprenticeship-standards/learning-and-skills-teacher (accessed 28 September 2024).

PeoplePlus (2022) [online] Available at: https://peopleplus.co.uk/education-in-prison (accessed 15 November 2024).

Success at School (nd) [online] Available at: www.successatschool.org (accessed 13 September 2024).

Taylor, B, Mills, M, Elwick, A, Pillinger, C, Gronland, G, Hayward, J and Hextall, I (2021) *Addressing Extremism Through the Classroom: A Research Report from the Centre for Teachers & Teaching Research*. London: UCL Institute of Education. [online] Available at: https://discovery.ucl.ac.uk/id/eprint/10133809 (accessed 19 September 2024).

The Glass House (nd) [online] Available at: www.theglasshouse.co.uk (accessed 28 September 2024).

3 The SEND learner in the further education and skills sector

Professional links

This chapter contributes to the following professional links:

The Diploma in Teaching mandatory content (DfE, 2024)

- 2.3 Range of support needs.
- 3.9 Individual support (including SEND and mental health).
- 4.11 Managing and supporting learners, including behaviour.

Learning and Skills Teacher Occupational Standards (IfATE, 2024)

- K4 Methods for creating and adapting inclusive learning resources.
- K5 Evidence-informed inclusive teaching, learning and assessment strategies.
- K11 Barriers to learning, and ways to overcome them and adapt teaching, learning and assessment.
- S4 Use a variety of teaching and assessment methods depending on the learning environment and learners' needs.
- S8 Design and use resources that are inclusive and add value to learners' development.
- S12 Use the results of initial and diagnostic assessment to plan learning and differentiated support at the start of and throughout the learner's journey.
- S18 Adapt communication style, method, and terminology to reflect the needs of the audience including individual learners, colleagues, stakeholders.
- B4 Act in a professional manner, and in a way that builds and maintains positive relationships with colleagues, students and stakeholders.

Professional Standards (ETF, 2022)

- 5 Value and champion diversity, equality of opportunity, inclusion and social equity.

→

- 11 Develop and apply your knowledge of special educational needs and disabilities to create inclusive learning experiences.
- 15 Plan and deliver learning programmes that are safe, inclusive, stretching and relevant to learners' needs.

Chapter objectives

At the end of this chapter you will be able to:

- identify different types of SEND and the legislation surrounding young people with SEND;
- define SEND and the social and medical models of disability;
- describe some of the SEND learners you may encounter and their characteristics;
- identify strategies for inclusivity within your classroom.

Introduction

The term SEND (special educational needs and disabilities) is not new and has been used for many years to describe learners who have learning disabilities. The SEND code of practice (DfE, 2022) sets out statutory guidance for all organisations working with young people 0–25 with SEND. It explains the duties of local authorities, schools, colleges and other health bodies under the Children and Families Act 2014. Within the FES sector the code applies to the following organisations:

- general FES colleges;
- specialist art and design and land-based colleges;
- sixth form colleges;
- 16–19 academies;
- special post-16 institutions.

It lists the following duties.

> - *The duty to co-operate with the local authority on arrangements for children and young people with SEN.*
> - *The duty to admit a young person if the institution is named in an Education Health and Care (EHC) plan.*
> - *The duty to have regard to this Code of Practice*
> - *The duty to use their best endeavours to secure the special educational provision that the young person needs.*
>
> (DfE, 2022, p 112)

Recently, Ofsted introduced a much stronger focus on SEND and supporting learners, with inspectors looking at the three I's of intent, implementation and impact through a SEND lens. They expect the curriculum to be well rounded and delivered in a way that supports SEND learners so that all learners, including those with SEND, acquire the knowledge and skills they need to succeed in life and transition into either further study or employment. It is therefore crucial that as a teacher in the FES sector you are aware of SEND learners and are using strategies that will meet the Ofsted requirements.

This chapter considers the different definitions of SEND and explores some of the conditions that you may experience in teaching these learners. It provides examples and ideas to help you ensure that your students with SEND are fully integrated and included in your sessions, promoting an inclusive and positive learning experience.

Definitions of SEND

There are currently two recognised approaches to defining and working with SEND learners, which as a teacher you need to be aware of. These are outlined below.

Social model of disability

The social model is generally the preferred model when thinking about disability. It was endorsed by the government in 2014 and is their recommended model for interaction with disabled people. This model concentrates on removing barriers that would impede a student's ability to interact in the classroom and is based around the distinction between impairment and disability. Impairment is defined as a characteristic or trait affecting a young person's appearance or functioning. With adjustments and interventions, teachers can minimise the impact it has on the learner and their inclusion within the classroom. It may manifest as psychological, physiological or anatomical.

Conversely, disability, according to the Equality Act 2010, is defined as follows:

> *A person has a disability for the purposes of the Act if he or she has a physical or mental impairment and the impairment has a substantial and long-term adverse effect on his or her ability to carry out normal day-to-day activities.*
>
> (Government Equalities Office, 2011)

Therefore, using this definition, a disability exists when a young person's activity and day-to-day life is severely impacted by their impairment.

For the purposes of this chapter, consider how any impairments may impact your learners and how you can make adjustments for them, remembering that an impairment may not always be visible to you.

Medical model of disability

The medical model of disability considers the impairment as the cause of a learner being unable to participate in the class and focuses on what they are unable to do rather than what they could do with adjustments. The learner, rather than the environment, is seen as the 'problem'.

Critical question ⓘ

» Considering your classroom and teaching practice, what barriers could there be that would impede a young person with an impairment? Explain your answers.

Table 3.1 provides some examples of barriers that may exist for a young person with a learning difficulty or disability. It also shows how the approach of the two different models, medical and social, differ for the way you may work with your learners.

Table 3.1 *Examples of ways to work with SEND learners*

Issue for the learner	Medical model	Social model
Communication with the teacher/peers	Student provided with magnifiers/amplifiers to help communication – medical equipment intervention.	Communication tailored –font size, audio, paper colour, provision of slides prior to sessions.
Classroom environment	Specialist products required. For example, hoists, specialist equipment.	Adaptation within the classroom to meet the learner's need – lighting and classroom layout, including the height of workspaces and desk layout to enable mobility for both learner and the tutor.
Education as a concept	Segregation and special learning environments. For example, specialist schools.	Accessible to all. SEND learners are integrated into mainstream education.
The learner	Assumption and stereotyping of the disability. A one-size-fits-all ideology.	Discussions take place around individual needs and the adaptations take these needs into account.

Critical question ⓘ

» In what ways does your current setting consider the SEND learner in terms of the medical versus social approach?

SEND in practice: common SEND needs in the further education and skills setting

This section explores different elements of SEND that you may encounter during your teaching. It examines how you may identify a SEND learner displaying these traits, with information on how you can best support them and provide an effective educational environment for their learning.

Social, emotional and mental health needs

Social, emotional and mental health (SEMH) needs refer to a category of special educational needs where children and young people face significant challenges in managing their emotions and behaviour. These difficulties often manifest as inappropriate responses and feelings in various situations (see Table 3.2 for an overview of SEMH learner characteristics).

Table 3.2 *SEMH learner characteristics*

Emotional regulation	Learners with SEMH needs may struggle to regulate their emotions effectively. They might experience anxiety, fear and feelings of being misunderstood.
Behavioural challenges	Common characteristics include disruptive, antisocial and uncooperative behaviour. Learners may exhibit temper tantrums, frustration, anger and verbal or physical threats.
Relationship difficulties	Building and maintaining relationships with peers and adults can be challenging for learners with SEMH needs. They may find it hard to connect with others.
Learning and coping	SEMH can impact a learner's ability to engage in learning and cope within an educational setting.

As a teacher you should look out for signs such as withdrawal, depression, anxiety, self-harm, stealing, truancy and vandalism, which while not conclusive may indicate that a learner is suffering with mental health issues.

Visual impairment

Visual impairment is the functional limitation of an eye or eyes or the vision system leading to loss of visual acuity and an inability to see objects as clearly as a healthy person (Mandal, 2023).

Within your practice you may experience learners with total or severe sight loss, partially sighted learners or learners who have more specific areas of sight loss, for example central or periphery vision loss.

It is crucial that you ensure that your visually impaired learners are offered inclusive and equal access to education, adhering to the legal requirement for equal rights and opportunities and providing spaces in which visually impaired learners can develop social skills and experience a sense of belonging.

CASE STUDY

Suleman has not disclosed having a visual impairment; however, he appears very clumsy in the class. He always says the teacher's writing is unclear and he cannot read it and as a result becomes quite distracted and at times disruptive. As his teacher, you have decided to observe him more closely to see if there is anything in particular that you could do to try and help him. You realise that when doing board work, Suleman struggles to copy information down in the time allowed and quite often he tries to use his friends' work to copy from rather than the board.

Critical question

» What as a tutor could you do to adapt to and support Suleman?

Discussion

You could consider:

- the physical environment – for example, do you or the organisation need to consider large-print signs?
- the classroom environment, including lighting, window blinds, use of black pens on the board, your position in the teaching space;
- providing a handout with large print for Suleman's use.

For example, you could develop revision sheets in a large font size. Ensure that your writing on the board is clear, and even adapt your lessons so that there is more discussion with Q&A, which will benefit all students and will enable you to check understanding and reinforce information. You could even consider colour and contrast if undertaking activities with the group and ensure that Suleman is seated near a natural light source to provide more illumination for him.

Hearing impairment

Hearing impairment refers to any degree of reduced ability to perceive sound. It can range from mild to severe and may be a short-term or a long-term condition. Depending upon the severity of the impairment, young people may be educated in a mainstream setting, with varying degrees of additional support, or in the most severe cases be in a special school or setting. However, it may be that you encounter an undiagnosed learner who is displaying certain behaviours that indicate they are experiencing hearing difficulties.

Critical question

» What specific behaviours may you encounter that could lead you to believe a learner may be struggling with their hearing?

Discussion

Although not exhaustive, you may have considered some of the following:

- asking you to repeat information;
- talking loudly;
- not responding to questions or directions;
- struggling to hear in noisy classrooms.

As a teacher there are several ways in which you could support your hearing-impaired learners, starting with the physical environment: your position in the room, the seating position and any ways in which you could reduce noise levels. In addition, there are a range of teaching methods that you could utilise: ensuring learners can always see your face when addressing them, speaking clearly, rephrasing, using visuals to provide key information and using facial expressions and gestures.

Critical question

» Revisit a lesson that you have recently planned and consider how you could adapt any input, tasks or activities to support a hearing-impaired learner.

Neurodiversity

Neurodiversity refers to the different ways the brain can work and interpret information. Most people are classed as *neurotypical*, which means that their brains function and process information in the way society expects. However, it is estimated that around one in seven people are neurodivergent (Business Disability Forum, nd). The term *neurodivergent* means that the brain functions, learns and processes information differently. The term *neurodiversity* usually refers to range of specific learning differences (see Figure 3.1), including:

- attention deficit hyperactivity disorder (ADHD);
- developmental co-ordination disorder (DCD), also referred to as dyspraxia;
- developmental language disorder (DLD);
- foetal alcohol spectrum disorder;
- Tourette's and tic disorders;
- specific learning difficulties/differences, eg dyslexia, dyscalculia.

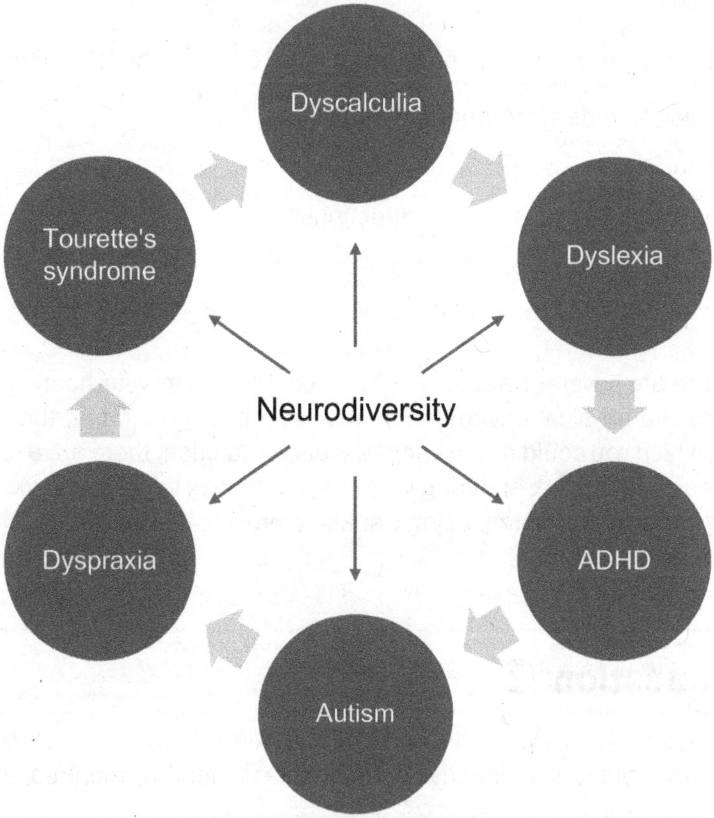

Figure 3.1 *The make-up of neurodiversity (adapted from Colley and Aquilina, nd)*

Within this make-up it is considered that:

- *8% of people in the UK are thought to have ADHD;*
- *10% of people in the UK are thought to have dyslexia;*
- *8% of people in the UK are thought to have dyspraxia;*
- *6% of people in the UK are thought to have dyscalculia;*
- *1% of people in the UK are thought to have an autistic spectrum condition;*
- *1% of people in the UK are thought to have Tourette's syndrome.*

(Colley and Aquilina, nd)

The next section focuses on some of these conditions and considers how you can support neurodivergent learners.

Dyslexia

Dyslexia is a specific learning difficulty which primarily affects reading and writing skills. However, it has much more of an impact on the learner in that it also affects the way they process and remember information. The official definition from the British Dyslexia Association (BDA, 2010) has been adapted from Rose (2009) and states that:

> *Dyslexia is a learning difficulty that primarily affects the skills involved in accurate and fluent word reading and spelling. Characteristic features of dyslexia are difficulties in phonological awareness, verbal memory, and verbal processing speed. Dyslexia occurs across the range of intellectual abilities. It is best thought of as a continuum and not a distinct category. Co-occurring difficulties may be seen in aspects of language, motor coordination, mental calculation, concentration, and personal organisation, but these are not, by themselves, markers of dyslexia.*
>
> (BDA, 2010)

Critical question ?

» Using the above definition, what may you see as potential signs that one of your learners is dyslexic?

Discussion

Although not an exhaustive list you may have considered some of the following:

- behaviour of the learner – daydreaming, easily distracted, difficulty in dealing with instructions;

→

- reading – reluctant to read aloud, mis-reads words, misses out sections of text;
- handwriting – legibility, incorrect spellings, letters reversed.

Within education the identification and support for dyslexia has been subject to reforms by the Department for Education, and in 2024 the British Dyslexia Association submitted recommendations to the Teachers' Standards for the compulsory sector based on research on how people learn, the subject, the curriculum and adaptive teaching. Take the opportunity to look at the report and how this can be used in the FES sector (BDA, 2024).

CASE STUDY

Simon has been at the college since September, having enrolled on a level 2 course from school. You notice that he finds it difficult to concentrate in your classes and when he is taking notes his handwriting is difficult to read and he writes very slowly. As his tutor, you suspect that he may be displaying signs of dyslexia, although he has no official diagnosis from school. Therefore, you decide that you will use some strategies that may help him and possibly others in the class. With the support of the college and your colleagues, you arrange for classes to be recorded, allowing Simon to revisit the session at his own speed. You also provide Simon with any PowerPoint presentations in advance of the class. As Simon also has difficulty with spelling and grammar, you discuss with him how he would like to you to give feedback and highlight any errors in his work. You choose to do this as you know from previous experience that some dyslexic students like the mistakes corrected, while others prefer for each mistake to be highlighted so that they can look at the mistake and identify what they did wrong.

Critical question

» As a trainee teacher is there anything else that you have observed your mentor doing that may help a dyslexic student?

Dyspraxia

According to the Dyspraxia Foundation (nd), dyspraxia is a condition affecting movement and co-ordination in children and adults and is also known as developmental co-ordination disorder (DCD).

It can manifest in several different ways, and students with dyspraxia may display different characteristics, including:

- co-ordination difficulties;
- poor concentration skills;
- poor listening skills;
- poor spatial awareness;
- poor motor skills;
- difficulty with social interaction and communication (verbal dyspraxia);
- difficulty in organising themselves or work.

In isolation these characteristics or traits may not signify that a student is dyspraxic, but there are some tell-tale signs that you could look out for when working with your class:

- disorganised and messy work;
- tendency to lose equipment;
- easily distracted;
- unable to multi-task;
- poor handwriting;
- difficulty concentrating.

A student with dyspraxia may also have other conditions which impact upon their ability to participate in the class, including dyslexia, dyscalculia, ADHD and Asperger's syndrome (Dyspraxia Foundation, nd).

Critical question ?

» How could you ensure that your classroom is dyspraxic friendly?

Discussion

The Dyspraxia Foundation has a wealth of resources in the form of fact sheets and help sheets for young people. Strategies that they suggest may be useful in your classroom include:

- making use of organisers, eg phone calendars and other apps, to help students with organisation skills;

→

- providing extra time for coursework and exams;
- recording sessions so that the student can re-watch or re-listen;
- using software packages that may help, eg touch-typing software.

Other things you may consider are ensuring you break down tasks into manageable chunks to avoid overload and confusion and providing writing frames to help a student organise their thoughts.

The following website has a range of strategies that you may wish to try with your FES student who is displaying signs of being dyspraxic: www.dyspraxiafoundation.org.uk/young-people.

Autism

Autism spectrum disorder (ASD) is a developmental disorder that affects communication and behaviour. Although autism can be diagnosed at any age, it is considered a neurodevelopmental disorder, and signs of autism typically appear during early childhood. Individuals with ASD may experience challenges in social skills, communication and behaviours. The term 'spectrum' indicates that autism manifests in different forms with varying levels of severity. According to the National Autistic Society (nd) the term autism is a condition that affects people in different ways, and each autistic person is unique with their own set of strengths and weaknesses. While autism in itself is not classed as a learning disability, it is estimated that around 4 per cent of autistic people will have a learning disability (National Autistic Society, nd).

However, the definitions and research around autism are changing constantly. The current thinking is that the spectrum of differences that an autistic learner may portray is very broad and that everyone with autism is different, with varying support needs that cannot be generalised for a classroom situation. Regardless of thinking on definitions, the fact remains that recent estimates by the government consider one in 100 people to be autistic, meaning that you are very likely to encounter an autistic learner within your teaching.

In 2021, the UK government published a five-year national strategy for autism with the following vision:

> *We want education settings to provide better and more inclusive support to autistic children and young people so that autistic people are better able to achieve their potential. We want more teachers and educational staff to understand the specific needs of their autistic pupils, ensuring that more school placements can be sustained. We also want to demonstrate that more autistic children have had their needs identified early on and that they are having positive experiences in education settings.*
>
> (DoH and DfE, 2021)

Critical questions

- » What are some of the characteristics that an autistic learner may display?
- » How may these manifest in your classroom?

Discussion

You may have considered some of the following: social interaction; obsessive behaviour; over sensitivity to certain situations; good rote memory skills; unable to make/maintain eye contact; unable to cope with change to a daily routine.

CASE STUDY

Students with autism are often some of the brightest students yet can experience a variety of barriers affecting their progression. Autism is a highly individual condition and the student's supports need to be carefully co-ordinated as a result. Sana is a very intelligent young woman who has been at her local college for two years and has aspirations of being a doctor. As a student she works very hard to achieve her goal, but struggles with hyper-sensitivity to noise and lighting, which makes it difficult for her to concentrate at times. She also struggles with the group tutorial activities and the associated noise within them. As her tutor there are several strategies and adjustments that you could use to try and help Sana manage her learning. You could find quiet work spaces, allow her to wear ear plugs in the classroom and provide individual rather than group sessions where appropriate. You could also work with your organisation's disability co-ordinator to provide additional support when required, for example at assignment submission periods.

Attention deficit hyperactivity disorder (ADHD)

Attention deficit hyperactivity disorder (ADHD) was first identified in 1994 by the American Psychiatric Association (APA). Within the condition there are three distinct areas that young people may exhibit:

1. inattention;
2. impulsiveness;
3. hyperactivity.

It is crucial that you can recognise possible signs of ADHD and have strategies for supporting an ADHD learner. The following list provides some pointers that you can use to help you identify of you have a learner with ADHD.

- Does the learner constantly get up to wander around the classroom?
- Do they struggle to pay attention in the class?
- Do they struggle to stay on task?
- Do they constantly call/shout answers out?
- Are they able to wait their turn during practical activities?

Any of these maybe an indication that a learner has ADHD. The ADHD Foundation has some excellent strategies for helping you to support teaching and learning in a positive and proactive way, including chunking activities, taking breaks to re-focus and using checklists.

Critical question ?

Go to the ADHD Foundation website www.adhdfoundation.org.uk and download the document on *Teaching and Managing Students with ADHD.*

» Considering your own practice, how can you use the ideas provided to develop your understanding of ADHD? What techniques could you employ to support inclusivity for the ADHD learner?

Working with broad areas of need

This next section considers some of the ways in which you can work with broad areas of need that come under the SEND umbrella. There are two areas that you need to consider when working with a SEND learner.

1. What underpinning research is there to support your strategies?
2. Do they work in the classroom?

However, you also need to be cognisant of the expectations of the SEND code of practice, which is applicable to all learners up to the age of 25. Cotterill (2023) discusses the notion of Quality First Teaching and the idea that what works well for SEND students will also work well for other learners. He advocates that as a strategy, Quality First Teaching should be the starting point for all teachers rather than just using the strategy for x or y. Quality First Teaching as a method is classed as the first stage of the Three Waves of Intervention model (see Figure 3.2).

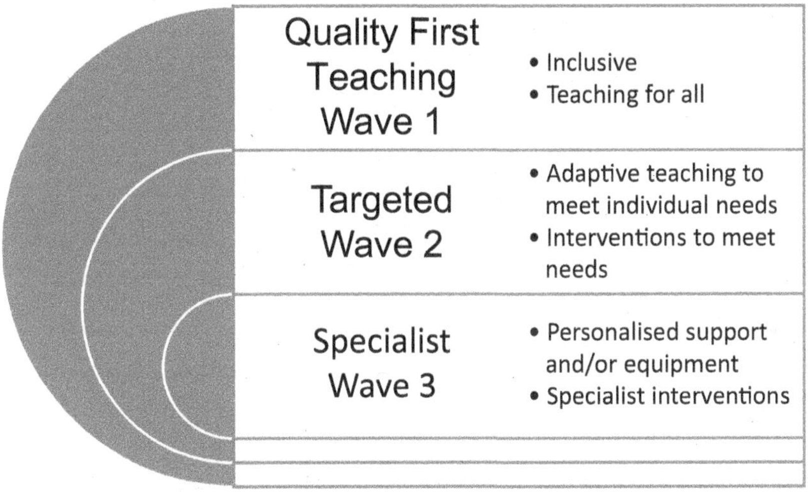

Figure 3.2 *Three Waves of Intervention model (adapted from Twinkl, nd)*

Three Waves of Intervention

Wave 1

Wave 1 of the model, Quality First Teaching, is the expectation that if you adapt your teaching through differentiation (or adaptive teaching in the new terminology) you will reach the majority of learners within your practice. As an inclusive approach Quality First Teaching advocates specific strategies that can be effective in the classroom (see Table 3.3).

Table 3.3 *Quality First Teaching strategies*

Strategy	**Rationale**
Clear learning objectives	Beginning each lesson with well-defined learning objectives can guide both you and your students, ensuring a focused and purposeful learning experience.
Set high expectations of all	Encourages a growth mindset and can help foster a positive learning environment.
Adaptive teaching	Recognise that learners have diverse needs and adapt your resources and tasks to support different abilities.
Questioning strategies	Make use of open-ended questions and use directed questioning to check learning.

⟶

Table 3.3 *(Cont.)*

Strategy	Rationale
Assessment strategies	Utilise formative strategies to check learning and help you identify learners who may be struggling.
Personalisation	Similar to adaptive teaching; tailor your teaching to individuals.
Create an environment of independent learning	Encourage autonomy and responsibility in your learners.

If, despite using some of the Quality First Teaching strategies identified in Table 3.3, your student is still falling behind, not achieving and not reaching the relevant expectations of the qualification, you start to move into Wave 2 of the model and consider targeted interventions for specific learners.

Wave 2

Wave 2 of the model focuses on the provision of additional teaching for cohorts of learners who have not developed mastery of core instruction or have exceeded agreed standards. Resources are targeted to support teachers at this level with approaches being timely, targeted, purposeful and time limited. The strategies used should be regularly monitored to gauge effectiveness and modified as necessary. In this stage, the teacher can monitor learner progress and data to identify learners who no longer require targeted intervention through a process of assess, plan, do and review through asking the following questions.

- What are we achieving?
- What is the learner doing?
- Are they fulfilling whatever the expectation is?
- Are they maintaining the development?

In Wave 2 the additional teaching and intervention sessions are typically planned alongside the Wave 1 activities and are combined with high-quality teaching to address specific needs. They are normally short-term focused teaching activities, often in particular areas, for example maths or English, and are continually monitored for effectiveness. There could be access to specialist resources within the setting, such as nurture groups, therapies and some one-to-one support.

Wave 3

The final wave in this three-part model is specialist intervention, addressing learners who have not responded to Wave 1 and 2 interventions or strategies. Not always, but usually, this type of learner may have an education, health and care (EHC) plan or will be under review for one. Teaching in this wave can be quite specialised and involves the use of intensive SEND pedagogical interventions and intensive teaching for short periods of time to support/ challenge to achieve or exceed agreed goals in the learner's learning plan. Wave 3 is usually where an external specialist may be asked to advise on more specialised support. Examples of Wave 3 support include specialist units within a setting, qualified SEND staff responsible for leading on any interventions and a special curriculum that learners may follow, such as lifeskills. Learners who do not respond to this third level of intervention in meeting their agreed goals will require more intensive assessment involving input from a multi-disciplinary team. Often this learner will be in a specialist SEND group, with specialist teachers. However, as a teacher in the FES sector it is important that you are aware of them and the interventions that may be required to support them.

Summary

This chapter has considered some of the more common instances of students with SEND that you may encounter in your own practice and discussed some of the characteristics that may manifest themselves within a learner in your classroom. As a teacher, you will often hear or suspect that your student has a learning difficulty or disability, and it is quite easy to label them as such according to the characteristics displayed. While labels can be important in terms of diagnosis and therefore opening access to specific resources, they do come with a caveat in that they can be 'sticky'; while you may suspect an underlying issue, the student may not have a diagnosis and as such has no access to those specific resources. Labels can also lead to stereotyping, prejudice or discrimination in the classroom. Therefore, it is our opinion that it is what you do with the label or suspicion that is important. By using strategies such as Quality First Teaching, you will ensure that you have an inclusive learning environment in which every student can grow and develop. In summary, having some awareness of learning difficulties and ways in which to support learners will enhance not only your practice but the learning experience of the student.

Check your understanding (level 5)

1. What are the two main models of disability?
2. What are your obligations under the SEND code of practice for learners in your classroom?
3. Name some of the traits or characteristics you may encounter when working with a neurodivergent learner.
4. Write down three strategies you could try to ensure that you are maintaining Quality First Teaching for an inclusive classroom.
5. What are the benefits of adaptive teaching when working with students who may be SEND students?

Developmental questions L6+7

1. Having considered various strategies to help your SEND learners, how would you adapt your curriculum input to ensure Quality First Teaching?
2. Critically evaluate one of the strategies that you have observed in your setting. How could you build upon this as a teacher?
3. Analyse how your pedagogical approaches to SEND learners can impact on their progression.
4. Using evidence-informed research, discuss how the recent developments in educational policy have impacted on your classroom practice.
5. Critique current theories of teaching and learning in relation to SEND learners.

Helpful websites and resources

In addition to the references in this chapter you may find the following of interest.

- Ofsted's evaluation of National Strategy intervention programmes: www.dera.ioe.ac.uk/id/eprint/326/1/An%20evaluation%20of%20National%20Strategy%20intervention%20programmes.pdf
- Department for Education (DfE) (2022) *SEND Code of Practice:0–25 Years* (Chapters 7 and 8). [online] Available at: www.gov.uk/government/publications/send-code-of-practice-0-to-25 (accessed 19 September 2024).
- www.adhdfoundation.org.uk
- www.disabilityrightsuk.org
- www.dyspraxiafoundation.org.uk/young-people
- www.et-foundation.co.uk/wpcontent/uploads/2022/12/Supporting_learners_with_additional_needs_-_23_Aug_2018.pdf – a link to working with young people in prisons who have additional needs.
- www.wholeschoolsend.org.uk – a resource for CPD hosted by Nasen.

References

ADHD Foundation: The Neurodiversity Charity [online] Available at: www.adhdfoundation.org.uk/ (accessed 28 September 2024).

British Dyslexia Association (2010) *Definition of Dyslexia*. [online] Available at: www.bdadyslexia.org.uk/dyslexia/about-dyslexia/what-is-dyslexia (accessed 29 September 2024).

British Dyslexia Association (2024) New Framework to Support Trainee and Early Career Teachers. [online] Available at: www.bdadyslexia.org.uk/news/new-framework-to-support-trainee-and-early-career-teachers (accessed 8 October 2024).

Business Disability Forum (nd) [online] Available at: www.businessdisabilityforum.org.uk (accessed 29 September 2024).

Children and Families Act 2014 [online] Available at: www.legislation.gov.uk/ukpga/2014/6/contents/enacted (accessed 29 September 2024).

Colley, M and Aquilina, J (nd) The Make Up of Neurodiversity. [online] Available at: https://adhdaware.org.uk/what-is-adhd/neurodiversity-and-other-conditions/ (accessed 29 September 2024).

Cotterill, T (2023) *Autism: A Student's Guide*. London: Sage.

Department for Education (DfE) (2022) *SEND Code of Practice :0–25 Years*. [online] Available at: www.gov.uk/government/publications/send-code-of-practice-0-to-25 (accessed 29 September 2024).

Department for Education (DfE) (2024) Diploma in Teaching (Further Education and Skills) qualification framework. [online] Available at: www.gov.uk/government/publications/further-education-initial-teacher-education/diploma-in-teaching-further-education-and-skills-qualification-framework (accessed 8 October 2024).

Department of Health and Social Care and Department for Education (DoH and DfE) (2021) *The National Strategy for Autistic Children, Young People and Adults: 2021 to 2026*. [online] Available at: www.gov.uk/government/publications/national-strategy-for-autistic-children-young-people-and-adults-2021-to-2026/the-national-strategy-for-autistic-children-young-people-and-adults-2021-to-2026 (accessed 29 September 2024).

Disability Rights UK (nd) [online] Available at: www.disabilityrightsuk.org (accessed 29 September 2024).

Dyspraxia Foundation (nd) Dyspraxia Foundation. [online] Available at: https://dyspraxiauk.com/dyspraxia-foundation (accessed 8 October 2024).

Dyspraxia Foundation (2022) *Dyspraxia Post 16 Strategies*. [online] Available at: www.dyspraxiacollective.co.uk/wp-content/uploads/2024/09/post-16-dyspraxia factsheet.pdf (accessed 19 September 2024).

Education and Training Foundation (ETF) (2022) *Professional Standards for Teachers and Trainers*. [online] Available at: www.et-foundation.co.uk/professional-standards/teachers (accessed 29 September 2024).

Equality Act 2010 [online] Available at: www.legislation.gov.uk/ukpga/2010/15/contents (accessed 19 September 2024).

Government Equalities Office (2011) Disability: Equality Act 2010. Guidance on Matters to Be Taken into Account in Determining Questions Relating to the Definition of Disability. [online] Available at: www.gov.uk/government/publications/equality-act-guidance/disability-equality-act-2010-guidance-on-matters-to-be-taken-into-account-in-determining-questions-relating-to-the-definition-of-disability-html (accessed 29 September 2024).

Institute for Apprenticeships and Technical Education (IfATE) (2024) *Learning and Skills Teacher*. [online] Available at: www.instituteforapprenticeships.org/apprenticeship-standards/learning-and-skills-teacher (accessed 29 September 2024).

Mandal, A (2023) What Is Visual Impairment? *News Medical Association*. [online] Available at: www.news-medical.net/health/What-is-visual-impairment.aspx (accessed 28 September 2024).

National Autistic Society (nd) [online] Available at: www.autism.org.uk (accessed 29 September 2024).

Ofsted (2009) *An Evaluation of National Strategy Intervention Programmes*. [online] Available at: www.dera.ioe.ac.uk/id/eprint/326/1/An%20evaluation%20of%20National%20Strategy%20intervention%20programmes.pdf (accessed 29 September 2024).

Rose, J (2009) *Identifying and Teaching Children and Young People with Dyslexia and Literacy Difficulties*. [online] Available at: www.thedyslexia-spldtrust.org.uk/media/downloads/inline/the-rose-report.1294933674.pdf (accessed 29 September 2024).

Twinkl (nd) What Is Quality First Teaching (QFT)? [online] Available at: www.twinkl.com.ph/teaching-wiki/quality-first-teaching-qft (accessed 29 September 2024).

4 The emotional health of the learner

Professional links

This chapter contributes to the following professional links:

The Diploma in Teaching mandatory content (DfE, 2024)

- 2.1 Getting to know your learners in FES.
- 2.3 Range of support needs.
- 2.7 Contemporary learning theory, neuroscience.
- 3.9 Individual support (including SEND, mental health).

Learning and Skills Teacher Occupational Standards (IfATE, 2024)

- K5 Evidence-informed inclusive teaching, learning and assessment strategies.
- K6 Strategies to engage and challenge all learners.
- K11 Barriers to learning, and ways to overcome them and adapt teaching, learning and assessment.
- S2 Identify, consider and take steps to minimise the impact of barriers to learning.
- S4 Use a variety of teaching and assessment methods depending on the learning environment and learners' needs.
- S9 Engage and inspire all learners.
- B5 Act in a manner that is ethical, fair, consistent and impartial, valuing equality, diversity and champion British values within professional boundaries.

Professional Standards (ETF, 2022)

- 1 Critically reflect on and evaluate your practices, values and beliefs to improve learner outcomes.

→

- 3 Inspire, motivate, and raise aspirations of learners by communicating high expectations and a passion for learning.
- 4 Support and develop learners' confidence, autonomy and thinking skills, taking account of their needs and starting points.
- 5 Value and champion diversity, equality of opportunity, inclusion and social equity.
- 11 Develop and apply your knowledge of special educational needs and disabilities to create inclusive learning experiences.

Chapter objectives

At the end of this chapter you will be able to:

- discuss potential causes of mental health and well-being concerns among young people;
- describe trauma-informed pedagogy, its emergence into the everyday vocabulary of teaching and its impact on classroom practice;
- identify behavioural issues such as oppositional defiant disorder (ODD) and conduct disorder (CD);
- describe a range of mental health issues found in young people including anxiety, depression, eating disorders and self-harm, along with their impact on barriers to learning;
- recognise and support young people with mental health issues;
- identify sources of suitable, commonly found support within FES settings.

Introduction

This chapter examines the diverse needs of learners with a focus on their mental and emotional health linked to current medical guidelines, including neuroscience, and pedagogical theories to assist in facilitating learning. It is split into two easy-to-follow sections, one covering the learner and the second covering the teacher/lecturer. The chapter focuses on discussing theories, information and strategies that will enable you to include these learners in your sessions.

Key definitions

So how do we define 'mental health issues' in the classroom? As a concept the term is quite complex and requires an understanding of what mental health is. The National Society for the Prevention of Cruelty to Children (NSPCC) suggests the following definition of mental health: '*mental health is an individual's cognitive, behavioural and emotional wellbeing. It's something we all have – including every child and young person*', and that the term mental health issues refers to '*mental health problems, conditions and mental illnesses. These issues may or may not be medically diagnosed*' (NSPCC, 2024).

Other definitions describe mental health issues or illness as disorders that can cause both psychological and behavioural issues with varying severity. Causes of mental health issues can be varied. While, as discussed earlier, the Covid-19 pandemic has been linked to an increase in mental health issues, causes such as substance abuse, brain injuries, infections and pre-natal damage are also factors that can have an impact. In addition, young people today have more exposure to online materials and experience more digital input than ever before. A 2021 report from the Education Policy Institute and The Prince's Trust reviewed over 5000 UK teenagers and concluded that heavy use of social media negatively impacted on their mental health. Frequent social media usage was associated with worse well-being and psychological distress scores on the survey, with findings that '*showed a significant relationship between heavy social media use at age of 14 and worse self-esteem and higher psychological distress at 17 (years of age)*', particularly among female students (Crenna-Jennings, 2021, p 38). As educators, we can only imagine what future technology and impact there will be as things such as artificial intelligence (AI) become more prevalent in society.

Section 1: the learner

Mental health concerns among further education sector learners and key definitions

The impact of the Covid-19 pandemic

Education has recently seen an increase in mental health issues among children and young people, with Kuyken (2023) identifying a large increase during the Covid-19 pandemic and subsequent lockdowns (March 2020 to December 2021). This research highlights the number of commonly diagnosed mental health illnesses among young people, and that depression rates have risen from 0.3 per cent to 8.5 per cent, social and emotional issues from 3.9 per cent to 7.5 per cent and probable/possible mental health difficulties from 4.5 per cent to 12.8 per cent.

The link between Covid-19 and the health of pupils is not unrecognised as an issue: the former head of Ofsted, Amanda Spielman, was quoted in October 2023 as saying the following post Covid-19: '*Poor behaviour and disruption in the classroom were contributing to anxiety and poor mental health among some pupils*' (Weale, 2023).

Other studies into learners' mental health as a direct result of the Covid-19 pandemic include a study by Ofsted (2020) that noted:

> *Older children have lost stamina in their reading and writing, some have lost physical fitness, others show signs of mental distress, including an increase in eating disorders and self-harm.*

A further study published by the Institute of Fiscal Studies and the Institute of Education (UCL, 2023) researched the impact of Covid-19 on children's emotional and social skills. Although it focused on young children it provides an insight into our FES learners of the future. This study suggests that 47 per cent of parents thought their children's emotional and social skills had worsened since the Covid-19 pandemic, with one example being the rise in children seeing a specialist, up from 5240 children in 2016–17 to 11,800 children in 2022–3.

A 2022 study conducted in Scotland with over 2000 college-aged learners found that over 64 per cent of participants had experienced low mental well-being, 37 per cent had experienced food insecurity (shortage of food partially due to the start of the cost of living crisis) and over 50 per cent had experienced moderate or high levels of anxiety, of which 55 per cent had hidden this from friends, family and lecturers due to fear of stigmatisation (Maguire et al, 2022). These studies suggest that the emotional and mental health of students has been affected by Covid-19 and that its legacy will filter into the FES sector for several years to come.

The specifics of a post-Covid learner

Resilience is often a word associated with emotional health issues and a desire to develop our learners' emotional health. It is hard to define resilience because as a trait it is extremely difficult to contextualise and see as a hidden character trait. The Mental Health Foundation (2023) defines resilience as '*our ability to cope with the normal stress of life as well as being able to bounce back from crises*'.

There has also been a shift in learners' skill sets in the post-Covid-19 period. Lots of research supports the emotional and mental health challenges that we have already covered within this chapter (Institute for Government, 2022; Maguire et al, 2022; Spours et al, 2022; UCL, 2023). However, we should attempt to view these changes as positive and embrace the new skill set. As Simmans (2023) notes, there are positives in the digital advances of these learners, allowing for more opportunities to showcase their adaptability. Many have become proficient in their own time management/self-motivation so should be capable of having more control over their own individualised learning plans.

However, we do have to be aware of the negative impact. If you look at the research conducted in primary and secondary schools after the pandemic, it will give you an insight into future trends for our FES sector. One such piece of research was commissioned by the Department for Education and conducted by Sheffield Hallam University/Ipsos UK on 63 senior leaders and questionnaires returned from over 1750 primary and secondary schools in the United Kingdom. This research found repeated references to well-being concerns, falling behavioural standards and a lack of social skills, with quotes from senior leaders such as '*Year 8 and Year 7 – mentally, socially, emotionally, they're still in primary. We are managing their behaviour more than their studying at the moment*' (Crossfield et al, 2023, p 43).

Table 4.1 is an extract from Department for Education lead research (DfE, 2022, p 12) which lists Covid-19 recovery challenges. It shows that pupils' emotional and mental health and well-being was a major concern for senior school leaders in 42 per cent of primary schools and 46 per cent of secondary schools. As previously mentioned, these are the FES learners of the future.

Table 4.1 *The biggest challenges schools faced in helping pupils recover their learning after the Covid-19 pandemic*

Primary		**Secondary**	
Large differences in progress between pupils	46%	Pupils' emotional and mental health and well-being	46%
Pupils' emotional and mental health and well-being	42%	Social distancing requirements	39%
School bubble closures	35%	School bubble closures	37%
Social distancing requirements	33%	Staff absences	33%
Staff absences	26%	Pupil absences	29%
Parental engagement/support	17%	Limited access to school equipment, resources or facilities	21%
Pupil absence	16%	Large differences in progress between pupils	19%
Pupil engagement	14%	Pupil behaviour	13%
Limited access to equipment/ resources/facilities	12%	Pupil engagement	12%
Pupil behaviour	8%	Parental engagement/support	8%

Source: Adapted from DfE (2022)

Other mental health concerns

Following the pandemic, we as educators are continuing see the effects of a range of mental health related issues in our classrooms. For example, behavioural issues, absenteeism, the need for counselling and therapy, and additional time for exams or coursework are all impacting staffing and resources (Patel, 2024). These effects are further corroborated by government figures for secondary school suspensions, which evidence a 37 per cent increase in permanent exclusions and a 25 per cent increase in temporary suspensions in England in 2022–23. As all young people need to be in education or employment up to the age of 18, some of these pupils will be progressing into the FES sector, bringing with them many of the challenges they faced in the school setting (Gov.UK, 2024b).

Mental health conditions

The previous section considered some of the reasons behind mental health issues. However, what may you as a teacher experience in your classroom? Table 4.2, while not exhaustive, gives an overview of some of the conditions and the symptoms that may be present in your learners.

***Table 4.2** Possible mental health issues in the classroom*

Disorder	Possible symptoms (but not limited to)
Anxiety	Fear and avoidance, irritability, difficulty concentrating, sleep disturbance, shaking and trembling.
Bipolar disorder	Extreme mood changes, depression, mania, rapid cycling from high to low, mixed state feelings, ie overactivity with a depressed mood.
Eating-related disorders: Anorexia nervosa Bulimia Orthorexia	Disrupted eating patterns, negative or obsessive thoughts about body size and shape, avoid eating in public or in front of others, vicarious pleasure in others' eating, weight fluctuations, excessively restricting foods or bingeing and purging, denial of the problem.
Depression	Sadness, loss of interest, irritation, low energy, difficulty concentrating, frequent crying, low self-esteem, alcohol and drug use, self-harm or suicidal thoughts.
Obsessive compulsive disorder (OCD)	Repetitive thoughts and actions, excessive handwashing, repetitive checking, hoarding, seeking reassurance, obsessions with symmetry or exactness.
Personality disorders	Distorted thinking and perceptions, problematic emotional responses, over- or under-regulated impulse control, difficulty functioning in social interactions and relationships.

Critical questions ?

» Read the following article '"We are all in the same storm but not in the same boat": The COVID pandemic and the Further Education Sector' (Spours et al, 2022). (This article is available from a range of online sources such as Taylor & Francis, Semantic Scholar or UCL Discovery.)

» Then consider how well you know your learners. Could your teaching benefit from more research around the individual learners to identify any potential mental health triggers and/or needs?

Discussion

Remember, not all learners are willing to disclose any concerns they have in the initial stages of a teaching programme. Extra disclosure normally occurs after the development of the initial rapport and trust between the learner and lecturer, so it would be wise to revisit your own institution's recording systems semi-regularly in case of any disclosures or updates as the year progresses.

Behaviour management

The world of behaviour management is evolving in education, so we need to focus on it and address the needs of our learners. Most learners will engage if provided with accessible learning materials and if they are interested in the content of the session. But on occasion we find some learners do not engage and that can be for a myriad of reasons, generally called 'barriers to learning'. Some of these barriers could be personal, such as not having had breakfast or having fallen out with a partner, and are specifically short term. However, there is an ever-expanding range of medical conditions that are being diagnosed that are generally grouped together as disruptive behaviour disorders (DBDs). DBDs refer to a group of behavioural and emotional problems characterised by a disregard for others and fall into three categories:

- *oppositional defiant disorders (ODD);*
- *disruptive behaviour disorders, non-specified (DBD NOS);*
- *conduct disorder (CD).*

(Nationwide Children's Hospital, 2024)

Some conduct disorders, such as attention deficit hyperactivity disorder (ADHD), are generally well known within society, but new diagnoses of disorders continue to appear. A condition that we are hearing more and more about in FES is that of oppositional defiant disorder (ODD), which is now believed to be found in 50 per cent of children with ADHD. ODD is a type of behaviour disorder which manifests as uncooperative, defiant and hostile attitudes (John Hopkins, 2024). It is considered manageable and potentially treatable, with two main theories as to why it occurs: developmental with issues surrounding independence or emotional attachment; and learnt theory via mirroring of negative reinforcement by parents or persons in position of power (John Hopkins, 2024). As an FES lecturer, you need to model best practice at all times to prevent unintended negative reinforcements as you subconsciously or consciously attempt to improve behaviour within your learning spaces.

Fundamentally, to quote Ginnis (2016, p 33) we must remember that there are differences between learners:

> *People are different, people react differently to the same circumstances, they have different likes and dislikes, they have different default behaviours, they perceive and process experiences differently.*

All of our learners will react differently. There is a saying that Neil remembers vividly from his own initial Teacher Education that his tutor told him: '*What works well for one group does not automatically work well for the next*'. We also need to remember, as quoted by Curzon and Timmons (2017, p 266), that there are numerous reasons for a reduction in behaviours. They list eight possible categories for a potential breakdown of discipline, writing before the impact of Covid-19, but the categories still remain pertinent, if not more so, in this post-Covid era given that class sizes appear to growing within all key stages, including Key Stage 5 (Weale, 2022).

Critical question ?

» How are you adapting your teaching to meet specific learners' needs? Take the time to reflect on a recent teaching session, either one delivered by you or one that you participated in. How was the session altered for the differing needs and abilities of the group to support the less able learners to achieve while at the same time pushing the more able learners to challenge and stretch them? (It might only be little adjustments like extra questions here and there or it might be more obvious, such as assigning tasks to learning support assistants in the room or providing additional harder/easy examples to work through. It all counts!)

Discussion

Conduct your own research on your area to find out how the Department for Education guidance on equality, diversity and inclusion is being addressed within your institution for learners and also, if possible, what your institution's own well-being policy is for staff for your own emotional and mental well-being.

Section 2: teacher interventions

Negative versus positive reinforcement and 'undoing' bad experiences

One of the biggest problems faced by a new teacher is getting to know your learners so that they feel able to be open with you. Relatively new research conducted by Mind UK (2024) shows that nearly two-thirds of people (64 per cent) '*put on a brave face*' to avoid talking about their mental health. This behaviour is more common among younger age groups, with

69 per cent of 16–24 year-olds using the tactic of '*bottling it up*', and it is this 'bottling up' that makes the lecturer role harder because without knowing the learner we cannot adapt sessions or topics which may act as triggers.

Government data shows that half of mental health disorders start before the age of 14, raising to 75 per cent by the age of 24 years, so while some learners enter our sector 'diagnosed', a further 25 per cent do not emerge until they are within our sector with emotional disorders, particularly anxiety and depression (Local Government Association, 2024). There are also specific anxieties linked directly to academic experiences, such as maths anxiety, whereby the thought of having to do maths can lead to physical symptoms of anxiety and those affected make a concerted effort to avoid situations where maths is required (National Numeracy Organisation, 2024). With the previous government's drive to improve literacy and numeracy among the UK population, compulsory GCSEs in English and maths until passed (or you leave FES), alongside their proposals for the new Advanced British Standard (Gov.uk, 2023a) that all FES learners must study maths and English to level 3, will only add to these anxiety triggers in the future if the new government continues with these proposals.

Anxiety can take many forms, from eating disorders such as anorexia, bulimia or binge eating disorder through to depression, which can be mild or severe. Bould et al (2017), in a study published in the *British Medical Journal*, define eating disorders as '*a group of conditions in which negative beliefs about eating, body shape, and weight accompany behaviours including restricting eating, binge eating, excessive exercise, vomiting, and laxative use*' (p 359). Bould et al also state that eating disorders are particularly common among adolescent girls, although they can also occur in boys and men.

There are an estimated 1.25 million people in the United Kingdom with eating disorders, and a disproportionate amount of those are under 25. Eating disorders are also commonly associated with other mental conditions such as anxiety or depression. Before the Covid-19 pandemic there had been a steady increase over the previous five years of those starting treatment, but that number spiralled from 8030 in 2019–20 to 12,460 in 2021–2. This is believed to be a direct result of the Covid-19 pandemic on the mental health of young people, with a further 80 per cent increase in those hospitalised, up from 13,200 in 2015–16 to 24,300 in 2020–1 (Children's Commissioner, 2023). It should also be noted that this is the number of people starting treatment; those unidentified or not starting formal treatment are not counted. As an FES teacher, it is paramount that you are aware of symptoms and changes in your students' behaviours to try to identify student concerns such as these within the cohorts you educate.

Trauma-informed pedagogy linked to adaptive teaching

According to *The SENCO Handbook*, a traumatic event is defined as

> *one that threatens injury, death or the physical integrity of self or other and also causes horror, terror or helplessness at the time it occurs. Traumatic events can include sexual abuse, physical abuse, domestic violence, community or*

> *school violence, medical trauma, motor vehicle accidents, acts of terrorism, war experiences, natural and human-made disasters, suicides and other traumatic issues.*
>
> (Martin-Denham and Watts, 2019, p 98)

As this definition is so wide it is quite hard to envision an FES class of up to 30 learners that will not have an affected pupil within it. A recent study of adults by the Office for National Statistics (2020) found that one in five people aged 18–79 years had experienced some form of abuse prior to the age of 16, while the 15–17 year-old age group, if they had suffered some form of abuse themselves, were most likely to then demonstrate/copy this behaviour themselves (Safer Lives, 2014). Governmental research also shows that in the UK, children who have been in care achieve poorer educational outcomes compared to those who have not been, along with one in ten pupils in 2021–2 (the latest available statistics) being identified by the government as being in need (Gov.UK, 2023b).

Adaptive teaching is a current buzzword in all aspects of teaching. In primary and secondary education, Professional Standard 5 covers '*adapting teaching to respond to the strengths and needs of all pupils*' (DfE, 2021), while Professional Standard 15 covers this in the FES Professional Standards (ETF, 2022). Adaptive teaching benefits are integral within its principles and are covered in the following extracts taken from the government's Initial Teacher Training and Early Career Framework. Although aimed at the primary and secondary sectors, it is increasingly used as a guidance document within the FES sector as the teacher/lecturer shortage continues to take effect, in order to make the FES sector as appealing as possible to all who might consider it (Gov.UK, 2024a):

- Provide opportunity to all pupils to experience success, including by maintaining high expectations for all, balancing input of new content (to prevent cognitive overload) so that learners master important concepts.
- Meet individual needs without creating unnecessary workload including making use of well-designed resources, building on pupils' previous knowledge, etc.
- Group pupils effectively (where possible) by applying high expectations to all groups.

Therefore, when planning sessions, we have moved substantially away from the '*all must, most should, some could*' style learning outcomes, which have been evidenced to create three pathways within a session for a cohort of 30 different learners rather than treating all learners as individuals and adapting the session to their specific needs (Eaton, 2022). A good short guide on understanding adaptive teaching has been created by Education Southwest (2023), a primary, secondary and FES trust partnership (see Table 4.3).

Table 4.3 *Understanding adaptive teaching*

Provide a measurable and challenging learning outcome and chunk the progress towards that outcome.	
Anticipate barriers • Different levels of prior knowledge. • Vocabulary. • A particular production skill such as writing. • A particular SEND. • Decoding written text. • Limited working memory. • Cultural experiences. • English as second/additional language. • A common misconception. • A lack of metacognitive knowledge. • Inherent complexity of resources/information.	Plan to address them • Read a text in advance. • Supply background knowledge. • Use pictures/video to contextualise upcoming information. • Teach relevant vocabulary, do not assume knowledge. • Introduce a concept via discussion. • Teach necessary learning behaviours. • Improve accessibility for all learners. • Plan to scaffold, with plans to reduce as learning occurs. • Produce a model to share. • Plan targeted support from TA/LSA/LSPs.
Assessment information informs subsequent planning and in-the-moment adaptations. • Other considerations. • How will you monitor responses? • Does the assessment method itself create barriers?	Use assessment to elicit evidence of learning • Questioning. • Tests. • Production tasks, eg writing, setting up experiments, painting, performing. • Talk. • Hinge questions. • Labelling diagrams. • Answers on sticky notes or mini-whiteboards etc.
Examples of in-the-moment adaptations • Adjust the level of challenge.	• Elicit via questions. • Allocate temporary groups to provide an additional scaffold.

→

Table 4.3 (*Cont.*)

• Change your language. • Clarify task or provide steps. • Clarify what 'good' looks like. • Highlight essential content. • Re-explain a concept or explain it in a different way. • Give additional (or revisit) examples and non-examples. • Use peer tutoring.	• Use assessment as a teaching method. • Use an analogy. • Set an intermediate goal. • Provide a prompt. • Structure a group attempt before an individual attempt. • Improve accessibility, eg proximity to teacher, visibility of whiteboard, read a text to the student.

Source: Adapted from Education South West, *Understanding Adaptive Teaching* V11 (2023)

Critical question

» Reflecting on your recent teaching, how could you have adapted your teaching to consider the emotional health of your learners?

Discussion

Make a point of reading/listening to the regional news, and then reflect on what news items could be impacting on your learners (eg floods, house fires, road traffic collisions, cost of living crisis, etc). You also need to remember that these traumatic incidents can happen at a point before or during the learners' FES journey. The ones on the news are the tip of the incidents that have been made public. Reflect and research other forms of trauma that may be affecting your learner cohorts.

CASE STUDY

A fellow trainee who is employed as a teacher in the FES sector has been given a regular timetable addition of a new cohort of level 2 learners. They are having problems getting the cohort to focus and work throughout the one-hour session, so they have come to you for advice as the low-level behaviour of a few individuals within the group is disrupting the learning of others. They have spoken to other teachers who have the same group and been told that those teachers have the same problem, but that they see it as '*there is always one or two problem learners in every group*' so they have not adapted anything they are doing. Your fellow trainee has tried behaviour controlling strategies and now feels that the issues encountered are down to the emotional health of the odd learner(s) that was not disclosed upon enrolment and has remained 'hidden' until now. They are at a loss of what to do now.

Critical questions ?

» What could you say or do to support your colleague?

» What research could you provide to your colleague to support them, with a focus on the emotional needs of their learners?

Emerging sector considerations

The FES landscape, as with any educational sector, is particularly dynamic and this is set to continue. The recommendations of the Lord Sainsbury report into technical education (Gatsby, 2016) recommended a simplification of qualifications within the post-16 landscape and led to a government post-16 skills plan (Gov.UK, 2018).

This review has led to several qualifications within the FES sector, particularly in FES colleges, with some awarding bodies moving from coursework-only models to having key modules with exams that are independently set and moderated as per GCSE or A level qualifications. The introduction of these exams and the additional externally moderated component of the new T levels could adversely affect learners with emotional or additional needs – the externally set and marked work 'caps' grades on the overall qualification, which means a poor result in this work could affect the overall outcome grade learners receive.

In addition, the T levels contain 45 days or 20 per cent of time on a placement with an employer (T levels website, nd) which could create an additional challenge for our learners and their needs. Before this change is completed, there is also talk of introducing another national-level qualification, the 'Advanced British Standard', which would focus on major and minor qualifications but must include English and maths. This may contribute further to learner and teacher anxiety as more changes appear to be forthcoming.

Signposting to learner services

Learner support services are paramount in an educational setting, and as a trainee or newly qualified teacher you should automatically receive safeguarding training on what to do if your learners need support. As a rule, anyone can make a safeguarding referral and it is critical that you are aware of your establishment's safeguarding points of contact. As well as referring learners, they are there to help and support you to find the best support for your learners. Most FES colleges have incredible pastoral support, such as an allocated pastoral tutor, an on-site or online counsellor, or a school or college chaplain (who is normally multi-faith). The learner services department also covers a range of housing, financial and other support needs, as well as being able to access and signpost to more pertinent external forms of support such as national charities or the local government support department. In short, help is always available and on call. Your role as a trainee or new teacher is to know your local point of contact, rather than having to know everything. They can then take over and assist you or the learner directly on how to move forward with your concern.

Summary

This chapter reviewed the emotional and mental health of learners, highlighting their visible and invisible additional needs. The only way you can truly understand your learners is by talking to them.

You may be provided with learner records from previous schools or tutors as they come to your classes, but FES learners have become robust in developing their own coping strategies, some of which go unnoticed. Without the rapport and mutual respect between learners and lecturers to physically hold discussions on these sometimes-awkward topics, you might never know how best to support your learners to empower and enable them to fully develop and achieve the best they can.

Achieving the best they can while in FES prepares them for their next steps into employment or further study. These discussions can also open up a world of support structures and networks that the learners can access throughout their lives as they make valuable contributions to the communities and societies that they are part of.

In addition, learner completion and success of their programmes of study are quantifiable measurements that our regulatory inspection bodies also want evidence of. Therefore, these conversations not only help the learners but also the educational establishment they belong to and so are of benefit to all involved.

Check your understanding (level 5)

1. What are the three main categories of disruptive behaviour disorders?
2. What percentage of mental health disorders start before 24 years of age?

3. What are the three main categories of eating disorders?
4. What routes are there within your educational placement or establishment to refer learners if you have safeguarding concerns?

Developmental questions L6+7

1. Before it is needed, take some to think how you would approach a learner who you suspect might have undisclosed emotional or mental health needs.
2. Revisit your teaching groups if in employment or placement. Then research further how you can adapt your sessions or delivery to take into consideration disclosed or undisclosed emotional or mental health needs.

Helpful websites and resources

- Mind – https://mind.org.uk
- Mental Health Foundation – https://mentalhealth.org.uk/explore-mental-health/factors-affect-mental-health
- National Health Service – www.nhs.uk/mental-health/advice-for-life-situations-and-events/how-to-help-someone-with-eating-disorder/

References

Bould, H, Newbegin, C, Stewart, A, Stein, A and Fazel, M (2017) Eating Disorders in Children and Young People. *British Medical Journal*, 5245: 359.

Children's Commissioner (2023) Young People with Eating Disorders in England on the Rise. [online] Available at: www.childrenscommissioner.gov.uk/blog/young-people-with-eating-disorders-in-england-on-the-rise (accessed 29 September 2024).

Crenna-Jennings, W (2021) *Young People's Mental and Emotional Health – Trajectories and Drivers in Childhood and Adolescence*. [online] Available at: https://epi.org.uk/wp-content/uploads/2021/01/EPI-PT_Young-people%E2%80%99s-wellbeing_Jan2021.pdf (accessed 29 September 2024).

Crossfield, J, Behailu, A, Stiell, B, Willis, B, Rutgers, D, Clarkson, L, McCaig, C, Ramaiah, B and Hallgarten, J (2023) *School Recovery Strategies: Year 2 Findings*. [online] Available at: https://assets.publishing.service.gov.uk/government/uploads/system/uploads/attachment_data/file/1131182/School_recovery_strategies_year_2_findings.pdf (accessed 29 September 2024).

Curson, L and Tummons, J (2017) *Teaching in Further Education: An Outline of Principles and Practice*. London: Bloomsbury.

Department for Education (DfE) (2021) *Teacher's Standards*. [online] Available at: https://assets.publishing.service.gov.uk/media/5a750668ed915d3c7d529cad/Teachers_standard_information.pdf (accessed 29 September 2024).

Department for Education (DfE) (2022) *School Recovery Strategies: Year 1 Findings*. [online] Available at: https://assets.publishing.service.gov.uk/government/uploads/system/uploads/attachment_data/file/1131182/School_recovery_strategies_year_2_findings.pdf (accessed 29 September 2024).

Department for Education (DfE) (2024) Diploma in Teaching (Further Education and Skills) qualification framework. [online] Available at: www.gov.uk/government/publications/further-education-initial-teacher-education/diploma-in-teaching-further-education-and-skills-qualification-framework (accessed 8 October 2024).

Eaton, J (2022) Moving from 'Differentiation' to 'Adaptive Teaching'. *Education Endowment Blog*, 19 October. [online] Available at: www.educationendowmentfoundation.org.uk/news/moving-from-differentation-to-adaptive-teaching (accessed 29 September 2024).

Education and Training Foundation (ETF) (2022) *Professional Standards for Teachers and Trainers*. [online] Available at: www.et-foundation.co.uk/professionalstandards (accessed 29 September 2024).

Education South West (2023) *Understanding Adaptive Teaching V11*. [online] Available at: https://d2tic4wvo1iusb.cloudfront.net/documents/Understanding-Adaptive-Teaching-v11.pdf?v=1680201249 (accessed 29 September 2024).

Gatsby Foundation (2016) *Report of the Independent Panel on Technical Education*. [online] Available at: www.gatsby.org.uk/uploads/education/reports/pdf/report-of-the-independent-panel-on-technical-education.pdf (accessed 29 September 2024).

Ginnis, P (2016) *The Teacher's Toolkit: Raising Classroom Achievement with Strategies for Every Learner*. Carmarthen: Crown Publishing.

Gov.UK (2018) *Post-16 Skills Plan and Independent Report on Technical Education*. [online] Available at: www.gov.uk/government/publications/post-16-skills-plan-and-independent-report-on-technical-education (accessed 29 September 2024).

Gov.UK (2023a) *A World-Class Education System – The Advanced British Standard*. [online] Available at: www.gov.uk/government/publications/a-world-class-education-system-the-advanced-british-standard (accessed 29 September 2024).

Gov.UK (2023b) *Outcomes for Children in Need, Including Children Looked After by Local Authorities in England*. [online] Available at: www.explore-education-statistics.service.gov.uk/find-statistics/outcomes-for-children-in-need-including-children-looked-after-by-local-authorities-in-england (accessed 29 September 2024).

Gov.UK (2024a) *Initial Teacher Training and Early Career Framework – January 2024*. [online] Available at: www.gov.uk/government/publications/initial-teacher-training-and-early-career-framework (accessed 29 September 2024).

Gov.UK (2024b) *Suspension and Permanent Exclusions in England*. [online] Available at: https://explore-education-statistics.service.gov.uk/find-statistics/suspensions-and-permanent-exclusions-in-england/2019-20 (accessed 29 September 2024).

Institute for Apprenticeships and Technical Education (IfATE) (2024) *Learning and Skills Teacher*. [online] Available at: www.instituteforapprenticeships.org/apprenticeship-standards/learning-and-skills-teacher (accessed 29 September 2024).

Institute for Government (2022) Timeline of UK Government Coronavirus Lockdown and Restrictions. [online] Available at: www.instituteforgovernment.org.uk/data-visualisation/timeline-coronavirus-lockdowns (accessed 29 September 2024).

John Hopkins Medicine (2024) Oppositional Defiant Disorder (ODD) in Children. [online] Available at: www.hopkinsmedicine.org/health/conditions-and-diseases/oppositional-defiant-disorder (accessed 9 October 2024).

Kuyken, W (2023) *Young People's Mental Health Deteriorated at Greater Rate During the Pandemic*. [online] Available at: www.ox.ac.uk/news/2023-09-21-young-people-s-mental-health-deteriorated-greater-rate-during-pandemic (accessed 29 September 2024).

Local Government Association (2024) *Children and Young People's Emotional Wellbeing and Mental Health – Facts and Figures*. [online] Available at: www.local.gov.uk/topics/children-and-young-people/children-and-young-peoples-mental-health (accessed 29 September 2024).

Maguire, C, Cameron, J, Cherman, V and Solomon, S (2022) *Thriving Learners: Initial Findings from Scottish Colleges*. [online] Available at: www.mentalhealth.org.uk/sites/default/files/2022-11/MHF_Thriving_Learners_Report.pdf (accessed 29 September 2024).

Martin-Denham, S and Watts, S (2019) *The SENCO Handbook: Leading Provision and Practice*. London: Corwin/Sage.

Mental Health Foundation (2023) *Resilience Across the UK During the Coronavirus Pandemic*. [online] Available at: www.mentalhealth.org.uk/our-work/research/resilience-across-uk-during-coronavirus-pandemic (accessed 29 September 2024).

Mind UK (2024) UK Hiding Behind a 'Brave Face' to Avoid Speaking About Mental Health. [online] Available at: www.mind.org.uk/news-campaigns/news/uk-hiding-behind-a-brave-face-to-avoid-speaking-about-mental-health (accessed 29 September 2024).

National Numeracy Organisation (2024) What Is Maths Anxiety? [online] Available at: www.nationalnumeracy.org.uk/what-issue/about-maths-anxiety (accessed 29 September 2024).

National Society for the Prevention of Cruelty to Children (NSPCC) (2024) *Child Mental Health: Recognising and Responding to Issues*. [online] Available at: https://learning.nspcc.org.uk/child-health-development/child-mental-health (accessed 29 September 2024).

Nationwide Children's Hospital (2024) Disruptive Behaviour Disorders. [online] Available at: www.nationwidechildrens.org/conditions/disruptive-behavior-disorders (accessed 29 September 2024).

Office for National Statistics (2020) Child Abuse in England and Wales, January 2020. [online] Available at: www.ons.gov.uk/peoplepopulationandcommunity/crimeandjustice/bulletins/childabuseinenglandandwales/january2020 (accessed 29 September 2024).

Ofsted (2020) *Children Hardest Hit by Covid Pandemic Are Regressing in Basic Skills and Learning*. [online] Available at: www.gov.uk/government/news/ofsted-children-hardest-hit-by-covid-19-pandemic-are-regressing-in-basic-skills-and-learning (accessed 29 September 2024).

Patel, A (2024) *Special Exam Requests Soar in Colleges*. [online] Available at: https://feweek.co.uk/special-exam-requests-soar-in-colleges (accessed 29 September 2024).

Safer Lives (2014) *In Plain Sight: The Evidence from Children Exposed to Domestic Abuse*. [online] Available at: www.safelives.org.uk/research-policy-library/in-plain-sight (accessed 29 September 2024).

Simmans, C (2023) *We Must Redefine Post-Covid Learners to Embrace and Celebrate Their Skills: Too Much of Our Post-Covid Narrative Is About What the Learners Have Lost Rather Than What They Have Gained*. [online] Available at: https://feweek.co.uk/we-must-redefine-post-covid-learners-to-embrace-and-celebrate-their-skills (accessed 29 September 2024).

Spours, K, Grainger, P and Vigurs, C (2022) 'We Are All in the Same Storm but Not in the Same Boat': The COVID Pandemic and the Further Education Sector. *Journal of Education and Work*, 35(8): 782–97.

T Levels website (nd) About T Levels. [online] Available at: www.tlevels.gov.uk/students/about (accessed 29 September 2024).

University College London (UCL) (2023) Half of Pupils Saw Social Skills Decline During Covid, Study Finds – Policy Makers Warn Pandemic Impact Stretches Beyond the Classroom. [online] Available at: https://schoolsweek.co.uk/half-of-pupils-saw-social-skills-decline-during-covid-study-finds (accessed 29 September 2024).

Weale, S (2022) Bigger Class Sizes Harming Pupils' Progress: Say 9 in 10 Teachers. *The Guardian*, 17 April. [online] Available at: www.theguardian.com/education/2022/apr/17/bigger-classes-harming-pupils-progress-say-9-in-10-uk-teachers (accessed 29 September 2024).

Weale, S (2023) Disruptive Behaviour in English Schools Worse Since Covid, Says Outgoing Ofsted Head. *The Guardian*, 6 October. [online] Available at: www.theguardian.com/education/2023/oct/06/disruptive-behaviour-in-english-schools-worse-since-covid-says-outgoing-ofsted-head (accessed 29 September 2024).

5 The learning process

Professional links

This chapter contributes to the following professional links:

The Diploma in Teaching mandatory content (DfE, 2024)

- 2.8 Role and currency of research and evidence.
- 2.9 Application of theory to practice.
- 2.10 Encouraging learners to be independent and aim high.
- 4.10 Application of evidence-based methods.

Learning and Skills Teacher Occupational Standards (IfATE, 2024)

- K1 The pedagogical theory and how to apply this theory to practice.
- K5 Evidence-informed inclusive teaching, learning and assessment strategies.
- K8 Techniques to involve learners in taking ownership of their own progress.
- S1 Integrate subject and pedagogic research into teaching activity to enhance teaching and support changes of practice.
- S5 Encourage learners to set challenging goals.
- S8 Design and use resources that are inclusive and add value to learners' development.
- B2 Underpin their practice by reference to professional standards and evidence-based teaching and learning.

Professional Standards (ETF, 2022)

- 3 Inspire, motivate, and raise aspirations of learners by communicating high expectations and a passion for learning.
- 9 Critically review and apply your knowledge of educational research, pedagogy, and assessment to develop evidence-informed practice.
- 14 Apply motivational, coaching and skill development strategies to help learners progress and achieve.

Chapter objectives ◎

At the end of this chapter you will be able to:

- an introduction to the complexity of conceptualising learning;
- key principles from foundational and contemporary theories of learning;
- the role of neuroscience in supporting teaching practice;
- common misconceptions about the findings of neuroscience research and their impact on teaching practice.

Introduction

Learning is a complex and dynamic process through which individuals acquire new knowledge, skills, attitudes or behaviours. Traditionally the learning process followed the four fundamental theories of learning: behaviourism, focusing on observable behaviours and the responses to environmental stimuli; cognitivism, emphasising internal mental processes such as thinking, memory and problem-solving; constructivism, suggesting how learners construct their own understanding and knowledge through experiences and reflecting on those experiences; and social learning theory, the proposition that learning occurs through observation, imitation, and modelling.

This chapter examines some of the more contemporary theories of learning and discuss how neuroscience and evidence-based and evidenced-informed research can support teaching practice, with examples to support you in the classroom, together with a critique of some of the more 'outdated' theories.

Activity ?

» Think about a time that you have learnt something. What did you learn and how did you learn it?

What is learning?

Some of the learning experiences which you might have considered include learning a skill (eg riding a bike), acquisition of knowledge (eg capital city of Italy) or a change in perspective or attitude (eg political preference). Some of the ways in which you might have learnt the skill or knowledge include discussions, observation, practice and responding to feedback. The purpose of this brief activity is to introduce you to the idea that learning is a broad concept, which is reflected in how academic attempts to define and characterise it continue to '*vary wildly*' (Barron et al, 2015, p 405) despite some recognised attempts as early as the Greek philosophers Aristotle and Plato.

Some of the complexity in conceptualising learning can be attributed to the range of disciplines to which it is of interest (eg education, psychology, neuroscience) because each discipline has a particular focus (or lens) through which it studies learning. For example, a large focus within neuroscience is the study of the structure and anatomy of the brain and, as such, learning is considered in terms of how it impacts/is impacted by those aspects of the brain. Not only is there inter-disciplinary disagreement in the way learning is understood and conceptualised but disagreement also prevails within disciplines (ie intra-disciplinary). Psychology provides a great illustration of intra-disciplinary disagreement; cognitive psychologists focus on the role of perception and information processing (ie organising, storing, retrieving) in learning, whereas social psychologists consider learning with a focus on interactions between people. The different perspectives, or lenses, that disciplines adopt to explore learning bring value to developing a holistic understanding. However, they are not helpful in creating a coherent understanding of the concept.

Despite the complexity in attempts to conceptualise and understand learning, there is some consensus that learning can be said to have occurred when there are long-term potential changes in the behaviour, skills, knowledge or attitudes of an individual which result from an experience. Brown et al (2014, p 2) provide the following broadly typical definition of learning: '*acquiring knowledge and skills and having them readily available from memory so you can make sense of future problems and opportunities*'.

Contemporary theories of learning

As discussed in more detail in Chapter 13, policymakers (ie government) are encouraging teachers to use evidence sourced through robust research (often externally produced through higher education institutions) in conjunction with other forms of knowledge to guide and inform their practice. This is commonly labelled as a drive towards evidence-informed education, and the argument is that use of research to inform teaching practice will enhance the quality of a teacher's practice and therefore student achievement will improve. Teacher support for this idea is quite consistent, with teachers commonly reporting that they value the role of research in guiding their practice (eg Coldwell et al, 2017; Nelson et al, 2017). However, support among academics for the drive towards evidence-informed education is less consistent (see Hammersley (2005) and Slavin (2002) for a comprehensive discussion). Academics' hesitancy is attributable to the problems and assumptions associated with this seemingly simplistic notion (further discussed in Chapter 13) but, for now, it is sufficient to note that '*evidence is a contested term and the relationship between research and practice is complex*' (Coldwell et al, 2017, p 19).

In 2024, the Department for Education published a document, *Expectations for the Delivery of Initial Teacher Education for FE*, stating a need for trainee teachers to understand '*how students learn*' through an understanding of '*the central evidence-based concepts that underpin effective teaching practice*'. Further evidence of the need for teachers to understand the evidence base around 'how students learn' can be seen in the ETF (2022) Professional Standards, the Diploma in Teaching mandatory content (ETF, 2023), and the Learning and Skills Teacher Occupational Standards (IfATE, 2024) listed at the outset of this chapter.

This requirement of teacher training programmes within FES is arguably somewhat overdue because the need for teachers within primary and secondary school settings to understand evidence-based principles of 'how pupils learn' forms a substantial part of the Core Content Framework for ITT (DfE, 2019).

One of the ways in which research can support teachers in their practice is through the construction of theory. Theories are abundant within the educational literature, and they often consist of a set of principles which collectively provide a perspective, account or explanation on an issue. The issue, in education, can relate to a teacher's practice in more direct (eg how students learn) or less direct (eg broader purpose of education) ways. The latter tend to be concerned with the education context in which practice takes place, thereby still potentially influencing a teacher's practice, albeit more distantly. In this chapter, we are interested in theories which provide an explanation of the learning process (ie 'theories of learning'); that is, how students absorb, process and retain knowledge. Teachers can use these theories to:

- increase the number of strategies available at their disposal;
- critique and validate current and previous practice;
- plan changes to practice with the goal of achieving specific pedagogical objectives;
- evaluate the effectiveness of their new practice/changed practice.

Within the relevant literature, there are broadly four seminal theories of learning which have been discussed comprehensively across teacher textbooks (see Bates (2019) for a concise discussion): behaviourism, cognitivism, constructivism and humanism. In practice, teachers combine these theories by incorporating principles of each at different times and in different situations that arise within the classroom.

The role of neuroscience in supporting teaching practice

Most commonly, it is educational research that teachers most commonly use to inform their practice, but this chapter considers the role of other disciplines, namely neuroscience, in creating useful knowledge that teachers can use to support their practice. We also consider the impact of teachers implementing commonly held misconceptions about the relationship between well-established neuroscience research findings and learning; in line with the relevant literature, these will be referred to as 'neuromyths'.

Some commentators argue that teachers need to better understand brain systems and processes involved in learning under the premise that this will support teachers' understanding of 'how students learn' and therefore enable the development of optimal teaching practices (Howard-Jones et al, 2020). This relatively recent area of study is commonly labelled 'educational neuroscience', but it is receiving varying degrees of support. Howard-Jones (2007) found that teachers reported being enthusiastic about the use of neuroscience findings to influence teaching practice to the extent that they would be more likely to influence their teaching methodology than curriculum content. However, the views of academics are more mixed; for example, Davis (2004) posits that 'learning states' are not those which are easily explorable through brain activity, while Bruer (2007, p 4) argues that a direct link between neuroscience and education is a '*bridge too far*'.

Evidence-based principles of learning derived from cognitive neuroscience

This section is split into five sub-sections; each subsection focuses on a principle of learning derived from cognitive neuroscience which has a robust evidence base that teachers can (and should) incorporate into their practice to enhance learning.

Chunking

Chunking is a strategy that can be used to break down large pieces of information into smaller, more manageable bits. As a strategy it can help learners process and remember information more easily. Table 5.1 provides some details about how it may help.

Table 5.1 *How chunking helps memory*

Improves memory	By chunking we are aligning learning with how our brains store and process information, which leads to better retention and recall.
Reduces cognitive load	Smaller chunks can be less overwhelming and therefore reduce cognitive load.
Enhances learning	It breaks down complex ideas into simpler parts, helping learners to grasp concepts quicker.
E- learning	In e-learning, chunking can make the 'bite-size' parts more engaging.

Activity ?

» In your teaching, how could you use chunking as a strategy effectively?

Discussion

You could have suggested the following.

- Dividing your course material into smaller, logical sections, with each chunk covering a single topic or concept.
- Use of headings and subheadings to organise your content. This helps learners quickly identify and navigate through different sections.
- Incorporate multimedia such as videos, images and infographics to complement text-based content. Multimedia can serve to chunk the information in a way that makes it more engaging and easier to digest.

→

- Be consistent with each chunk. For instance, start with an introduction, followed by the main content, and end with a summary or key takeaways.
- Avoid overwhelming learners with too much information at once. Aim for brevity and clarity, ensuring that each chunk is concise and focused.
- Provide summaries at the end of each chunk to reinforce the main ideas.

Cognitive load theory

Cognitive load theory (CLT) (Sweller, 1988) suggests that our working (ie short-term) memory is only able to process a small amount of information at any one time, yet it is responsible for processing information from our various senses simultaneously, and they are constantly receiving input. Consequently, our working memory must be highly selective as to which sensory input (ie information) it attends to and processes further. Input not meeting the threshold for further attention is lost.

Activity ?

» Think about a lesson where you, as a student, found the subject matter so complex that it was hard to grasp.

Discussion

CLT goes some way to explaining why that might have happened. It is an instructional framework that focuses on avoiding overloading the working memory by optimising the way information is presented to learners to enhance their understanding, retention and subsequent achievement. If the working memory is overloaded, then potentially important information being received can be lost thereby negatively affecting student achievement.

Working memory has a maximum duration of about 20 seconds and an ability to hold roughly seven chunks of information (Miller, 1956), with a maximum concurrent processing (eg organising, contrasting, comparing) limit of two to four chunks of information.

CLT identifies three types of cognitive load.

1. Intrinsic load: The inherent difficulty of the material and tasks.
2. Extraneous load: Unnecessary information or activities, such as noise or irrelevant activity or stimuli.

3. Germane load: The cognitive effort required to process, understand and assimilate new material with existing schemata (ie clusters of information).

Cognitive overload occurs when the combination of intrinsic, extraneous and germane load becomes overwhelming for the learner and results in difficulty processing new information.

The following instructional strategies can be implemented to optimise the loads placed on learners during learning periods.

- **Reduce extraneous load:** Simplify the presentation of information to avoid unnecessary complexity. Ensure clarity in verbal delivery, learning materials and tasks. Lack of clarity in instruction puts too high a load on the working memory, and so too much time is spent problem-solving the instructions as opposed to new schema formation. For example, lessons that use PowerPoint with excessive writing and the teacher talking at the same time can inadvertently generate excessive cognitive load and lead to working memory failures. (Chandler and Sweller, 1991).
- **Manage intrinsic load:** Break down complex information into smaller, manageable chunks. Sequencing – presenting parts of a concept in sequence – can reduce the intrinsic load of the whole (van Merriënboer et al, 2006). However, this only works with certain types of content. Chunking – breaking content down into smaller yet still meaningful units – can help reduce this load.
- **Increase germane load:** Use techniques like worked examples, scaffolding and practice to help learners process and understand the material. Reflection – reflecting on a concept and connecting new content with past experiences – can assist with the creation of more complex schemas. Interleaving – presenting similar but distinct concepts, terms or principles together – can assist with discrimination learning and thereby avoid the construction of incorrect schemas (Rohrer, 2012). Worked examples – providing explanations with solutions – can help with the creation of schema, particularly with novice learners

Activating students' prior knowledge before sharing new information with them has also been found to be beneficial in managing working memory limitations. By retrieving relevant knowledge from a student's long-term memory, students can bring crucial information to their working memory, which better enables assimilation of new information to build upon what they already know. Activating student prior knowledge is an evidence-based teaching strategy (see Marzano et al (2000) for a comprehensive discussion). By applying the aforementioned techniques, teachers can create more effective learning environments that help students grasp and retain new information more efficiently.

Dual coding

Dual coding theory can be traced back to the practical use of images to aid memory but, largely owing to the work of Paivio 1960–80, it has evolved into a theory that explains how we process and encode sensory information into our memory. Several dual coding strategies, discussed later in this section, have subsequently been constructed to balance the influx of sensory information and optimise utilisation of the working memory.

Dual coding theory assumes that our working memory entails two internal cognitive processing systems: a verbal system that processes linguistic (ie language) information and a non-verbal system that processes non-linguistic (eg images) information. Beyond the collective capacity issues within our working memory, each of the aforementioned cognitive systems has individual capacity limits. As such, overloading information through one modality (eg verbal) can overwhelm that 'channel' and leave others (eg visual) under-utilised. Paivio and Beggs (1971) theorised that linguistic input forms cognitive structures in the verbal system, while non-verbal input forms cognitive structures in the non-verbal system. Although these systems are independent, they work in parallel and are interconnected, meaning that information from those inputs can be processed simultaneously. Engaging both cognitive systems enables information to be processed more thoroughly and alleviates some limitations around the capacity of the working memory.

Think of a motorway as representing a student's working memory, with each lane representing a sensory input. There are a limited number of cars that can fit on it without causing a traffic jam. Dual coding lets us make use of all available lanes and there are ways to widen these lanes. For example, student prior knowledge can impact these lanes; those with more prior knowledge can usually make sense of a wider range of lesson content representations (eg vocabulary, visual cues).

You can make use of dual coding theory in the classroom by essentially combining lingual and non-lingual learning materials during lessons. Most commonly, this is likely to involve supplementing verbal content delivery with visual representations (eg diagrams, concept maps, timelines). Alternatively, you could facilitate student discussions around a visual resource or ask students to manipulate objects or materials while receiving verbal instruction. Importantly, students must understand the relationship between the lingual and non-lingual learning materials they are exposed to. This understanding does not happen haphazardly and, although particular visuals often align better with particular subjects (eg diagrams to represent concepts of biology), careful and deliberate teacher planning is essential.

A common query from trainee teachers is around how different dual coding is from learning styles (to be discussed later in this chapter). Essentially, they differ in that the former relates to how the brain processes information, while the latter relates to student preferences about how they learn best. Cuevas and Dawson (2018) compared the effectiveness of implementing principles of learning styles versus dual coding on 204 university students' ability to process and retain visual and auditory information. Participants' preferred learning style had no relationship with the amount of information retained, regardless of whether information was presented in ways which align with their preferred learning style or not. However, strongly supporting dual coding theory, those in the visual and audio condition retained twice as much information as those in the audio-only condition. Similarly supportive findings for dual coding theory have been obtained beyond knowledge retention, including on knowledge acquisition (Schnotz, 2012), topic understanding (Dogomeo and Aliazas, 2022) and literary comprehension (Smith and Weinstein, 2016).

Spaced learning

The spaced learning principle states that learning will be more effective if it happens in four 15-minute learning periods separated by breaks rather than condensed into a single 60-minute period, for example. Spaced learning is usually pitted in research against massed practice; spaced learning entails the allocated learning time being split across an extended period, whereas massed (or blocked) learning involves condensing allocated learning time into fewer, prolonged learning periods. A classic application of this can be seen in student approaches to revision; the spaced learning hypothesis contends that revision will be more effective if spaced over an extended pre-exam period (eg 15-minutes per day for four days prior to an exam) rather than condensing it into a single slot (eg a solid 60-minute revision period on the day before an exam).

This principle originates in the work of German psychologist Herman Ebbinghaus in the late 1800s and his experimental work on human memory. Essentially, he found that rehearsing information slowed down the rate at which memory of the information decayed (ie was forgotten). According to Donovan and Radosevich (1999, p 795), spacing learning has since become '*one of the most strongly accepted ideas within task performance and learning literatures*'. Vlach and Sandhofer (2012, p 1138) reinforce this, suggesting that '*the spacing effect is arguably the most replicable and robust finding from experimental psychology*'.

Understanding how the spacing effect works requires a brief and simplified look into how memory works. When information is learned (eg the start date of the Second World War), a memory is encoded into the brain through the formation of neuronal networks. Over time, those networks (ie learnt information) decay and become less accessible if the information is not rehearsed. Attempting to retrieve the information once it has become less accessible reconstructs and strengthens the neuronal networks, thereby increasing the likelihood of it being consolidated into long-term memory and making the information more accessible. Importantly, the learning periods must be effortful; immediate repetition is not sufficiently cognitively challenging and consequently less effective.

This approach to learning has been shown to be effective in enhancing acquisition and retention of vocabulary (eg Bloom and Shuell, 1981), facts and word lists (eg Zechmeister and Shaughnessy, 1980). Cepeda et al (2006) conducted a meta-analysis of 254 studies totalling over 14,000 participants. They found that students who applied spaced learning scored roughly 10 per cent better on verbal recall tests than students who learned through condensed periods (ie massed learning). The strength of evidence supporting the spaced approach to learning is reflected by its increasingly regular presence in teacher texts (eg Hattie, 2009; Dean et al, 2012; Didau, 2015; Perry et al, 2021).

The optimal amount of time between learning periods is yet to be firmly established. However, Cepeda et al (2008) recommend reviewing learned information in intervals of approximately 25 per cent of the time between initial learning and the summative exam.

There are several ways which teachers can adapt curriculum delivery to make best use of this principle, such as by planning short and frequent review sessions over an extended period of time. An advantage of introducing more spacing is that it generally involves changes in timing but not necessarily in materials or lesson content. With that said, these strategies can sometimes be difficult for teachers to implement in practice due to external influences (eg curricula and timetabling pressures) (Pashler et al, 2007), and it creates gaps in learning which teachers need to fill with other learning (Didau, 2015).

Interleaving

Spaced learning, as we have seen, promotes spreading learning over an extended period. Interleaving endorses and builds upon that idea to propose that related topics within a given subject should be learned in parallel. This approach contrasts with a more traditional linear approach of learning a topic in isolation and entirety before moving on to the next. A straightforward example of interleaving might appear in learning of an additional language where a teacher could mix vocabulary from relatable topics (eg animals and colours) rather than teaching words from a single topic at a time.

Interleaving and spaced learning both: a) discourage a massed (or 'blocked') structure and delivery of a curriculum, and b) insist that a topic should be uncomfortably challenging but manageable for learners during initial learning and when revisited. The challenge is essential because it promotes the encoding of new information and makes future recall easier by adding depth to the student's understanding. More specifically, research shows that deeper understanding involves an enhanced ability to discriminate between concepts and corresponding causes, effects and the broader context.

Interleaving may appear deceptively detrimental in the short term compared to massed learning (because less time will have been dedicated to studying any single topic), but research is developing a consensus across practical and academic learning that it will yield greater long-term achievement (Didau, 2015). For example, Rohrer and Taylor (2007) recruited college students to compare the effect of interleaving versus block learning on how to calculate the volume of four geometric solids. Students all attended three sessions spaced one week apart after being allocated to one of two groups: 'inter-leavers' or 'blockers'. For both groups, the first and second sessions were practice sessions and the third was a test. Each of the two practice sessions also included tutorials and practice problems but, importantly, differed in their structure. The 'inter-leavers' read all tutorials before beginning to solve practice problems. For the 'blockers', each tutorial was followed immediately by practice problems relating to that tutorial. Both groups were given the same amount of learning time, saw the same tutorials and completed the same practice problems. Interestingly, practice performance was 29 per cent better in the 'blockers' group, but in the test that performance was reversed with 'inter-leavers' performing 43 per cent better. Rohrer and Taylor (2007) attribute the superior test performance to the 'inter-leavers' knowing not only how to solve each kind of problem but also which procedure (ie formula) to use. Firth et al (2021) reinforce the positive effect of interleaving learning on both recall and the ability to transfer learned material to new learning in their meta-analysis. All 17 studies included in their meta-analysis revealed a positive effect for interleaving learning, with overall effect sizes of Hedge's $g = 0.65$ for impact on recall and $g = 0.60$ for transferring learned material (both considered medium-to-large effects).

An interleaving approach partially resolves the quandary of 'filling the gaps' left by spacing learning; however, it requires a skillful teacher to identify and plan an appropriate structure of curriculum structure. That challenge is exasperated by some lacking clarity about the optimum: a) cycle for interleaving and b) relatedness of concepts being interleaved. Elaborating on the former, there are various structured and unstructured ways that you can cycle through learning material, and it is unclear which is most effective. Hypothetically, we will call the topics to be learned A, B and C. A random cycle could look like ACBAABAC, whereas a more structured approach might look like AABBCCAABBCC, but this could be adjusted depending upon how many topics are included in the cycle and how much time you want to spend on each topic in each interval.

Progressing to the latter, Yan and Sana (2021) found that if the topics being interleaved are too different then learning can become confusing and the potentially positive impact of interleaving can be lost. Conversely, if the topics being interleaved are too similar, then the learning can feel 'blocked' and lack the necessary cognitive challenge, and again the positive effects of interleaving may be lost. Some other restraints, largely similar to those discussed for spaced learning, are also prevalent here. For example, curricula and timetabling pressures might dictate delivery.

CASE STUDY

Implementing interleaving in a plumbing apprenticeship course

Adil is a senior instructor at a vocational training centre. He had observed that plumbing apprentices often struggle to retain and apply various plumbing techniques and concepts over time. To address this, he decided to implement interleaving as a teaching strategy.

His main objective was to improve apprentices' retention and application of plumbing skills by interleaving different types of tasks and concepts within each training session.

He started off by conducting a skills assessment to determine the apprentices' baseline proficiency in various plumbing tasks, such as pipe fitting, soldering and troubleshooting leaks.

Instead of focusing on one skill at a time (blocked practice), Adil then designed training sessions that included a mix of different plumbing tasks. For example, a single session might include pipe fitting, installing fixtures and diagnosing common plumbing issues.

→

He ensured that the apprentices engaged in hands-on practice with a variety of tasks during each session. For instance, they might spend 20 minutes on pipe fitting, followed by 20 minutes on fixture installation and then 20 minutes on troubleshooting leaks.

Apprentices also worked in small groups to solve practical plumbing problems that required the application of multiple skills. This collaborative approach encouraged them to think critically and make connections between different tasks.

Adil also gave his apprentices the opportunity to engage with independent learning, including a variety of tasks to be completed at home, ensuring that apprentices practised a range of skills regularly.

To check that the strategy was working effectively Adil then administered weekly formative assessments that included a mix of tasks from different areas of plumbing. This helped reinforce the interleaving approach and provided ongoing evaluation of apprentices' skills.

The results from adopting this strategy were overwhelming and proved to be an effective strategy for improving apprentices' understanding and retention of plumbing skills. By mixing different types of tasks within each training session, Adil helped his apprentices develop a deeper and more flexible understanding of plumbing.

The apprentices demonstrated better retention of plumbing techniques and concepts over time. They were able to recall and apply knowledge from different areas more effectively. In addition, by regularly encountering a variety of tasks, apprentices developed stronger problem-solving skills and were better equipped to handle complex plumbing issues and they therefore reported feeling more confident in their abilities and appreciated the variety in their training sessions and assessments

Common misconceptions about the findings of neuroscience research and their impact on teaching practice

As we have seen, beyond the role of educational research-based knowledge being used to influence teachers' practice, there is growing interest in the application of neuroscience research findings in teaching practice (Gabrieli, 2016). For example, the Royal Society (2011, p 9), a '*Fellowship of many of the world's most eminent scientists*', suggests that neuroscience could be a '*tool for science-based education which can help assess the impact of different educational approaches*'. This has resulted in the creation of a sub-discipline within neuroscience, labelled as educational neuroscience, and the establishment of related academic journals (eg *Trends in Neuroscience and Education*) and research centres (eg Cambridge Centre for Neuroscience in Education).

For Bowers (2016, p 600), '*the most fundamental claim associated with educational neuroscience is that new insights about the brain can improve classroom teaching*'. This growing interest is partly attributable to the increasing explicit calls for teachers to better understand 'how students learn', and some argue that cognitive neuroscience can support teachers to this end. However, owing to the immense complexity of neuroscience, persistent misconceptions remain within the teaching community about the relationship between the brain and learning – commonly labelled as 'neuromyths'. Neuromyths are broadly considered to be a consequence of '*misconceptions generated by misunderstanding, a misreading, or a misquoting of facts scientifically established*' (OECD, 2002, p 111). Dündar and Gündüz (2016) broadly reinforce this in their argument that the permeation of neuromyths through education and into teaching practice can usually be traced back to misread, misconstrued or exaggerated neuroscience findings.

For Winch et al (2015, p 211) supporting teachers in being able to accurately identify truly research-based knowledge from 'false knowledge' (eg neuromyths) is an important step in '*sharpening their critical interpretation of research evidence*'. Although beyond the scope of this chapter, false knowledge encountered by teachers is not exclusively sourced from neuroscience. For example, Fuson (2009, p 343) discusses how misinterpretations of powerful figures in education such as Vygotsky and Piaget have also led to teacher '*practices that are counterproductive*' for students.

There are some within academia (eg Goswami, 2008; Carew and Magsamen, 2010) who subscribe to the promise of educational neuroscience for influencing teachers' practice but, perhaps consequent to several criticisms at the prospect (see Bowers (2016) for a comprehensive discussion), there are equally many critics (eg Geake, 2008; Macdonald et al, 2017). Arguably the most pertinent of those is Bowers' (2016, p 601) observation that: a) '*there are no examples of neuroscience motivating new teaching methods that are effective*', and b) educational neuroscience has failed to produce any knowledge that could be, or has been, derived from behavioural research.

In 2002, the OECD published the following list of prominent neuromyths permeating education and the teaching community.

- We only use 10 per cent of our brain.
- Either the left or right cerebral hemisphere is dominant.
- Students will achieve better if teaching aligns with their preferred learning styles (VAK).
- Regular and plentiful intake of water improves brain function and achievement.
- IQ is distributed across various multi-intelligences.

Below is an overview of the basic conception, premise and evidence base of the above claim relating to learning styles because this remains perhaps the most prevalent and influential in the lifelong learning sector. For a thorough examination of the above claims in light of relevant neuroscience research, Geake (2008) would be a good recommendation.

Students will achieve better if teaching aligns with their preferred learning styles

VAK (visual, auditory, kinaesthetic) is perhaps the most well-known learning styles model, and it posits that learning is optimised when a teaching approach aligns with a student's preferred learning style (also known as the *meshing hypothesis*). For visual learners, the meshing hypothesis states that learning is most efficient when they are presented with information in a visual form (eg diagrams, pictures), auditory learners might benefit most from hearing information to be learned, and kinaesthetic learners from a 'hands-on' approach.

There is some evidence that aligning the teaching approach to a student's preferred learning style can improve proxy measures of achievement such as student attitudes towards learning (Lovelace, 2005). However, the over-arching consensus is that robust scientific evidence linking improved attainment to learning styles is absent (Pashler et al, 2007). It is important to understand that 'evidence' is to some extent an arbitrary term and the bar at which evidence becomes sufficiently 'robust' within academic research is high, albeit slightly inconsistent. Without going into excessive detail, empirical (ie quantitative, data-driven) research is often favoured in terms of 'robustness' because it necessitates researchers maintaining tight controls in the research process to demonstrate reliability and validity. These controls include:

- selection of participants (ie sample);
- research environment;
- stimuli (ie tools and instruments) used;
- procedure followed by participants;
- approach to data analysis.

In implementing these controls, ecological validity can be compromised; that is, the likelihood of the findings obtained being replicated in a natural environment (eg a classroom). This is because increased control over the research process contributes to creating a contrived environment which can result in participants behaving differently than they would in a natural environment (ie the 'Hawthorne effect'). However, without maintaining tight control over the research, then the research is unlikely to be considered sufficiently 'robust' to influence policy around teaching practices. For a comprehensive discussion about the process and challenges which educational researchers endure, some of which have been introduced above, we would recommend reading Fraenkel and Wallen (2009).

Despite consensus within the academic community that determining a student's dominant learning style and educating them accordingly is not an evidence-based teaching approach, the practice remains widely adopted by teachers. In 2014, the Wellcome Trust surveyed 1200 teachers from different educational contexts and, consistent with earlier findings (eg Dekker et al, 2012), found that the learning styles neuromyth was the most pervasive: 76

per cent of teachers indicated that the VAK model influences their practice. Similar findings have been obtained internationally (McDonald et al, 2017) and they are likely a consequence of teachers reporting that they believe aligning teaching strategies to a student's preferred learning style is an evidence-based approach. Using large samples of teachers, the Education Endowment Foundation (Nelson et al, 2017) and Clarke (2020) found that only 75 per cent and 68 per cent of them, respectively, subscribed to the VAK model.

In addition to a lack of empirical supporting evidence, there are conceptual issues which make the learning styles notion problematic. Attempts to classify learning styles have been ongoing for some time with little coherence; Ausubel (1968) identified 18 different styles, Hill (1972, in Mullally, 1977) identified 29 'cognitive styles', and Oxford and Anderson (1995) identified 20 learning dimensions. Secondly, the separation within the brain that the VAK model implies is implausible because neuroscience has shown that sensory modalities within the brain are highly inter-related (ie it will see when it hears and touches) (Kayser, 2007). A third conceptual issue is inconsistency of individual learning styles across time and measures (ie student self-report vs established learning styles questionnaires vs teacher evaluations of student learning styles).

Subscription to the learning styles neuromyth creates problems for teachers and students; for example, time and likely money may be invested to identify a student's preferred learning style (Dündar and Gündüz, 2016). It can also result in labelling or 'shoe boxing' students as particular 'types' of learners, which can subsequently limit exploration in future learning and impair motivation to apply oneself or adapt as required across situations beyond the classroom.

As with many neuromyths, proliferation of the learning styles notion is largely attributable to a distant and misinterpreted relationship with neurological research, intuitive appeal and commercialisation. There is also an intuitive appeal because: a) it is largely undisputed that individuals have preferences in how they learn, and b) it implies that all students can learn well in the right environment. This could be misconstrued as aligning with current thinking that teachers should recognise differences between learners and practise adaptive teaching. Finally, educational institutions have paid a lot of money for learning style assessment instruments, training and applying the methods so there are commercial interests in keeping the idea alive.

How prevalent are neuromyths within the teaching community and how do we dispel them?

Boser (2019) found that 97 per cent and 77 per cent of 214 'college-level' staff agree with the learning styles and right-brain/left-brain neuromyths mentioned above, respectively. These findings are broadly consistent with related research (for example Geake, 2008; the Wellcome Trust, 2014; and Clarke, 2020) which provide further evidence of teachers utilising practices driven by neuromyths. Macdonald et al (2017) report that a common characteristic among teachers who subscribe to neuromyths is an underestimation of the complexity of learning and cognition. A classic example of this would be teachers' oversimplification of teaching and learning; for example, a teacher's belief that a single teaching approach will be effective for all learners (eg aligning learning styles).

One might assume that additional training in education and neuroscience would dispel neuromyths, but the picture is less clear. Several studies (eg Dekker et al, 2012; Macdonald et al, 2017) have shown that teachers are generally little better able to identify neuromyths than the general public, which might suggest that initial teacher training programmes have been ineffective in this aspect. Similarly, little difference has been observed between trainee teachers and experienced teachers, which might indicate that institutional CPD programmes are similarly not plugging this knowledge gap.

Other teacher demographics, including age, subject specialism and number of years' experience, also fail to predict ability to identify neuromyths (eg Clarke, 2020). There is some, albeit inconsistent, evidence of a positive correlation between the ability to identify neuromyths and exposure to academic neuroscience literature (Macdonald et al, 2017), level of education (Macdonald et al, 2017; Clarke, 2020) and seniority of a teacher's role (Nelson et al, 2017; Clarke, 2020). There are two noteworthy points here: a) the significance and magnitude of the positive correlations discussed are highly varied across research, and b) teachers with more favourable demographics (eg higher level of education) remain unable to reliably identify neuromyths. The above findings suggest that some progress may be obtained from teachers pursuing higher levels of education through postgraduate study (see Chapter 11 for further discussion about the benefits of postgraduate study). More responsibility is also being placed on teacher training programmes to develop trainee teachers' research literacy, engage with academic literature and therefore better equip them to discern evidence-based teaching approaches from those which are not. This increased responsibility can be seen in the related Diploma in Teaching mandatory content and ETF Professional Standards highlighted at the outset of this chapter. Institutional CPD programmes also have a role to play in ensuring that they examine the evidence base underpinning teaching strategies before rolling them out.

Summary

This chapter has discussed some of the learning theories that you may come across in your teaching. Some of these theories are now considered outdated, but it is still important that you are aware of them and are able to critique them because they remain influential in aspects of education to varying extents. The further reading at the end of this chapter has some excellent sections on learning theories that were once more widely influential. In addition, this chapter has highlighted that teachers' explicit knowledge of well-established educational research findings and neuromyths appears to be '*highly variable*' but that they generally '*show a weak conceptual understanding of current research knowledge*' (Nelson et al, 2017, p 24), which is a difficult challenge to overcome.

Check your understanding (level 5)

1. List three principles derived from cognitive neuroscience that you can use in your practice to enhance learning.
2. Describe some of ways in which you could chunk your classes and programmes.
3. What do you understand by interleaving?
4. How could you reduce cognitive load for your students?

Developmental questions

1. What are the potential criticisms of VAK?
2. How can we go about dispelling neuromyths which permeate education?

Further reading

- Geake, J G (2009) *The Brain at School: Educational Neuroscience in the Classroom*. Maidenhead: Open University Press.
- Jordan, A, Carlile, O and Stack, A (2008) *Approaches to Learning: A Guide for Teachers*. Maidenhead: Open University Press.
- Scales, P (2013) *Teaching in the Lifelong Learning Sector*. Maidenhead: Open University Press.

References

Ausubel, D P (1968) *Educational Psychology: A Cognitive View*. New York: Holt, Rinehart, & Winston.

Barron, A, Hebets, E A, Cleland, T, Fitzpatrick, C, Hauber, M and Stevens, J (2015) Embracing Multiple Definitions of Learning. *Eileen Hebets Publications*, 59. http://digitalcommons.unl.edu/bioscihebets/59

Bates, B (2019) *Learning Theories Simplified*. 2nd ed. Los Angeles, CA: Sage.

Bloom, K and Shuell, T (1981) Effects of Massed and Distributed Practice on the Learning and Retention of Second-Language Vocabulary. *The Journal of Educational Research*, 74(4): 245–8.

Boser, U (2019) What Do Teachers Know About the Science of Learning? *The Learning Agency*. [online] Available at: www.the-learning-agency.com (accessed 29 September 2024).

Bowers, J S (2016) The Practical and Principled Problems with Educational Neuroscience. *Psychological Review*, 123(5): 600–12.

Brown, P C, Roediger, H L III and McDaniel, M A (2014) *Make It Stick: The Science of Successful Learning*. Cambridge. MA: Harvard University Press.

Bruer, J (2007) The Brain/Education Barrier. *Science*, 317: 1293–1300.

Carew, T J and Magsamen, S H (2010) Neuroscience and Education: An Ideal Partnership for Producing Evidence-Based Solutions to Guide 21st Century Learning. *Neuron*, 67: 685–8.

Cepeda, N J, Pashler, H, Vul, E, Wixted, J T and Rohrer, D (2006) Distributed Practice in Verbal Recall Tasks: A Review and Quantitative Synthesis. *Psychological Bulletin*, 132(3): 354–80.

Cepeda, N J, Vul, E, Rohrer, D, Wixted, J T and Pashler, H (2008) Spacing Effects in Learning: A Temporal Ridgeline of Optimal Retention. *Psychological Science*, 19(11): 1095–1102.

Chandler, P and Sweller, J (1991) Cognitive Load Theory and the Format of Instruction. *Cognition and Instruction*, 8(4): 293–332.

Clarke, S (2020) *Teachers' Awareness of and Attitude to Research, School Research Culture, and Student Achievement: A Pragmatic Examination*. PhD thesis, Edge Hill University.

Coldwell, M, Greany, T, Higgins, S, Brown, C, Maxwell, B, Stiell, L, Willis, B and Burns, H (2017) Evidence-informed Teaching: An Evaluation of Progress in England. Research report. Department for Education.

Cuevas, J and Dawson, B L (2018) A Test of Two Alternative Cognitive Processing Models: Learning Styles and Dual Coding. *Theory and Research in Education*, 16(1): 40–64.

Davis, R L (2004) Olfactory Learning. *Neuron*, 44(1): 31–48.

Dean, C B, Hubbell, E, Pitler, H and Stone, B (2012) *Classroom Instruction That Works: Research-Based Strategies for Increasing Student Achievement*. Alexandria, VA: ASCD

Dekker, S, Lee, N, Howard-Jones, P and Jolles, J (2012) Neuromyths in Education: Prevalence and Predictors of Misconceptions Amongst Teachers. *Frontiers in Psychology*, 3 (429): 1–8.

Department for Education (DfE) (2019) *Initial Teacher Training (ITT): Core Content Framework*. London: DfE.

Department for Education (DfE) (2024) Diploma in Teaching (Further Education and Skills) qualification framework. [online] Available at: www.gov.uk/government/publications/further-education-initial-teacher-education/diploma-in-teaching-further-education-and-skills-qualification-framework (accessed 8 October 2024).

Didau, D (2015) *What If Everything You Knew About Education Was Wrong?* Carmarthen: Crown House Publishing.

Dogomeo, J and Aliazas, J (2022) Dual Coding Cognition in Devising Infographics for an Enhanced Students' Scientific Knowledge. *International Journal of Science, Technology, Engineering and Mathematics*, 2(4): 1–17.

Donovan, J J and Radosevich, D J (1999) A Meta-Analytic Review of the Distribution of Practice Effect: Now You See It, Now You Don't. *Journal of Applied Psychology*, 84(5): 795–805.

Dündar, S and Gündüz, N (2016) Misconceptions Regarding the Brain: The Neuromyths of Preservice Teachers. *Mind, Brain, and Education*, 10(4): 212–32.

Education and Training Foundation (ETF) (2022) *Professional Standards for Teachers and Trainers*. [online] Available at: www.et-foundation.co.uk/professionalstandards (accessed 29 September 2024).

Education and Training Foundation (ETF) (2023) Diploma in Teaching (Further Education and Skills) Education Framework. [online] Available at: www.gov.uk/government/publications/further-education-initial-teacher-education/diploma-in-teaching-further-education-and-skills-qualification-framework (accessed 15 November 2024).

Firth, J, Rivers, I and Boyle, J (2021) A Systematic Review of Interleaving as a Concept Learning Strategy. *Review of Education*, 9: 642–84.

Fraenkel, J R and Wallen, N E (2009) *How to Design and Evaluate Research in Education*. 7th ed. New York: McGraw-Hill.

Fuson, K C (2009) Avoiding Misinterpretations of Piaget and Vygotsky: Mathematical Teaching without Learning, Learning without Teaching, or Helpful Learning-path Teaching? *Cognitive Development*, 24(4): 343–61.

Gabrieli, J D E (2016) The Promise of Educational Neuroscience: Comment on Bowers. *Psychological Review*, 123(5): 613–19.

Geake, J (2008) Neuromythologies in Education. *Educational Research*, 50(2): 123–33.

Goswami, U (2008) Principles of Learning, Implications for Teaching: A Cognitive Neuroscience Perspective. *Journal of Philosophy of Education*, 42: 381–99.

Hammersley, M (2005) The Myth of Research-Based Practice: The Critical Case of Educational Inquiry. *International Journal of Social Research Methodology*, 261(8): 317–30.

Hattie, J (2009) *Visible Learning: A Synthesis of Over 800 Meta-analyses Relating to Achievement*. Abingdon: Routledge.

Howard-Jones, P, Jay, T and Galeano, L (2020) Professional Development on the Science of Learning and Teachers' Performative Thinking: A Pilot Study. *Mind, Brain, and Education*, 14(3): 267–78.

Howard-Jones, P, Pickering, S and Diack, A (2007) *Perceptions of the Role of Neuroscience in Education*. London: Innovation Unit.

Institute for Apprenticeships and Technical Education (IfATE) (2024) *Learning and Skills Teacher*. [online] Available at: www.instituteforapprenticeships.org/apprenticeship-standards/learning-and-skills-teacher (accessed 28 September 2024).

Jonassen, D and Grabowski, B (1993) *Hill's Cognitive Style Mapping*. Abingdon: Routledge.

Kayser, C (2007) Listening with Your Eyes. *Scientific American Mind*, 4: 24–29.

Lovelace, M K (2005) Meta-Analysis of Experimental Research Based on the Dunn and Dunn Model. *The Journal of Educational Research*, 98(3): 176–83.

Macdonald, K, Germine, L, Anderson, A, Christodoulou, J and McGrath, L (2017) Dispelling the Myth: Training in Education or Neuroscience Decreases but Does Not Eliminate Beliefs in Neuromyths. *Frontiers in Psychology*, 8: 1–16.

Marzano, R, Gaddy, B and Dean, C (2000) What Works In Classroom Instruction. [online] Available at: www.researchgate.net/publication/265663591_What_Works_In_Classroom_Instruction/citation/download (accessed 22 November 2024).

Miller, G A (1956) The Magical Number Seven, Plus or Minus Two: Some Limits on Our Capacity for Processing Information. *Psychological Review*, 63(2): 81–97.

Mullally, L (1977) Educational Cognitive Style: Implications for Instruction. *Theory into Practice*, 16(4): 238–42.

Nelson, J, Mehta, P, Sharples, J and Davey, C (2017) *Measuring Teachers' Research Engagement: Findings from a Pilot Study*. Education Endowment Foundation. [online] Available at: https://educationendowmentfoundation.org.uk/projects-and-evaluation/evaluation/eef-evaluation-reports-and-research-papers/methodological-research-and-innovations/measuring-teachers-research-engagement (accessed 29 September 2024).

Organisation for Economic Co-operation and Development (OECD) (2002) *Understanding the Brain: Towards a New Learning Science*. Paris: OECD Publishing.

Oxford, R L and Anderson, N (1995) State of the Art: A Crosscultural View of Language Learning Styles. *Language Teaching*, 28: 201–15.

Paivio, A and Begg, I (1971) Imagery and Associative Overlap in Short-term Memory. *Journal of Experimental Psychology*, 89(1): 40–5.

Pashler, H, Bain, P, Bottge, B, Graesser, A, Koedinger, K, McDaniel, M and Metcalfe, J (2007) *Organizing Instruction and Study to Improve Student Learning*. Washington, DC: National Center for Education Research.

Perry, T, Lea, R, Jørgensen, R, Cordingley, P, Shapiro, K and Youdell, D (2021) *Cognitive Science Approaches in the Classroom*. Education Endowment Foundation.

Rohrer, D (2012) Interleaving Helps Students Distinguish Among Similar Concepts. *Educational Psychology Review*, 24(3): 355–67.

Rohrer, D and Taylor, K (2007) The Shuffling of Mathematics Problems Improves Learning. *Instructional Science*, 35(6): 481–98.

Royal Society (2011) *Brain Waves Module 2: Neuroscience Implications for Education and Lifelong Learning*. London: Royal Society.

Schnotz, W (2012) Integrated Model of Text and Picture Comprehension. In Mayer, R E (ed) *The Cambridge Handbook of Multimedia Learning* (pp 72–103). 2nd ed. Cambridge: Cambridge University Press.

Slavin, R E (2002) Evidence-Based Education Policies: Transforming Educational Practice and Research. *Educational Researcher*, 31(7): 15–21.

Smith, M and Weinstein, Y (2016) Six Strategies for Effective Learning. [online] Available at: www.learningscientists.org/blog/2016/8/18-1 (accessed 15 July 2024).

Sweller, J (1988) Cognitive Load During Problem Solving: Effects on Learning. *Cognitive Science*, 12: 257–85.

Van Merriënboer, J J, Kester, L and Paas, F (2006) Teaching Complex Rather Than Simple Tasks: Balancing Intrinsic and Germane Load to Enhance Transfer of Learning. *Applied Cognitive Psychology*, 20(3): 343–52.

Vlach, H A and Sandhofer, C M (2012) Distributing Learning Over Time: The Spacing Effect in Children's Acquisition and Generalization of Science Concepts. *Child Development*, 83(4): 1137–44.

Wallen, N E and Fraenkel, J R (2001) *Educational Research: A Guide to the Process* (2nd ed). Lawrence Erlbaum Associates Publishers.

Wellcome Trust (2014) How Neuroscience is Affecting Education. [online] Available at: https://wellcome.org/sites/default/files/wtp055240.pdf (accessed 29 November 2024).

Winch, C, Oancea, A and Orchard, J (2015) The Contribution of Educational Research to Teachers' Professional Learning: Philosophical Understandings. *Oxford Review of Education*, 41(2): 202–16.

Yan, V X and Sana, F (2021) Interleaving Retrieval Practice Promotes Science Learning. *Psychological Science*, 33(5): 782–8.

Zechmeister, E B and Shaughnessy, J J (1980) When You Know That You Know and When You Think That You Know But You Don't. *Bulletin of the Psychonomic Society*, 15: 41–4.

Part 3 Teachers and teaching

6 The further education and skills teacher

Professional links

This chapter contributes to the following professional links:

The Diploma in Teaching mandatory content (DfE, 2024)

- 1.6 Ensuring and maintaining subject expertise.
- 2.8 Role and currency of research and evidence.
- 3.1 The role of a teacher.
- 3.2 What makes a good teacher?
- 3.3 Working with and learning from other teachers.
- 3.4 Other sources of support.

Learning and Skills Teacher Occupational Standards (IfATE, 2024)

- K1 The pedagogical theory and how to apply this theory to practice.
- K2 How to support contextualised opportunities to develop English and maths.
- K10 How to promote and foster a safe and supportive learning environment.
- K14 The requirements and implications of organisational policies and procedures, such as internal and external regulatory bodies and frameworks.
- K15 Techniques to develop collaborative relationships.
- K19 Ways to access personal and professional development, and to maintain sector and/or subject specific currency.
- S17 Comply with internal and external regulations, legislation and guidance, such as: teaching, learning and assessment, recording, storing and sharing information relating to learners.
- S18 Adapt communication style, method, and terminology to reflect the needs of the audience including individual learners, colleagues, stakeholders.

→

- S21 Continually update and maintain their own knowledge and skills as a teaching professional and a subject specialist as part of managing their own continual professional development (CPD).
- S22 Be proactive in seeking and responding to feedback from varied sources including learner voice, peers, colleagues, employers and stakeholders to improve own practice.
- S23 Manage workload through preparation and prioritisation, time management, and responsiveness to change.
- S24 Act within the statutory frameworks which set out their professional duties and responsibilities.
- B1 Be resilient and adaptable when dealing with challenge and change, maintaining focus and self-control.
- B2 Underpin their practice by reference to professional standards and evidence-based teaching and learning.
- B3 Committed to continuous professional development.
- B4 Act in a professional manner, and in a way that builds and maintains positive relationships with colleagues, students and stakeholders.
- B5 Act in a manner that is ethical, fair, consistent and impartial, valuing equality, diversity and champion British values within professional boundaries.
- B6 Model sustainable practices and promote sustainable development principles, values and goals in relation to their subject specialism.

Professional Standards (ETF, 2022)

- 6 Develop collaborative and respectful relationships with learners, colleagues and external stakeholders.
- 7 Engage with and promote a culture of continuous learning and quality improvement.
- 12 Understand your teaching role and responsibilities and how these are influenced by legal, regulatory, institutional and ethical contexts.

Chapter objectives

At the end of this chapter you will be able to:

- identify and explain your teaching role and responsibilities of a teacher in the FES sector;

- discuss how the FES teaching role and responsibilities are influenced by legal, regulatory, institutional and ethical contexts;
- describe ways of working with and learning from other professionals;
- identify other sources of support;
- explain what dual professionalism means for your practice;
- identify ways to improve and develop the role of the dual professional.

Introduction

The FES sector encompasses a broad and incredibly diverse part of the education system. It comprises multiple types of providers, including:

- general FES colleges;
- sixth form colleges;
- specialist colleges, eg land-based colleges, art, design and performing art colleges;
- independent training providers;
- local authority providers;
- third sector providers;
- employer providers;
- adult community education providers.

The sector offers a wide range of courses and options, including academic, vocational, adult education and community courses. Therefore, the FES teacher plays a critical role in educating and training a diverse range of students, from young adults who have finished secondary education to older adults looking to upskill or change careers (ETF, 2020).

The role and responsibilities of a teacher

The role of a teacher is essentially about making sure that purposeful learning is taking place to prepare learners for successful careers, lifetime skills and growth in life (DfE, 2021). It also involves the teacher modelling their behaviour; maintaining and enhancing their own practice and knowledge by integrating reflective practice; CPD and learning; and keeping up to date with pedagogical and subject knowledge and skills.

Here are some key roles and responsibilities of the FES teacher, based on the cycle of a learner's journey (see Figure 6.1).

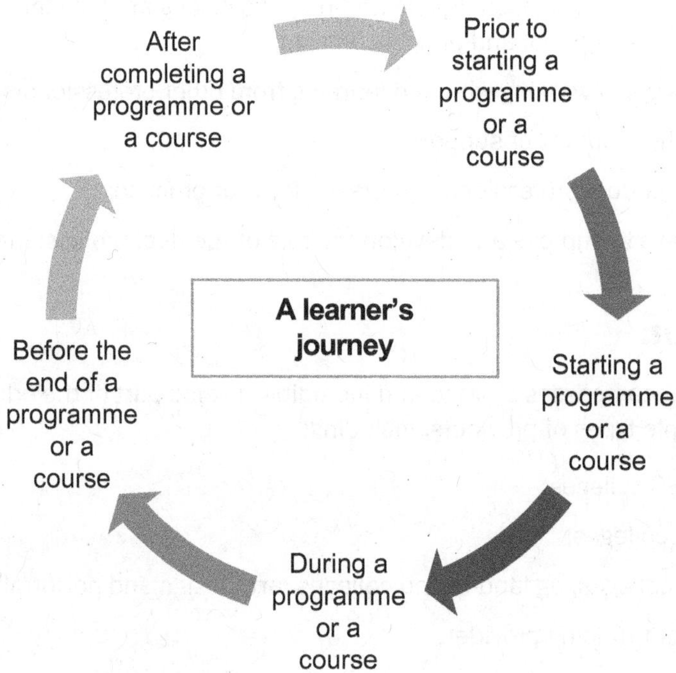

***Figure 6.1** A learner's journey*

Source: Author's own

- **Prior to starting a programme or a course:** At this stage, learners might be enquiring about a programme or a course. They might have already applied for what they would like to study. As an FES teacher, you need to be familiar with your organisation's policies, processes and procedures in relation to learner applications and interviews. You might not be directly involved at this stage, but you can liaise with other professionals and start identifying learners' needs through their applications and interviews. This forms part of the initial assessment process to identify the needs of your learners, your organisation and your role as a teacher. The information obtained contributes to curriculum planning, preparation for resources and assessment arrangement.

  At this stage, you will start preparing schemes of work, session plans and any equipment or resources required for the duration of the curriculum. You will liaise and work with other professionals (eg managers, learning support officers, teaching support officers and/or student support officers) to identify and prepare for the learning support that needs to be in place. You will also ensure that you are up to date with any internal or external requirements, such as the awarding organisation's specification or any changes with assessment requirements, in order to plan the curriculum.

- **Starting a programme or a course:** This is an important part of a programme. As an FES teacher, you will work with colleagues to plan, deliver and facilitate the induction programme to prepare learners for the programme or course. At this stage, a range of initial and diagnostic assessment activities are carried out to determine learners' starting points with their subject and general knowledge, as well as their aspirations. This is an important part of the learner's journey, as creating a safe and inclusive environment starts with how learners are inducted. FES teachers play an essential role in creating such an environment to nurture and motivate the learners.

- **During a programme or a course:** Based on the schemes of work, FES teachers will plan, prepare, teach, train and facilitate learning by applying a range of teaching, learning and assessment approaches, techniques and activities. You will also lead and manage a positive learning environment by developing and inspiring learners to stay motivated and engaged. This requires different sets of skills and practice such as mentoring, coaching, active listening and pastoral strategies to meet individual needs. FES teachers model their behaviour by adhering to the internal and external organisations' policies and procedures, legislations and codes of practice.

  Internal quality assurance (IQA) is essential to any organisation. It is a system to monitor and ensure consistent, good-quality education throughout the learner's journey. FES teachers often have multifaceted roles such as being a teacher, trainer, personal tutor, assessor and internal quality assurer. Therefore, FES teachers need to have appropriate training and understanding of IQA and the assessor's role and responsibilities.

  Throughout the programme, FES teachers seek formal and informal feedback regularly from learners and other professionals to inform, improve and enhance their own practice. This can be achieved through collecting learner feedback, formal evaluation surveys or from inspection feedback.

- **Before the end of a programme or a course:** FES teachers need to manage formative and summative assessment throughout the programme. The results of the assessment provide insights into learners' progress in their subject knowledge, skills and behaviours. Before the end of a programme or course, it is helpful to evaluate the programme or course with colleagues and learners. This contributes to the overall quality improvement process and can inform future development of the curriculum.

  Learners need support and guidance about their development and progression relating to career choice and to continue their growth. FES teachers play an essential role in ensuring that learners receive appropriate information, advice and guidance about their next steps.

- **After completing a programme or a course:** It is often perceived that the learner's journey ends at the completion of a programme or course. It is helpful to identify learner progress and involve past achievers to speak to current or future learners. It is also a celebration of the programme and course. FES teachers can also liaise with past achievers who have potentially become employers themselves and can provide valuable industrial knowledge and information.

Critical questions ?

» If you are interested in teaching or are an early career teacher, what do you consider your roles and responsibilities?

» If you are an experienced teacher, do you agree with the roles and responsibilities identified in this chapter? Have there been any differences or changes in your roles and responsibilities between the start of your career and now?

Activity ?

» Create a summary, a timeline or an image of your own journey into teaching.

» If you are teaching already, what advice would you give to an early career teacher or someone who is interested in becoming a teacher? If you are new to teaching, what questions would you ask an experienced teacher?

What makes a good teacher?

Teaching is beyond making sure that learners pass their exams or achieve their qualifications. FES teachers, like people in any other profession, need to adhere to a set of professional standards. At the heart of FES teaching, professional behaviours, values and attributes should underpin the professional practice of FES teachers. Professionalism is the core of what motivates FES teachers to strive and thrive.

The Learning and Skills Teacher Occupational Standards (IfATE, 2024) state that a learning and skills teacher:

- *needs to be flexible, innovative, and adaptable, changing their behaviour and teaching style to suit the environment and level of their students;*
- *needs to have a sound understanding of pedagogy and regularly engage with robust evidence of effective teaching and learning methods and practice relevant to their subject area(s);*
- *typically has significant autonomy and needs to demonstrate consistently high standards of personal and professional conduct and is accountable for their professional development;*
- *may be responsible for the managing of others, as well as managing budgets.*

There are ten occupational duties mapped with knowledge, skills and behaviours that learning and skills teachers need to demonstrate and evidence through the apprenticeship programme.

The ETF Professional Standards (2022) consist of 20 standards that are categorised into three domains:

- **Professional values and attributes:** *Seven standards to help you develop your own judgement of what works and does not work in your teaching and training.*
- **Professional knowledge and understanding:** *Five standards which highlight the importance of subject knowledge, teaching expertise, knowledge sharing, supporting learners with educational difficulties, and professional responsibilities.*
- **Professional skills:** *Eight standards which support you to master planning, motivation, coaching and assessment strategies to enable your learners to make excellent progress.*

From the above standards, similar characteristics and qualities can be identified in what a 'good' FES teacher is, including the following.

- *Love and enthusiasm for the taught subject.*
- *Mastery skills and knowledge in teaching practice and subject specialism.*
- *A passion for continuing professional development and learning.*
- *A duty of care to learners, colleagues, and other professionals.*
- *A good communicator.*
- *A good organiser.*
- *Having high expectations for the learners.*
- *Modelling professional behaviour and attitudes such as respect, integrity, adaptability, and inclusivity.*

(Machin et al, 2023, pp 33–4)

In a report by the Commission on Adult Vocational Teaching and Learning (CAVTL) (2013), four characteristics of excellent adult vocational teaching and learning are identified.

- *A clear line of sight to work on all vocational programmes.*
- *'Dual professional' teachers and trainers who combine occupational and pedagogical expertise, and are trusted and given the time to develop partnerships and curricula with employers.*
- *Access to industry-standard facilities and resources reflecting the ways in which technology is transforming work.*
- *Clear escalators to higher level vocational learning, developing and combining deep knowledge and skills.*

(CAVTL, 2013, p 15)

Biesta's three dimensions of education (2010), as represented in Figure 6.2, offers another lens to look at what makes a good FES teacher.

- **Vocational curriculum content and qualification:** FES teachers need to acquire and develop a deep understanding of subject-specific knowledge and skills required for their roles, enabling them to impart this knowledge and skills effectively to their learners as they work towards their qualifications or programmes. It is equally important for FES teachers to develop the art and craft of teaching that suits the needs of the learners and the subject they teach.
- **Vocational values:** The FES sector prides itself on the importance of a strong work ethic, characterised by the commitment to perform tasks well and to do a good job (Sennett, 2008).
- **Practical wisdom:** FES teachers need to be able to draw upon practical wisdom, such as problem-solving, adaptability, creativity, collaboration and critical thinking, to deal with any unforeseen circumstances independently or collectively (Gregson et al, 2020).

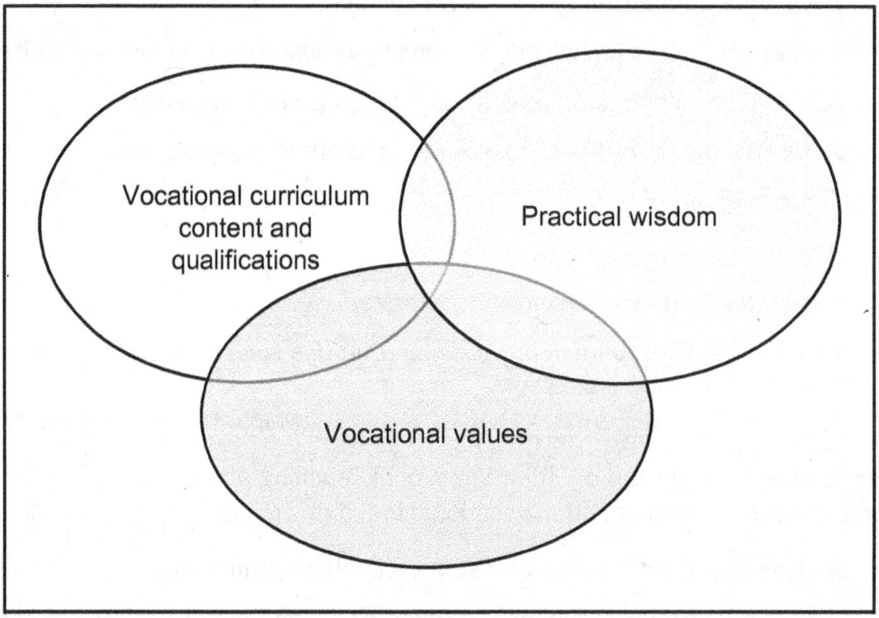

***Figure 6.2** Three dimensions of education in FES*

(Adapted from Gregson et al's (2020) *Reflective Teaching* and Biesta's (2010) *Good Education in an Age of Measurement*)

Critical questions ?

» What is your experience as a learner? How might the experience impact on your role as an FES teacher?

» What makes a good FES teacher?

» Based on Figure 6.2, what does each dimension mean to you in your role and the subject you teach? Discuss with your colleagues and find out if there are similarities or differences.

Working with and learning from other teachers

Aligned with the professional values and attributes of an FES teacher, teachers are lifelong learners. CPD and learning are the essential ingredients to enable FES teachers to thrive (Gregson et al, 2020). FES teaching is not only about teaching your own subject but also about learning from other subject specialists and teachers.

There are different ways to work with and learn from other teachers.

- **Collaborative teaching and learning:** Teachers can greatly benefit from sharing good practice with their peers. By co-designing curriculum or even co-teaching sessions, teachers can learn from each other and blend diverse teaching styles and experiences. This practice not only enriches the learners' experiences but also enables teachers to learn from each other and fosters professional growth and innovation (Wiliam, 2016). There is increasing evidence about how collaborative professional development can support teachers' critical thinking and autonomy in developing personalised learning, such as joint practice development (JPD) (Gregson et al, 2015; ETF, 2018; Chen, 2022).
- **Developing and enhancing subject-specific knowledge and practice:** Connecting and working with colleagues from the same subject area can be of huge benefit to each other by sharing good ideas and practice and identifying concerns or areas for improvement. Crawley (2015, p 489) summarises four working models of the *connected professional*, including the practical connection, the democratic connection, the civic connection and the networked connection. He emphasises that '*participating in decisions affecting their professional lives and environments, with peers and with the engagement of the wider community*' is one of the characteristics of the FES teaching professional (Crawley, 2015, p 494).
- **Cultivating a research culture and innovation in teaching:** Engaging in research projects with colleagues can lead to significant innovation in teaching. Collaborative research allows FES teachers to focus on their context-focused issues or concerns (LSRN, 2024). This not only improves teaching practices but also contributes to the academic field of education, with a focus on the FES sector.

Critical questions

» What are the potential challenges of implementing collaborative teaching strategies and how can they be overcome?

» What role should FES teachers play in educational research, and how can you be better involved?

Activity

» Ask your colleagues about what and how they develop their pedagogical and subject-specific knowledge and skills. Find out about the common themes of how they keep up to date with dual professionalism.

Other sources of support

Teachers do not need to know everything, but they need to be aware of how, when and where to seek support. This can be based on teachers' own needs or those of the learners. It is essential to set the professional boundaries of the teaching role when working with learners and other professionals.

FES teachers can and should be aware of the internal and external support that is available to them. Internally, it is important to know your rights as a teacher, such as your employment contract, your legal rights and expectations from your employer (Machin et al, 2023).

Some useful external organisations or resources to support your role as an FES teacher include the following.

- **Association of Colleges (AoC)** (www.aoc.co.uk): Represents and supports FES colleges in England, advocating for the interests of colleges and their students at the national level.
- **Department for Education (DfE)** (www.gov.uk/government/organisations/department-for-education): A department of the UK government responsible for child protection, education, apprenticeships and wider skills in England.
- **Edge Foundation** (www.edge.co.uk): An independent education charity dedicated to shaping the future of education by promoting technical, practical and vocational learning.
- **Education and Training Foundation (ETF)** (www.et-foundation.co.uk): A government-funded initiative dedicated to the professional development and continuous improvement of teachers and trainers in the English FES sector. ETF also provides information, advice and guidance for professionals considering or currently working within the FES sector.

- **Gatsby** (www.improvingtechnicaleducation.org.uk): A charitable foundation set up by David Sainsbury to improve education and skills in science, technology, engineering, mathematics and technical education.
- **Learning and Skills Research Network** (https://lsrn.wordpress.com): A network of practitioners, researchers and policymakers who share an interest in research in the learning and skills sector of education.
- **National Education Union (NEU)** (https://neu.org.uk): The largest education union in the UK, representing teachers, lecturers and support staff in schools, colleges and educational support services.
- **Office for Standards in Education, Children's Services and Skills (Ofsted)** (www.gov.uk/government/organisations/ofsted): An independent organisation responsible for inspecting a range of educational institutions, including state schools and some independent schools, as well as local services, to achieve excellence in the care of children and young people, and in education and skills for learners of all ages.
- **Society for Education and Training (SET)** (https://set.et-foundation.co.uk): The professional membership body for teachers and trainers in the post-16 education and training sector, dedicated to the professional development and recognition of those working in education.
- **University and College Union (UCU)** (www.ucu.org.uk): A union representing academics, lecturers, trainers, instructors, researchers, managers and postgraduate students involved in HE and FES throughout the UK.
- **Union Learn** (www.unionlearn.org.uk): A branch of the Trades Union Congress (TUC) that promotes lifelong learning and skills development among the workforce, supporting union learning and the spread of high-quality and accessible learning in the workplace.

Critical questions ?

» What support services and guidance does your employer/organisation provide?

» How does your employer support your CPD and learning? What are your opportunities for career progression?

The dual professional

The term 'professionalism' represents a complex and debated concept that has no direct and simple definition. It has different meanings for different people in varied contexts, particularly in the vast and diverse FES sector. FES teachers take different routes to their teaching careers in the sector. They might enter the sector as a teacher who began their career in education, having followed a path from school-based experiences to university and teacher training. Some are considered as 'second career' teachers who possess industrial and vocational experiences but may not have FES teaching experiences or practices. A significant proportion of FES teachers are identified as second career teachers. These individuals have transitioned to teaching after establishing successful careers in other professional sectors, bringing with them a wealth of relevant qualifications and extensive experience in industrial or commercial settings. This career shift arguably necessitates a psychosocial transformation and the cultivation of a new professional identity tailored to the educational context. Consequently, to fulfil their roles effectively, these FES teachers must adopt a dual or multiple identity and professionalism, prioritising their expertise in the subject matter while also embracing the competencies required of a professional teacher (Senior, 2015). No matter which routes FES teachers take to enter the FES sector, it is undoubtedly the case that they are dual professionals – '*teachers and trainers with occupational expertise and experience, who can combine this with excellent teaching and learning practice*' (CAVTL, 2013, p 8).

The notion of a 'dual professional' was initially recognised in 2007 by the Institute for Learning (IfL), a voluntary professional body for teachers and trainers in the post-compulsory education and training sector in England. The IfL introduced a model for professionalism in 2007 (see Figure 6.3) which puts continuing professional development and learning (CPDL) at the centre of its model. However, it is also debatable what types of CPDL really drive the quality of education in FES. Dual professionalism is abbreviated to 'Dual prof' in this model.

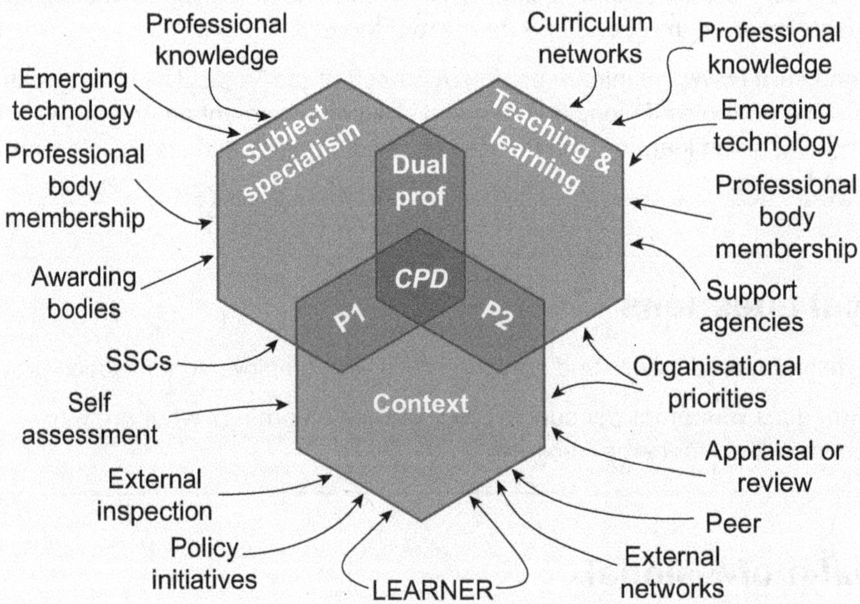

***Figure 6.3** Institute for Learning model of dual professionalism (IfL, 2007) (now ETF)*

Senior (2015) proposed a different framework for the 14–19 Diploma, and this framework has been further developed and adapted to the FES sector. In the landscape of the FES sector, the concept of dual professionals has become increasingly prominent. These individuals are characterised by their dual expertise in both their subject specialism and pedagogical skills, enabling them to effectively bridge, connect and collaborate between industry and the classroom.

Dual professionals in the FES sector often begin their careers outside the realm of education, possessing substantial industry experience which they later bring to their teaching roles. This unique blend of real-world experience and educational acumen makes them invaluable to vocational education, where practical skills and up-to-date industry knowledge are paramount.

The integration of dual professionals into the FES sector enhances the learning experience by providing students with insights grounded in actual practice. These teachers not only teach but also enrich the curriculum with contemporary practices, innovations and real-life challenges from their respective fields. Their firsthand experience helps in cultivating a workforce that is more attuned to the current demands and future needs of the industry.

However, transitioning from industry to education poses challenges, primarily in adapting to educational environments and pedagogies. The development of teaching skills is crucial for these professionals to effectively convey their specialised knowledge. Institutions often support this transition through professional development programmes focused on teaching methodologies, educational technologies and student engagement strategies.

Policymakers have recognised the value of dual professionals and have implemented strategies to attract and retain such talent in the FES sector. This includes incentives like qualification bursaries, training grants and structured mentorship programmes that ease the transition for industry experts moving into teaching roles.

The future of the FES sector increasingly depends on its ability to integrate dual professionals, adapt to evolving industry trends and prepare students for a rapidly changing global economy. Continued investment in professional development and support for dual professionals will be critical in maintaining the relevance and efficacy of vocational education and training programmes. Figure 6.4 is an adapted framework about the dual professionalism by Senior (2015).

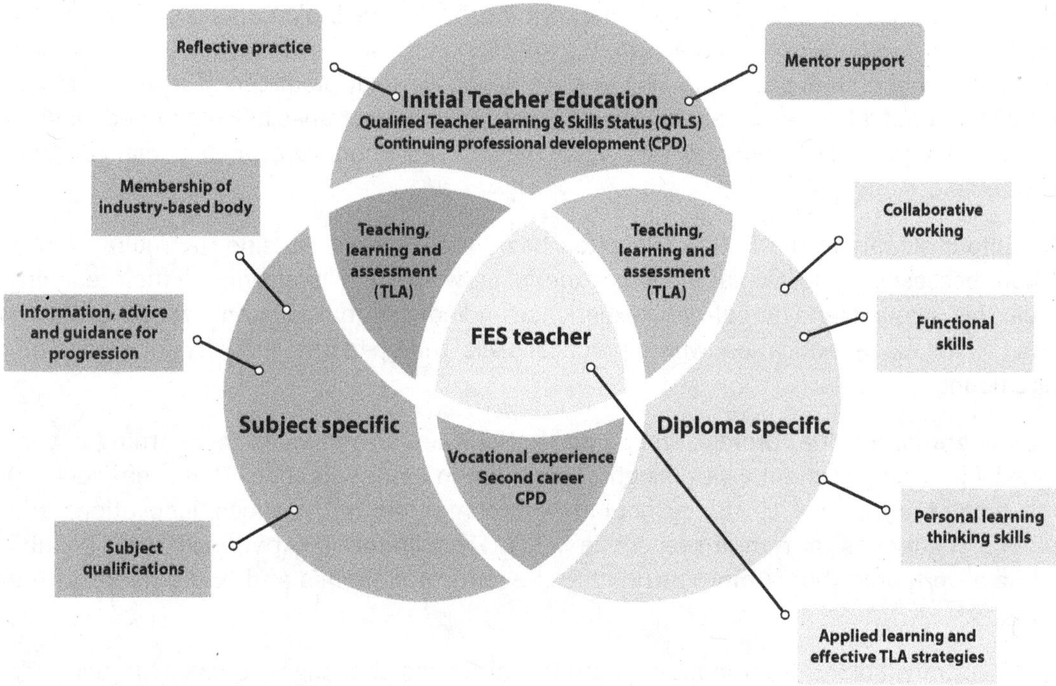

Figure 6.4 *The dual professional (adapted from Senior, 2015)*

CASE STUDY

Gosia is a new teacher in the FES sector. Her journey into teaching is rooted in a strong background in electrical engineering. After completing an apprenticeship in this field, Gosia worked as an electrical engineer for eight years. During this period, she gained valuable industry experience and even supported apprentices, providing her with some initial exposure to the educational aspect of her profession.

Subsequently, Gosia transitioned to self-employment, continuing her work as an electrical engineer for another four years. Her experience in running her own business further honed her skills and provided her with a diverse range of practical insights.

Recognising her passion for teaching and supporting the next generation of engineers, Gosia decided to formalise her teaching skills. She completed a level 3 teaching qualification, which equipped her with the foundational knowledge and pedagogical skills required for her new role in education.

Now, Gosia is timetabled to teach level 2 learners on the study programme for electrical engineering. She is keen on developing her industrial and pedagogical skills and knowledge in order to teach and support the learners but is unsure of where and how to start.

Critical questions

- How do you interpret the concept of dual professionalism, and what impact does it have on your professional practice?
- In what ways can your role as the dual professional be further developed and enhanced?
- What challenges might Gosia face in adapting her practical skills to a classroom setting?
- What strategies can she use to ensure her learners benefit from her dual expertise?
- How can the institution support her ongoing development in both areas?
- In what ways can Gosia balance the demands of maintaining her technical skills in electrical engineering with developing her pedagogical skills and knowledge in her teaching role?
- How can she stay up to date with the latest industry advancements to ensure her teaching remains relevant and impactful?

Activity

- Read and complete *Activity 4: SOAR Analysis to Underpin Your Development Plan* in the Dual Professional Toolkit produced by the Education and Training Foundation (ETF, 2018). When you complete the activity, discuss your plan with your peers.

  www.et-foundation.co.uk/wp-content/uploads/2020/04/Dual-Professional-toolkit_2.pdf

Summary

This chapter has provided an understanding of your roles and responsibilities as an FES teacher, as well as how you can improve and enhance your knowledge and practice as a dual professional. This chapter also has provided support you in exploring how you work with learners, other teachers and professionals internally and externally.

Check your understanding (level 5)

1. What are the key roles and responsibilities as an FES teacher?
2. What are the different ways to work with other teachers and professionals?
3. What support services are you aware of, internally and externally, as an FES teacher?
4. How can you improve and develop your role as a dual professional?

Developmental questions L6+7

1. How important is collaboration with colleagues and other stakeholders in the FES sector? Provide some examples of how you could work more collaboratively to enhance learner outcomes.
2. How could you handle ethical dilemmas that may arise in your teaching practice, particularly those related to statutory compliance?
3. How could you stay up to date with changes in legislation and statutory requirements in the FES sector?
4. What professional development activities could you access to enhance your understanding of statutory frameworks?

Further reading

- Jones, S (2022) *Great FE Teaching: Sharing Good Practice*. London: SAGE Publications.
- Tully, P (2022) Joining the dots: Theorising Professionalism in the English Further Education Sector. *Research in Post-Compulsory Education*, 27(1): 66–97. https://doi.org/10.1080/13596748.2021.2011510

References

Biesta, J J (2010) *Good Education in an Age of Measurement*. New York: Routledge.

Commission on Adult Vocational Teaching and Learning (CAVTL) (2013) *It's About Work...: Excellent Adult Vocational Teaching and Learning.* [online] Available at: www.et-foundation.co.uk/wp-content/uploads/2023/09/CAVTL-one-year-on-review.pdf (accessed 5 October 2024).

Crawley, J (2015) Growing Connections – the Connected Professional. *Research in Post-Compulsory Education*, 20(4): 476–98.

Chen, I (2022) *Working and Learning Together: The Lived Experiences of Further Education Teachers Engaging with Joint Practice Development as a Model of Collaborative Enquiry for Professional Learning*. PhD thesis, University of Sunderland. ProQuest Dissertations and Theses Global.

Department for Education (DfE) (2021) *Skills for Jobs: Lifelong Learning for Opportunities and Growth*. [online] Available at: www.gov.uk/government/publications/skills-for-jobs-lifelong-learning-for-opportunity-and-growth (accessed 29 September 2024).

Department for Education (DfE) (2024) Diploma in Teaching (Further Education and Skills) qualification framework. [online] Available at: www.gov.uk/government/publications/further-education-initial-teacher-education/diploma-in-teaching-further-education-and-skills-qualification-framework (accessed 8 October 2024).

Education and Training Foundation (ETF) (2018) *The Dual Professional Toolkit: A Guide for Those Looking to Move Toward Dual Professionalism*. [online] Available at: www.et-foundation.co.uk/wp-content/uploads/2020/04/Dual-Professional-toolkit_2.pdf (accessed 29 September 2024).

Education and Training Foundation (ETF) (2020) *So What Is the FE Sector?* [online] Available at: www.et-foundation.co.uk/wp-content/uploads/2020/08/200729-ETF-FE-Sector-Guide-RGB-v10.pdf (accessed 29 September 2024).

Education and Training Foundation (ETF) (2022) *Professional Standards for Teachers and Trainers*. [online] Available at: www.et-foundation.co.uk/professional-standards/teachers (accessed 29 September 2024).

Education and Training Foundation (ETF) (2023) *New Level 5 Full FE Teaching Qualification*. [online] Available at: www.et-foundation.co.uk/resources/teacher-education/qualifications-in-education-and-training (accessed 29 September 2024).

Gregson, M, Nixon, L, Pollard A and Spedding T (eds) (2015) *Readings in Reflective Teaching in Further, Adult and Vocational Education*. London: Bloomsbury.

Gregson, M, Duncan, S, Brosnan, K, Derrick, J, Husband, G, Nixon, L, Spedding, T, Stubley, R and Webber Jones, R (2020) *Reflective Teaching in Further, Adult and Vocational Education*. London: Bloomsbury.

Institute for Apprenticeships and Technical Education (IfATE) (2024) *Learning and Skills Teacher*. [online] Available at: www.instituteforapprenticeships.org/apprenticeship-standards/learning-and-skills-teacher (accessed 29 September 2024).

Institute for Learning (IfL) (now ETF) (2007) *Model of Dual Professionalism*.

Learning and Skills Research Network (LSRN) (2024) *Staying with the Troublemakers: A Celebration of Research in FE*. [online] Available at: https://lsrn.wordpress.com/2024/05/01/staying-with-the-troublemakers (accessed 29 September 2024).

Machin, L, Hindmarsh, D, Murray, S and Richardson, T (2023) *A Complete Guide to the Level 5 Diploma in Education and Training*. St Albans: Critical Publishing.

Sennett, R (2008) *The Craftsman*. London: Penguin.

Senior, L (2015) *The Rise and Demise of the 14–19 Diploma*. PhD thesis, University of Derby. ProQuest Dissertations and Theses Global.

Wiliam, D (2016) *Leadership for Teacher Learning: Creating a Culture Where All Teachers Improve So That All Students Succeed*. West Palm Beach, FL: Learning Science International.

7 Planning for teaching and learning

Professional links

This chapter contributes to the following professional links:

The Diploma in Teaching mandatory content (DfE, 2024)

- 1.1 Curriculum development.
- 1.4 Required wider or prerequisite knowledge.
- 2.7 Contemporary learning theory, neuroscience.
- 2.8 Role and currency of research and evidence.
- 2.9 Application of theory to practice.
- 3.5 Rigorous curriculum thinking.
- 3.7 Planning and delivering sessions.
- 3.10 Teacher expectations of learners including classroom management.
- 3.11 Face to face and remote delivery.
- 3.12 Assessment and feedback.
- 4.5 Curriculum planning and review.
- 4.6 Lesson planning and adaptations.
- 4.7 Planning and conducting assessment.
- 4.9 Assessment feedback and advice or guidance.
- 4.10 Application of evidence-based methods.
- 4.11 Managing and supporting learners, including behaviour
- 4.14 Developing expertise
- 4.15 Updating and CPD

→

- 4.16 Professional responsibilities
- 4.17 Working with colleagues

Learning and Skills Teacher Occupational Standards (IfATE, 2024)

- K1 The pedagogical theory and how to apply this theory to practice.
- K3 The principles of designing, planning, and organising curriculum.
- K5 Evidence-informed inclusive teaching, learning and assessment strategies.
- K9 Principles and practices of assessment and feedback.
- K10 How to promote and foster a safe and supportive learning environment.
- S4 Use a variety of teaching and assessment methods depending on the learning environment and learners' needs.
- S11 Provide ongoing learner feedback.
- S19 Engage learners to establish standards of behaviour, mutual respect and safe working.
- S20 Challenge learners to address inappropriate behaviour or viewpoints.
- B2: Underpin their practice by reference to professional standards and evidence-based teaching and learning.
- B3 Committed to continuous professional development.
- B4 Act in a professional manner, and in a way that builds and maintains positive relationships with colleagues, students and stakeholders.
- B5 Act in a manner that is ethical, fair, consistent and impartial, valuing equality, diversity and champion British values within professional boundaries.

Professional Standards (ETF, 2022)

- 6 Develop collaborative and respectful relationships with learners, colleagues and external stakeholders.
- 7 Engage with and promote a culture of continuous learning and quality improvement.
- 9 Critically review and apply your knowledge of educational research, pedagogy, and assessment to develop evidence-informed practice.
- 13 Promote and support positive learner behaviour, attitudes and well-being.
- 19 Apply appropriate and fair methods of assessment and provide constructive and timely feedback to support learning and achievement.

Chapter objectives

At the end of this chapter you will be able to:

- explore and identify key principles of rigorous curriculum thinking and inclusive practice;
- explain what a person-centred approach means and how it can be integrated in practice;
- identify approaches for managing positive classroom behaviour and maintaining an inclusive learning environment;
- identify and explain different types of assessment methods and their purpose and applications;
- create resources to support both face-to-face and digital delivery methods;
- identify and explain ways to provide constructive feedback to enhance learner progress and achievement;
- apply strategies to support individual learner needs and promote engagement;
- identify and explain reflective practice for continuous improvement in teaching;
- describe different ways to critically evaluate one's teaching methods and learner outcomes;
- identify opportunities for continuing professional development (CPD) and value its importance.

Introduction

The FES sector is diverse and multicultural with staff and learners from different backgrounds and life experiences. This is pertinent to plan an inclusive and person-centred curriculum to meet the needs of your learners. In this chapter, you will learn about the principles of curriculum design to effectively plan and deliver inclusive and engaging lessons, manage classrooms, utilise assessment strategies, and continuously improve through reflective practice and professional development. This chapter is designed to provide you with practical suggestions for your teaching and is closely related to Chapters 8, 9, 10 and 11.

Rigorous curriculum thinking and curriculum for inclusive practice

Planning is an essential part of good practice in teaching, learning and assessment, and designing an inclusive curriculum is the foundation of the planning process. A good starting point is to define what curriculum is, but this can be problematic and it is hard to reach a uniform definition. This is because curricula very often evolve over time, influenced by policy changes and driven by different sets of standards in the context of the educational sector (Tummons, 2012).

The curriculum in the FES sector is an evolving and responsive entity, continuously reviewed and updated to reflect changes in educational research, stakeholder feedback, and political, societal and economic factors. It includes mechanisms for regular evaluation, curriculum innovation and professional development for professionals in the sector. There is not a simple definition of curriculum.

As a teacher working in the sector, you can use the following questions to explore and identify what your understanding of curriculum is.

- What is your understanding of the term 'curriculum' in the context of further education and skills?
- What is your role and responsibilities in the sector? How do you contribute to the curriculum?
- What programme or course do you teach, train or assess? Who are your learners?
- What knowledge, skills and behaviour do your learners need to acquire on the programme or course?
- How do you teach, train, facilitate and motivate your learners to acquire the knowledge, skills and behaviour for the programme or course?
- How are your learners assessed and how do they receive feedback to develop their knowledge, skills and behaviour?
- What else do you need to consider and include in the curriculum to enrich your learners' experiences and enhance their learning?

Once you have thought through your answers to the above questions, let's explore in Table 7.1 some different definitions based on the purpose and perspective of curricula.

Table 7.1 *Purpose, perspective and definition of different curricula*

Purpose and perspective	Definition
Content based	The curriculum is a structured set of courses and learning resources designed to teach specific knowledge and skills to learners. It includes the subjects taught, the content delivered and the educational resources used (Stoller, 2004).
Competency based	The curriculum focuses on developing specific competencies and skills required for particular careers or industries. It emphasises hands-on training, practical applications and the attainment of proficiency in key areas.
Inclusive practice	The curriculum ensures that all learners, regardless of their abilities, backgrounds or circumstances, have equitable access to education. It incorporates differentiated instructions, adaptive learning resources and supportive measures to meet diverse needs (University of Cambridge, 2024).

Table 7.1 *(Cont.)*

Purpose and perspective	Definition
Learner centred	The curriculum is designed around the needs, interests and goals of learners. It prioritises personalised learning experiences, allowing learners to progress at their own pace and engage in self-directed learning activities (Nunan, 1988).
Outcome oriented	The curriculum is structured to achieve specific educational outcomes, such as qualifications, certifications and measurable skill levels. It focuses on ensuring that learners attain the desired results and are prepared for FES or employment (Spady, 1994).
Holistic and integrated	The curriculum integrates academic, vocational and personal development aspects to provide a holistic education. It includes core subjects, practical training and life skills development to prepare learners for all aspects of life and work.
Flexible and adaptive	The curriculum is designed to be flexible and adaptable to changes in technology, industry demands and learner needs. It allows for adjustments and updates to keep the content relevant, current and effective.
Experiential learning	The curriculum emphasises experiential learning, where learners gain knowledge and skills through real-world experiences, such as apprenticeships, internships and project-based learning. It focuses on learning by doing.
Collaborative	The curriculum is developed and delivered through collaboration between educational institutions, industry partners and other stakeholders. It ensures that the education provided is relevant, practical and aligned with market skills needs.
Reflective practice	The curriculum encourages continuous reflection and improvement by both teachers and learners. It includes regular assessment, feedback mechanisms and opportunities for professional development to enhance teaching and learning practices.

You may find that some of the above definitions are quite often based on the behaviourist view of education, or some are situated in social learning theories (Tummons, 2020). However, it is important to think critically about curricula in different educational and cultural contexts. Chapters 8, 10 and 11 further examine and explore how to transform curricula by understanding decolonisation and its influence on curricula and subject-specific considerations. Different curriculum models are introduced in Chapter 10 to consolidate practical approaches to curriculum planning.

Inclusive practice is not just about teaching and supporting learners with learning difficulties and/or disabilities. It is about having a deep understanding of how various factors like race, ethnicity, gender identity, class, language, religion, ability, sexuality, mental health, age, education and body size can intersect to create different forms of discrimination, prejudice and domination (Crenshaw, 1989, 1991). According to the Oxford English Dictionary, belonging to multiple communities with overlapping identities creates complex experiences of both oppression and privilege, significantly affecting individual lives. Figure 7.1 represents the complexity and the extent of what your learners may experience and how these different factors may impact or influence your thinking. Using an intersectionality lens, teachers and trainers examine their own beliefs and assumptions, reflecting on their own practice to support learners by developing and creating an inclusive curriculum.

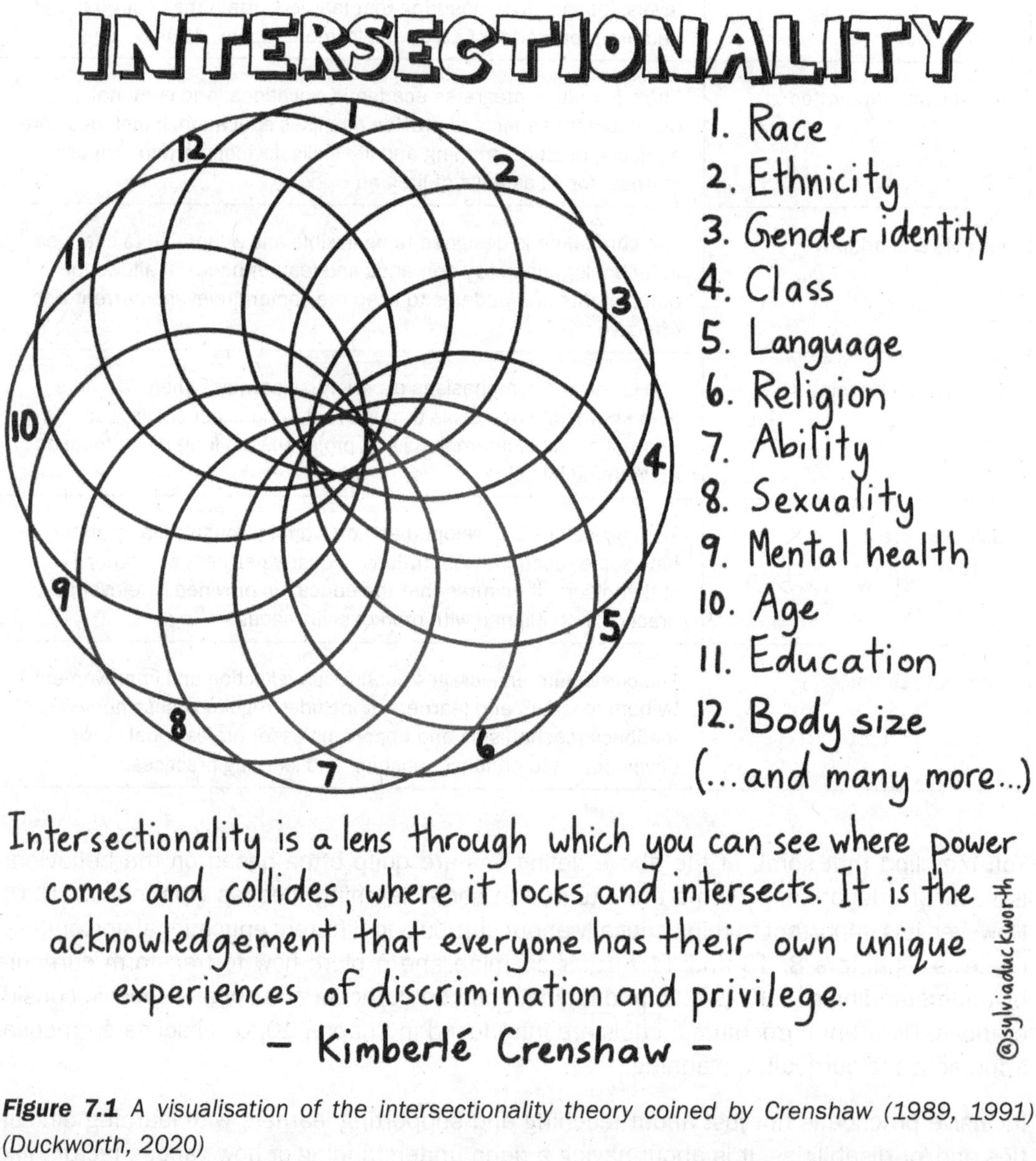

Figure 7.1 *A visualisation of the intersectionality theory coined by Crenshaw (1989, 1991) (Duckworth, 2020)*

Inclusive and adaptive teaching is never easy, but there are frameworks and strategies that may help with designing and planning an inclusive curriculum. It requires continuing reflection and critical evaluation to adjust and adapt the curriculum and resources to meet the needs of the learners.

Universal Design for Learning (UDL) is a useful framework for curriculum design, initially developed in the 1990s and then introduced in 2012 by CAST. UDL is an approach to teaching and learning that gives all students equal opportunity to achieve their full potential in learning.

The goal of UDL is to use a variety of teaching methods to remove any barriers to learning. It is about building in flexibility that can be adjusted for all learners' strengths and needs. You may wish to revisit Chapter 3 on SEND as this approach can be especially helpful for learners who have not been formally diagnosed or learners whose first language is not English.

The UDL guidelines contain extensive details. Each of the three areas (engagement, representation, and action and expression) includes several parameters, each with checkpoints that offer direction on specific aspects of that guideline. Please refer to Figure 7.2 for the UDL graphic organiser. Based on the UDL guidelines (CAST, 2024), teaching and learning should be designed to accommodate the needs of every learner.

- **Multiple means of engagement:** The UDL guidelines refer to this as the why of learning. In practice, multiple means of engagement involve energising learners by offering varied learning environments, both face to face and online, as well as opportunities for both collaborative and individual work. The emphasis is on providing choices to learners in their learning methods and captivating their interest with relevant and authentic learning experiences.
- **Multiple means of representation of learning materials:** The UDL guidelines call this the 'what' of learning. 'Multiple means of representation' means offering learning content in various formats so that learners can choose their preferred method to acquire information and knowledge. For example, you might provide a text to read along with a podcast or a video covering the same material. Alternatively, learners might be encouraged to explore a subject using resources they find on their own.
- **Multiple means of action and expression in learning:** The UDL guidelines describe this as the 'how' of learning. 'Multiple means of action and expression' is about giving learners options to demonstrate their learning in different ways. This could include writing an essay, creating a podcast, producing an information booklet or recording a video presentation.

Figure 7.2 *Universal Design for Learning guidelines version 3.0 (CAST, 2024)*

The Universal Design for Learning Guidelines (UDL)

The goal of UDL is **learner agency** that is purposeful and reflective, resourceful and authentic, strategic and action-oriented.

	Design multiple means of engagement
Access	**Design options for welcoming interests and identities** (7)
	• Optimise choice and autonoy (7.1)
	• Optimise relevance, value, and authenticity (7.2)
	• Nurture joy and play (7.3)
	• Address biases threats, and distractions (7.4)
Support	**Design options for sustaining effort and persistence** (8)
	• Clarify the meaning and purpose of goals (8.1)
	• Optimise challenge and support (8.2)
	• Foster collaboration, interdependence, and collective learning (8.3)
	• Foster belonging and community (8.4)
	• Offer action-oriented feedback (8.5)
Executive Function	**Design options for emotional capacity** (9)
	• Recognise expectations, beliefs, and motivations (9.1)
	• Develop awareness of self and others (9.2)
	• Promote individual and collective reflection (9.3)
	• Cultivate empathy and restorative practices (9.4)

	Design multiple means of representation
Access	**Design options for perception** (1)
	• Support opportunities to customise the display of information (1.1)

Figure 7.2 *(Cont.)*

	• Support multiple ways to perceive information (1.2)
	• Represent a diversity of perspectives and identities in authentic ways (1.3)
Support	**Design options for language and symbols** (2)
	• Clarify vocabulary, symbols, and language structures (2.1)
	• Support decoding of text, mathematical notations, and symbols (2.2)
	• Cultivate understanding and respect across languages and dialects (2.3)
	• Illustrate through multiple media (2.5)
Executive Function	**Design options for building knowledge** (3)
	• Connect prior knowledge to new learning (3.1)
	• Highlight and explore patterns, critical features, big ideas, and relationships (3.2)
	• Cultivate multiple ways of knowing and making meaning (3.3)
	• Maximise transfer and generalization (3.4)

	Design multiple means of action and expression
Access	**Design options for interaction** (4)
	• Vary and honor the methods for response, navigation, and movement (4.1)
	• Optimise access to accessible materials and assistive and accessible technologies and tools (4.2)
Support	**Design options for expression and communication** (5)
	• Use multiple media for communication (5.1)
	• Use multiple tools for construction, composition, and creativity (5.2)
	• Build fluencies with graduated support for practice and performance (5.3)
	• Address biases related to modes of expression and communication (5.4)

→

Figure 7.2 *(Cont.)*

Executive Function	**Design options for strategy development** (6)
	• Set meaningful goals (6.1)
	• Anticipate and plan for challenges (6.2)
	• Organise information and resources (6.3)
	• Enhance capacity for monitoring progress (6.4)
	• Challenge exclusionary practices (6.5)

Critical questions ?

» Revisit and reflect on the questions at the start of this section. Has your understanding of curriculum design and planning changed or deepened? Why and how?

» Read the following article: www.fenews.co.uk/fe-voices/the-intersectionality-of-theory-of-mind-in-21st-century-education-insights-for-inclusion (Hoole, 2023). Explore the concept of intersectionality and its impact on curriculum design and inclusive practice. How can you apply an intersectional lens to identify and address the unique needs of learners from different backgrounds and life experiences?

Activity ?

» Visit the UDL website and download the key questions for consideration (CAST, 2020) when planning lessons via the link: www.cast.org/products-services/resources/2020/udl-guidelines-key-questions-planning-lessons

» Write down your answers to the key questions and discuss your answers with your colleagues. What would you do differently in your lesson planning?

Person-centred approach

The person-centred approach was first defined within the field of humanistic psychology, particularly in the work of Rogers (1961). This approach emphasises the core belief that every learner has the capacity for growth and self-direction.

Person-centred planning integrates principles from diverse psychological frameworks, including social learning theory, personal construct theory and positive psychology. This methodology promotes self-awareness, individualised learning, self-efficacy, resilience and a sense of belonging. Numerous practitioners acknowledge person-centred approaches as tangible implementations of positive psychology concepts, exemplified by solution-focused work and appreciative inquiry. Furthermore, professionals often identify parallels between person-centred practices and the applications of social psychology that are frequently employed within educational contexts. Some of the key theories include the following.

- **Social learning theory** was developed by Albert Bandura in 1977 and further expanded by scholars including Carol Dweck. This theory posits that people learn behaviours, skills and attitudes through observing others, imitating their actions and modelling their behaviour. Social learning theory emphasises the importance of social influences and cognitive processes in the development of new behaviours. The role of intrinsic motivation is important in fostering the learners' sense of pride, satisfaction and achievement. Dweck (2006) emphasises the significance of embracing a 'growth mindset', wherein mistakes and challenges are viewed as essential components of meaningful learning experiences.
- **Personal construct theory** offers a framework for comprehending the ideas that shape everyone's unique perception of the world. Learners strive to understand their environment and predict future events, thus formulating theories referred to as 'personal constructs'. These personal constructs serve as cognitive lenses through which events are interpreted. Understanding these constructs facilitates meaningful listening and enhances comprehension of individuals on a personal level.
- **Positive psychology** emphasises the positive aspects of human life, such as happiness, well-being and human flourishing. Martin Seligman, a leading figure in this field, described positive psychology as '*the scientific study of optimal human functioning, which aims to discover and promote the factors that allow individuals and communities to thrive*' (Seligman and Csikszentmihalyi, 2000, p 5).

Here are the key principles in the person-centred approach.

- **Unconditional positive regard:** Treat every learner with respect and value, regardless of their background or behaviour.
- **Empathy:** Strive to understand and share the emotions and perspectives of learners.
- **Congruence:** Be honest and authentic in interactions with learners, creating a trusting and open learning environment.

Activity ⑦

» How could you implement the person-centred approach in your learning environment?

Discussion

Here are some suggestions as to how this approach can be integrated into your curriculum design and development.

- **Creating a supportive, motivating and safe learning environment:** It is important to establish a classroom culture that promotes equality, mutual respect, safety and trust. This requires investing time in listening to your learners and identifying what their starting points are. Learners who enter the FES sector have varied experiences from their past, and it is important to identify their needs and what they are aspiring to accomplish. The Education and Training Foundation has published a guide called *Creating Spaces to Think in Further Education* (Mycroft and Sidebottom, 2022) which provides a helpful framework and practical strategies for creating a thoughtful and caring environment for all. You will have an opportunity to explore the guide further in the chapter task.
- **Student voice and choice:** You should encourage learner participation in decision-making processes related to their learning. When planning a curriculum, it is essential to provide opportunities for learners to choose topics, projects and methods of assessment that interest them and align with their goals.
- **Building strong relationships:** One of the essential parts of creating an inclusive environment is about building strong, supportive relationships with learners to understand their individual needs, interests and aspirations. A helpful strategy is using regular, meaningful communication to stay connected with learners and provide personalised support.
- **Individualised learning plans:** Teaching professionals should develop personalised learning plans that cater to each learner's strengths, needs and learning preferences. Learners are encouraged and supported to set achievable and personalised goals that need to be regularly reviewed.

Based on the above principles, some practical strategies are listed in Table 7.2.

Table 7.2 *Person-centred approaches and practical strategies*

Person-centred approaches	Practical strategies
Active listening and effective communication	• Practise active listening techniques to fully understand learners' perspectives and needs. • Use open-ended questions and reflective statements to facilitate deeper conversations with learners.

Table 7.2 *(Cont.)*

Person-centred approaches	Practical strategies
Flexible teaching methods	• Employ a variety of teaching methods and adapt them to meet the diverse needs of learners. • Use project-based learning, experiential learning and other learner-centred approaches to make learning more engaging and relevant.
Assessment for Learning	• Use formative assessment methods to provide ongoing feedback that supports student learning and growth. • Involve learners in self-assessment and peer assessment to help them take ownership of their learning process.
Promoting self-advocacy and independence	• Encourage learners to set their own learning goals and develop self-advocacy skills. • Support learners in developing the confidence and skills needed to take responsibility for their learning and personal development.

It is essential for teaching professionals to engage in CPD and reflection to deepen understanding and practice of the person-centred approach.

Some of the practical ways to engage with CPD include participation in workshops, seminars and peer learning groups that focused on person-centred education. It is helpful to regularly reflect on teaching practices and interactions with learners to identify areas for improvement by using learner feedback to inform and enhance teaching methods and classroom practices. Another useful way to develop and enhance person-centred practice is to work collaboratively with colleagues to share best practices and support each other in implementing person-centred approaches. Planning an inclusive and person-centred curriculum requires a whole-team approach, using collaborative planning and problem-solving to address challenges and enhance learner outcomes.

Critical questions ?

Download and read the introduction, Chapter 1 and 2 in the guide called *Creating Spaces to Think in Further Education* (Mycroft and Sidebottom, 2022): www.et-foundation.co.uk/wp-content/uploads/2022/04/OTLA-AP-guide-CreatingSpaces-31.03.22-FINAL.pdf

» What is your understanding of the ten components (appreciation, attention, difference, ease, encouragement, equality, feelings, incisive questions, information and place)?

→

» How could you introduce and integrate the Thinking Environment approaches to your practice?

Planning and delivering sessions

> *'By failing to prepare, you are preparing to fail.'* – Benjamin Franklin
>
> *'A man who does not plan long ahead will find trouble at his door.'* – Confucius
>
> *'Our goals can only be reached through a vehicle of a plan, in which we must fervently believe, and upon which we must vigorously act. There is no other route to success.'* – Pablo Picasso

The above quotes suggest that planning and preparation is the key to manage and be ready for our everyday life. Through planning and preparation, teachers and trainers ensure the smooth delivery of teaching/training sessions or practical workshops to meet the needs of learners in the FES sector. There is a range of planning processes and documentation that require careful consideration (see Figure 7.3).

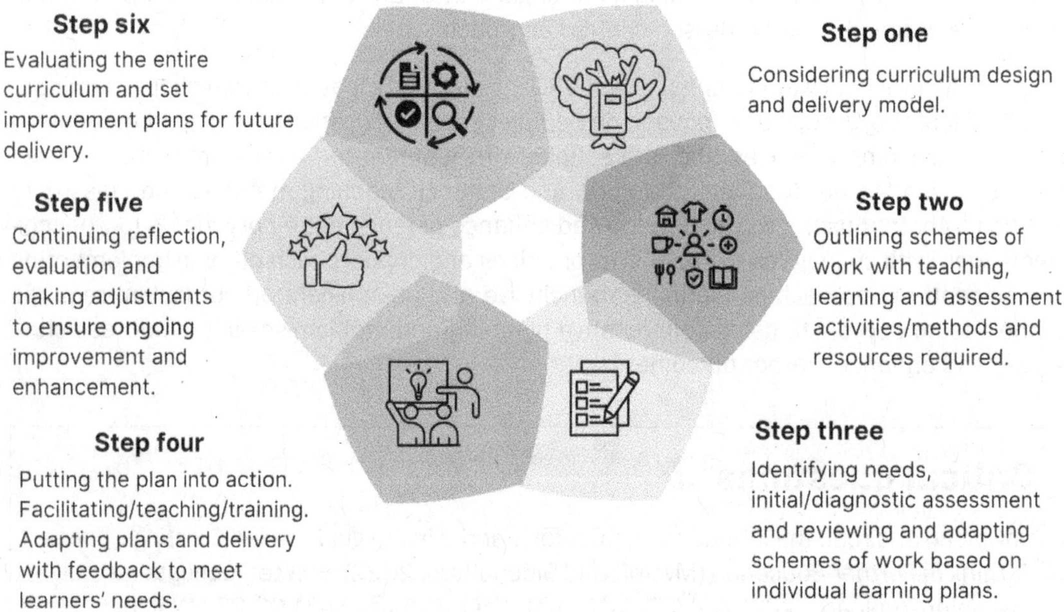

Figure 7.3 *The six-step planning and delivery process*

Source: Author's own

Step one: considering curriculum design and delivery model

In the initial step, it is important to begin by designing a curriculum that aligns with educational outcomes and the needs of the target learner group. Select a delivery model (eg in-person, online, blended) that best suits the content and the learners' circumstances. Also consider factors such as the structure of the programme, the sequence of topics, end point assessment requirements, and the integration of theoretical and practical elements to ensure comprehensive coverage of the subject matter.

Step two: outlining schemes of work with teaching, learning and assessment activities/methods and resources required

In the next step, develop detailed schemes of work that outline the topics to be covered in each session, the teaching and learning activities, assessment methods and the resources required. Ensure that these schemes incorporate a variety of instructional strategies to cater to different learning needs, and include formative and summative assessments to monitor learner progress.

Step three: identifying needs, initial/diagnostic assessment and reviewing and adapting schemes of work based on individual learning plans

In this step, conduct initial and diagnostic assessments to identify the specific needs, strengths and areas for improvement for each learner. Use this information to review and adapt the schemes of work, creating individualised learning plans that address the unique needs of each student. This step ensures that all learners are supported appropriately and can achieve their potential.

Step four: putting the plan into action; facilitating/teaching/training; adapting plans and delivery with feedback to meet learners' needs

This is the implementation stage and involves facilitating, teaching or training as planned. Use a variety of instructional techniques to engage learners actively and monitor their progress continuously. Be prepared to adapt the lesson plans and delivery methods based on real-time feedback and observations to better meet the learners' needs and enhance their understanding.

Step five: continuing reflection, evaluation and making adjustments to ensure ongoing improvement and enhancement

It is essential to regularly reflect on the effectiveness of your teaching and the learners' progress. This can be achieved by collecting and analysing feedback from learners, peers and self-assessment to identify areas for improvement. This is followed by making necessary adjustments to the teaching strategies, materials and activities to ensure ongoing enhancement of the learning experience.

Step six: evaluating the entire curriculum and setting improvement plans for future delivery

At the end of the course or programme, conduct a comprehensive evaluation of the entire curriculum; assess the overall effectiveness of the curriculum design, delivery model and outcomes. Based on the evaluation, set specific improvement plans for future delivery, ensuring that the curriculum continues to evolve and meet the changing needs of learners and/or educational outcomes.

These steps are formed as a starting point for teaching professionals and on a continuing basis for improvement and enhancement.

CASE STUDY

Amelia, a new teacher, has recently joined an FES college. She is enthusiastic but feels overwhelmed with the task of planning her curriculum for the upcoming term. She does not know where to start her planning and spends a lot of time trying to locate resources.

As Amelia's colleague, what hints and tips could you offer to her? How can you support her based on the above planning and delivery process?

Developing inclusive resources to meet learner needs

Inclusive resources and materials are essential to support and motivate learners. Effective design and use of resources can increase learner engagement, encourage curiosity and enrich the course/programme (Avis et al, 2019).

Inclusive resource design ensures that educational materials and activities are accessible, engaging and effective for all learners, regardless of their diverse backgrounds and abilities. You may find that this chapter links closely to Chapter 4, with more specific exploration of the emotional health of the learner and pedagogies related to supporting learners with specific learning needs. Table 7.3 shows the key principles for the design and development of inclusive resources.

Table 7.3 *Key principles for the design and development of inclusive resources*

Key principles	Description	Examples
Accessibility	Ensure all resources are accessible to learners with disabilities. This includes using readable fonts, providing text descriptions for images and ensuring compatibility with assistive technologies.	Screen reader-compatible documents, captioned videos, large print materials.
Inclusivity	Design resources that reflect and respect the diverse cultural, linguistic and social backgrounds of learners. Avoid stereotypes and ensure representation.	Diverse case studies, multilingual resources, culturally relevant examples.
Clarity and simplicity	Present information in a clear, organised and straightforward manner. Avoid unnecessary complexity to reduce cognitive load.	Use bullet points, headings and concise language; provide step-by-step instructions.
Engagement	Create interactive and engaging resources that cater to different learning styles and keep learners motivated.	Interactive simulations, gamified learning activities, multimedia presentations.
Flexibility	Develop adaptable resources that can be modified to suit various learning paces and styles. Allow for personalisation and differentiation.	Customisable templates, adjustable difficulty levels, varied activity formats.
Feedback and assessment	Integrate regular opportunities for feedback and assessment to monitor progress and address individual learning needs.	Formative quizzes, peer feedback sessions, self-assessment checklists.
Supportive learning environment	Foster an inclusive and supportive environment that encourages collaboration and mutual respect among learners.	Group work guidelines, inclusive discussion prompts, clear communication channels.
Cultural sensitivity	Ensure resources are culturally sensitive and promote an understanding of different perspectives and experiences.	Global case studies, culturally diverse reading materials, inclusive language.
Continuous improvement	Regularly review and update resources based on feedback and changing needs to maintain their relevance and effectiveness.	Feedback surveys, resource audits, ongoing professional development.

There are different types of resources and an increasing choice of digital tools and technology available for use (see Table 7.4).

Table 7.4 *Types of resources and examples*

Types of resources	Description	Examples
Textbooks	Traditional print or digital books used to provide comprehensive coverage of a subject.	Subject-specific textbooks, ebooks.
Handouts	Printed or digital documents provided to learners to supplement lessons.	Lecture notes, summaries, worksheets.
Presentation slides	Visual aids used to support lectures and presentations.	PowerPoint slides, Google Slides, Prezi presentations.
Multimedia resources	Materials that use a combination of text, audio and video to enhance learning.	Educational videos, podcasts, interactive simulations.
Interactive whiteboards	Digital whiteboards used to display and interact with digital content.	Smartboards, digital annotation tools.
Online learning platforms	Web-based platforms that host courses and learning materials.	Moodle, Canvas, Blackboard.
Open educational resources (OERs)	OERs are a fantastic type of instructional material because they are free to reuse, adapt and share. They have been created and led by educational professionals.	OERs can include various materials such as lesson plans, quizzes, online articles, digital media, databases, simulations, and more. These resources are accessible in extensive collections or via search engines, and they can vary from single images to comprehensive courses.
Assessment tools	Resources designed to evaluate learner understanding and progress.	Quizzes, tests, online assessment tools like Kahoot!, Quizizz, Socrative.
AI-generated tools	Tools for drafting and editing text, images and other media.	There is a range of tools available such as ChatGPT, Copilot and Midjourney.
Specialist equipment	Tools and materials used for hands-on experiments and practical learning.	Circuit tester, lab kits, 3D printer.
Manipulatives	Physical objects used to teach concepts through hands-on experience.	Maths blocks, geometric shapes, science models.

Table 7.4 *(Cont.)*

Types of resources	Description	Examples
Software applications	Computer programs designed to support learning in specific areas.	Coding software, design software (AutoCAD, Photoshop).
Mobile apps	Educational applications accessible via smartphones and tablets.	Duolingo, Khan Academy, Quizlet.
Books and articles	Supplementary reading materials for deeper understanding of subjects.	Academic journals, articles, reference books.
Case studies	Detailed examination of specific situations used to illustrate concepts.	Business case studies, medical case studies.
Simulations	Digital or physical models used to replicate real-world processes or systems.	Flight simulators, business simulation games.
Games and gamified learning	Resources that use game mechanics to enhance engagement and learning.	Educational games, gamified learning platforms.
Flashcards	Cards with information used for quick review and memorisation.	Vocabulary flashcards, formula flashcards.
Posters and charts	Visual aids that summarise and display information prominently.	Educational posters, infographics, flowcharts.
Study guides	Compiled materials to aid in review and exam preparation.	Revision notes, practice exams, study tips.
Workbooks	Books containing exercises and activities for practice and reinforcement.	Language workbooks, maths practice books.
Field trips and visits	Materials and guides used to support educational trips and excursions.	Field trip guides, activity sheets, observation checklists.

One approach to encouraging person-centred and inclusive learning is project-based learning (PBL). PBL involves engaging individual or group learners to work together on a real-world project. This is a process that involves public presentation of a final product, such as a publication, artwork, service or object. Throughout this process, learners create multiple drafts and prototypes, make informed choices, and demonstrate the concepts and skills they have acquired. With teacher approval, learners can select any project type, provided it aligns with the curriculum and relates to a real-life context.

PBL enhances motivation, self-directed critical thinking and problem-solving skills. Learners develop the ability to research and integrate knowledge from various sources and disciplines, thereby acquiring lifelong skills (Cole, 2024).

Activity ?

» Work with your colleagues to identify opportunities to integrate PBL in your context and curricular planning. What are the opportunities and activities that you have explored and how can you integrate them in your context?

Teacher expectations of learners, including classroom management

Before we explore further the theories and practices related to classroom management, what is your understanding, attitude and belief about human behaviour?

- Do you think human behaviour is learned?
- Do you think behaviour is influenced by the environment and how it is influenced?
- Can humans learn new behaviour and unlearn old behaviour? Why? Why not?

Human behaviour encompasses the potential and manifested abilities of individuals or groups to react to internal and external stimuli throughout their lifespan in the mental, physical and social dimensions (Hutchison and Charlesworth, 2024).

In the FES sector, it is especially challenging to manage classrooms with learners who may struggle to transition from the more 'disciplined and prescriptive' environments to learning independently with self-control and motivation. FES learners are dynamic, including post-14 learners from schools, apprentices, offenders and adult learners. FES teaching professionals often find themselves teaching or training mixed age and experience groups, who each have different reasons for learning, as well as varying expectations and motivations (Vizard, 2012). Thus, it is important to consider how to make an inclusive and positive learning environment where expectations and boundaries are established with clear communication channels.

Classroom management encompasses a range of strategies and techniques that teachers utilise to promote effective learning by reducing distractions and disruptions. It involves all actions taken by a teacher to encourage learner involvement, co-operation and a productive learning environment. Effective classroom management strategies help minimise behaviours that hinder learning, thereby reinforcing practices that support educational progress (Dix, 2017).

Additionally, classroom management includes record-keeping and organising non-academic tasks essential for documenting teaching and learning processes. This involves tracking class attendance, maintaining records of learner progress, and managing the display and storage of instructional materials.

Crucially, classroom management focuses on learner engagement, preparing learners to become self-directed and responsible for their learning. This includes setting their own learning goals, managing their time effectively, and fostering positive relationships with peers and teachers in the classroom (Open University, 2020).

Armitage et al (2016) summarise three key concepts in managing classrooms.

1. **Clarity:** It is important to ensure that you communicate to learners clearly about your role, attitude and expectations; model desired behaviour to set an example for learners; and ensure instructions and explanations are straightforward and unambiguous to avoid misunderstandings. Seeking feedback from learners to build an open and secure learning environment is essential to developing a positive relationship between you and learners.
2. **Consistency:** Consistency in expectations and setting boundaries is key to creating a stable learning environment. It is also important to apply policies and consequences fairly and regularly, ensuring all students understand and trust the classroom management system. Consistent behaviour from the teacher helps in building reliability and respect among learners.
3. **Challenge:** It increases learner engagement by providing appropriate levels of challenge to stimulate their motivation and growth. This can be achieved by setting new, stimulating tasks and supporting learners in overcoming difficulties, promoting resilience and a growth mindset (Dweck, 2006).

Face-to-face and remote delivery

The Department for Education (DfE) (2021) published a literature review on online and blended delivery pedagogy and assessment in FES, following the Covid-19 pandemic. To begin with, it is essential to understand the following terminology and what it means in educational settings.

- **Face-to-face or in-person delivery:** This model of delivery is often described as traditional teaching, which focuses on a range of physical and synchronous activities. The advantages of this type of teaching is that learners value the direct social interactions and immediate feedback that face-to-face classrooms provide. This format allows for real-time questioning and instant clarification, which many learners find beneficial. The traditional classroom setting fosters a sense of belonging and community among learners. This environment supports peer interactions and collaborative learning experiences, which can enhance motivation and engagement.
- **Remote delivery:** There are various definitions of remote delivery. This can include remote education, digital remote education, blended learning and asynchronous

education. According to Hamer and Smith (2021, p 4), remote education is a broad term that '*encompasses any learning that happens outside of the classroom, with the teacher not present in the same locations as the pupils [learners]*'. There is nothing remote about remote delivery because it requires careful planning and curation of curricula and resources. The same principles of a quality curriculum still apply to remote delivery.

- **Blended learning:** Blended learning provides '*a combination of face-to-face learning and digital activities and content that facilitate any time/any place learning*' (Hamer and Smith, 2021, p 18). This model of learning is often presented in a 'flipped classroom' where learners receive learning content and resources remotely, followed by in-person practice and tutorials.

Regardless of the delivery mode, the fundamental pedagogical principles remain unchanged. The focus should always be on the learner, ensuring that teaching practices are effective and inclusive (DfE, 2021). It is critical to maintain a strong teacher presence and facilitate interactions between teachers and learners as well as among learners for both online and blended learning environments. Making use of emerging technologies, such as mobile pedagogy, and immersive technologies, such as augmented reality and virtual reality, holds promise for enriching learning experiences.

The success of either mode hinges on the quality of teaching, access to technology and the ability to adapt to learners' needs. Blended learning, which strategically combines both methods, offers a flexible and inclusive approach that can enhance educational outcomes in FES. Further exploration and explanation about digital and online pedagogies is provided in Chapter 9.

Assessment and feedback

Assessment is an integral part of the teaching and learning cycle. There are internal and external requirements with respect to assessment. A good starting point is to identify your initial understanding about assessment.

- What is assessment?
- Why do you assess?
- What is the difference between assessment, testing and accreditation?
- Do you perceive assessment primarily as a means of qualification attainment, or do you emphasise its role in evaluating overall outcomes and achievements?
- What specific assessment methods do you currently employ to ascertain the extent of your learners' comprehension and progress?
- How do you deliver feedback to learners in a manner that fosters their understanding and guides them in improving, developing and enhancing their learning?

Based on the above questions, you will explore the definition, purpose and key concepts of assessment and how to integrate assessment in the planning process.

Hamilton and Hillier (2006, p 212) summarise that:

> *assessment is a process of identifying what has been learnt, either recently or over a length of time, whereas accreditation is the award of credit, leading to qualifications, of learning which can be shown through the successful achievement of learning outcomes.*

This definition differentiates assessment from testing and accreditation. Assessment is a process through which teaching professionals collect information regarding the effectiveness of teaching and learning, as well as the suitability of the course or curriculum being used. While assessment may include assigning marks or grades, it encompasses much more. It is vital to the educational process because it informs teaching professionals' decisions on selecting and approaching learning tasks. Additionally, assessment provides insights into which areas of the curriculum require revision.

Based on the purpose of assessment, Clarke (2008) introduced the following concepts.

- **Assessment of Learning:** This type of assessment is often described as summative assessment, which include tests and grades. This type of assessment is often based on standards, measurement or criteria and normally occurs at the end of a task, unit, module or course. The main purpose of this type of assessment is to identify individual learners' level of learning. It is important to use a mixture of assessment types to accommodate different learning needs and provide fair and equitable opportunities for learners.
- **Assessment for Learning (AfL):** Formative assessment methods are used to provide ongoing feedback that supports student learning and growth. AfL involves learners in self-assessment and peer assessment to help them take ownership of their learning process. This type of assessment is usually not graded. Conversely, AfL makes learners' skills and understanding visible, provides feedback and determines the next steps in advancing each learner's learning. Learners and teachers co-construct in a dialogue to improve both learning and teaching. Some of the key principles to design AfL include:
  - setting clear expectations and monitoring progress;
  - identifying particular needs of learners or groups;
  - selecting and adapting materials and resources;
  - creating differentiated teaching strategies and learning opportunities;
  - providing immediate feedback and direction to support individual learners to move forward.

AfL focuses on learner engagement and motivation. Strategies in planning and using AfL include:

- determining what learners know and can do;
- facilitating the learners' understanding of what they are to learn and what is expected of them;

- identifying confusions, preconceptions or gaps in learning;
- identifying progress and needs (learning outcomes);
- determining the next steps in advancing learning;
- responding to learners' questions, concerns and requests;
- providing timely, action-oriented feedback and advice to learners on how to improve their work such as feed forward;
- helping learners understand their strengths and gaps and to plan their own learning.

Further exploration of AfL is provided in Chapter 10.

- **Assessment as Learning:** This type of assessment is usually formative and ungraded. For example, teaching professionals would elicit students' learning and metacognitive processes (Flavell, 1976), before then creating opportunities for students to monitor and critically reflect on their learning and identify next steps. Metacognition is the process of thinking about thinking. There are two key concepts of metacognition: metacognitive knowledge and self-regulation. Metacognitive knowledge refers to what an individual learner knows about themselves, such as strengths and areas for improvement and strategies for learning and problem-solving. Self-regulation involves the conscious strategies and tools we employ to manage our thinking processes. *Assessment as Learning* is used to empower learners to self-regulate their learning behaviour.

When planning for assessment in curricula, it is paramount to consider the purpose of different assessments. During the learning process, students learn about themselves as learners and become aware of how they learn. Some examples and teaching strategies to develop learner autonomy and independence include:

- assisting students in setting their own goals and tracking their progress;
- providing examples and models of high-quality work that align with curriculum outcomes;
- demonstrating and instructing in the skills of self-assessment;
- collaborating with learners to establish clear criteria for good practice in learning;
- offering frequent and challenging opportunities for practice, enabling learners to build confidence in self-evaluation;
- observing learners' metacognitive processes and their learning and providing constructive feedback;
- fostering a safe environment where learners can take risks and readily find support.

Other strategies involve:

- encouraging learners to use self and peer assessments, along with exemplars and criteria, to reflect on tasks;

- reflecting on learning strategies to both support and challenge progress, making adjustments as necessary;
- actively engaging in and documenting their own learning through self-reflection and goal setting;
- taking responsibility for their learning and keeping track of future goals and directions.

There are many different assessment types and methods. In Table 7.5, you can locate the most common methods and strategies when planning curricula.

Table 7.5 *Assessment types, methods and strategies*

Assessment types	What does it mean?	Practical methods and strategies
Formative assessment	Ongoing assessments, reviews and observations during the learning process.	Exit tickets, quizzes, observations, polls
Summative assessment	Evaluation at the end of a unit or programme by comparing it against standards or benchmarks.	Final exams, end-of-term projects, standardised tests
Initial and diagnostic assessment	Pre-assessment to determine students' knowledge, skills and misconceptions before instruction.	Pre-tests, diagnostic quizzes, KWL charts
Peer assessment	Students assess each other's contributions using a predefined set of criteria.	Peer review forms, collaborative rubrics
Self-assessment	Students evaluate their own learning and progress.	Self-reflection journals, checklists, rating scales
Criterion referenced	Tests that measure student performance against a fixed set of criteria or learning standards.	Rubrics, skill checklists, competency tests
Informal assessment	Unstructured, spontaneous assessments often conducted in a casual manner.	Observations, informal questioning, class discussions
Formal assessment	Structured assessments with pre-determined criteria and standards.	Written exams, assignments, projects
Holistic assessment	Several criteria are assessed from multiple tasks, aspects or units and often when learners carry out tasks in a work environment.	Digital portfolios, physical portfolios, professional discussions

The reflective teacher

In education, reflective practice has become a crucial aspect of demonstrating professionalism and ongoing professional development. This importance stems from the often-tacit nature of professional knowledge, which can be challenging to articulate explicitly. Through reflection, teaching professionals can reveal implicit knowledge by critically thinking about and questioning their assumptions, resulting in significant changes in both their thinking and practice (Moon, 2004).

Dewey (1933, p 118) in *How We Think* introduces the concept of reflective thought and defines it as:

> *active, persistent, and careful consideration of any belief or supposed form of knowledge in the light of the grounds that support it and the further conclusion to which it tends ... it includes a conscious and voluntary effort to establish belief upon a firm basis of evidence and rationality.*

Dewey's concept of 'reflective experience' relies on the intentional cultivation of thoughts that link actions to their consequences (Dewey, 1916).

Reflective practice is '*a state of mind, and ongoing attitude to life and work, the pearly grit in the oyster of practice and education; danger lies in it being a separate curriculum element with a set of exercises*' (Bolton and Delderfield, 2018, p 1). It is the ability to reflect on your own experiences and actions in order to engage in a process of continuous learning. Reflective practice is a way of studying your own experiences to improve the way you teach. Critical reflection is '*the sustained and intentional process of identifying and checking the accuracy and validity of your teaching assumptions*' (Brookfield, 2017, p 3). It is very useful for teachers who want to carry on professional learning throughout their teaching career. The act of reflection is a great way to increase confidence and become a more self-critical and autonomous professional (Appleyard and Appleyard, 2015). FES teachers, just like any other professionals, have a duty of care to enhance their skills and knowledge via a process of continuous reflective practice, as it is an integral part of maintaining professional practice and status.

It is important for teaching professionals to observe their own behaviour, feelings, thoughts, skills, attitudes, assumptions and biases from different perspectives. This offers teachers a more thorough understanding of dilemmas or scenarios in their classroom and promotes new ways of thinking. Some of the benefits of reflective practice are the following.

- It can help teachers recognise and continue good practices.
- It can make teachers become aware of aspects of current practices that could be improved.
- It can help teachers identify areas that require considerable attention.

Appleyard and Appleyard (2015, p 16) identify six key features of reflective practice:

- *It is cyclical.*
- *It is ongoing.*

- *It is multi-sourced.*
- *It is recorded.*
- *It is objective and logical.*
- *It requires an open mind and curiosity.*

There are different reflective models and theories that can help teaching professionals to evaluate and reflect on their practice. David Kolb (1984) proposed a four-stage model that describes how learners acquire knowledge through experience(s). This experiential learning cycle consists of four stages: concrete experience, reflective observation, abstract conceptualisation and active experimentation, as represented in Figure 7.4. You can enter the cycle at any stage, but the process is continuing and iterative, allowing for ongoing learning and development.

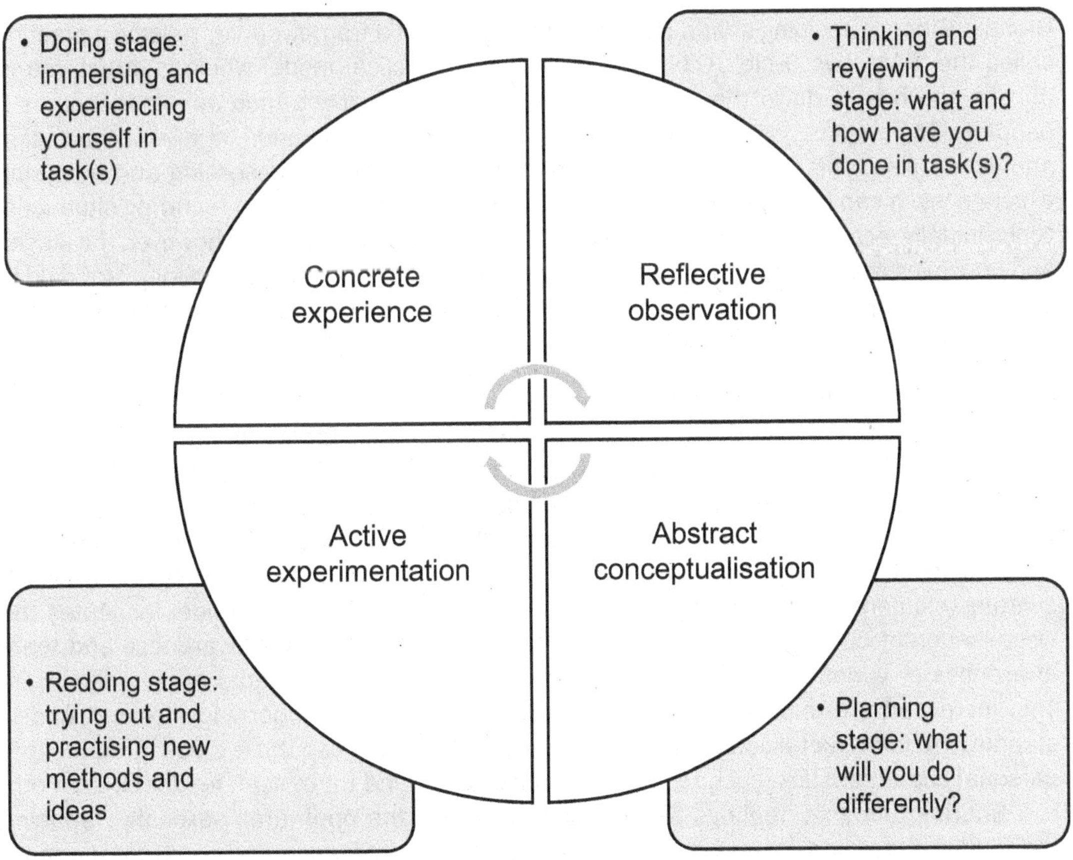

Figure 7.4 *Kolb's experiential learning cycle (1984)*

The four stages of Kolb's experiential learning cycle include the following.

1. **Concrete experience (CE):** This stage involves having direct or firsthand experience. It is the 'doing' phase where you actively engage in an activity.
2. **Reflective observation (RO):** After the experience, you step back to reflect on what happened. This stage involves observing and thinking about the experience from different perspective.
3. **Abstract conceptualisation (AC):** In this stage, you form abstract concepts and generalisations based on your reflections. You develop theories, ideas or conclusions that can explain the experience.
4. **Active experimentation (AE):** You use the new ideas or concepts that have been developed to test their validity in new situations. This stage involves planning and trying out what you have learned.

Graham Gibbs, a sociologist and psychologist, developed a framework for reflective practice called the 'Reflective Cycle' (Gibbs, 1988). This is a cyclical model which is structured in phases and breaks down the experience, allowing you to reflect upon an experience as it happens. The cycle covers six stages: description, feelings, evaluation, analysis, conclusion and action plan. This model provides a practical framework for processing and analysing experiences. It can be effectively applied to both isolated incidents and recurring situations. Gibbs initially recommended this model for use with repetitive scenarios; however, the stages and principles are equally applicable to singular experiences. When utilised for a standalone event, the action plan may adopt a broader perspective, focusing on the application of the derived conclusions to future contexts.

Another reflective model is described as Johari's Window (see Figure 7.5). The term 'Johari' is derived from the names of psychologists Joseph Luft and Harry Ingham, who developed the model in 1955. The Johari's Window is structured into four principal quadrants: the open area, encompassing aspects known to both the individual and others; the blind area, which includes elements known to others but not to the individual; the hidden area, comprising aspects known to the individual but not to others; and the unknown area, which contains elements unknown to both the individual and others. This model facilitates the visualisation of one's personality and can be used to enhance self-awareness and team awareness of various characteristics, preferences, abilities, strengths and weaknesses. This increased awareness can subsequently improve team rapport, loyalty and understanding. To construct a Johari Window, one should follow these three steps: first, identify personal characteristics; second, define specific goals; and third, seek feedback from others. Sharing thoughts, feelings and opinions enlarges the open area vertically, reducing the hidden area, and fosters greater understanding, acceptance and trust among team members.

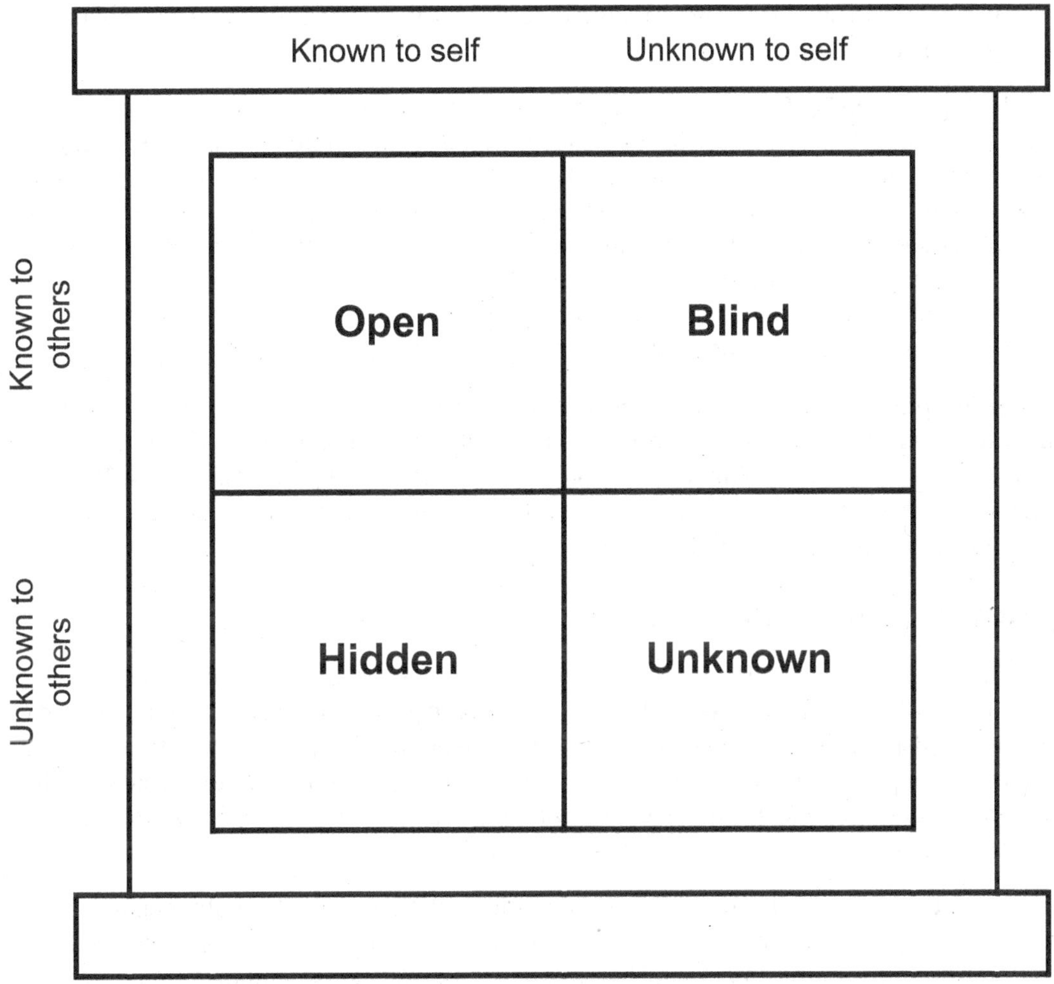

Figure 7.5 *Johari's Window (1955)*

Source: Adapted from Esposito et al, 1978

Brookfield (2017) suggests that the value of teaching can be discovered through critical reflection, which he views as essential for excellent teaching. Critically reflective teachers continually refine their 'authentic voices' and pedagogic principles, recognising the worth and dignity of their work. This reflection brings multiple benefits, such as self-assuredness, goal achievement and reflective learners. Brookfield proposes four lenses for reflection: autobiographical, learners' perspectives, colleagues' experiences and theoretical literature. Self-reflection, rooted in teachers' experiences, is the foundation for identifying areas for improvement. Understanding learner experiences is crucial for responsive teaching and equity. Engaging with peers provides feedback, innovative solutions and a sense of shared challenges. The scholarly literature enhances teachers' understanding of broader educational contexts. Excellent critical practice involves not just collecting feedback but also implementing changes, documenting progress and fostering democratic learning environments.

Brookfield emphasises that the continuous effort to improve teaching is the hallmark of exceptional educators.

Schön (1983, 1987) offers a fresh perspective on professional practice by introducing the concept of 'reflection-in-action'. Schön believes that effective professionals possess an intuitive, often 'tacit' knowledge they can reflect on even while they work, allowing them to manage unique and uncertain situations. He distinguishes between traditional technical rationality, which focuses solely on problem-solving, and his approach, which includes problem setting and framing issues interactively. He explains 'knowing-in-action' as the spontaneous and often tacit knowledge professionals use without conscious thought, and 'reflecting-in-action' as the process of thinking about and adjusting one's actions in real time.

Reflective practice necessitates dedicated time, space and conscious effort within our daily routines. In the field of education, it is a fundamental component of our professional development and the ongoing pursuit of enhancing our teaching methodologies. The aforementioned models and theories provide a valuable foundation for teaching professionals, encouraging them to examine their practices from various perspectives.

Effective communication

Effective communication is vital in teaching, extending beyond classroom instruction to include identifying and discussing learning and progress. The most successful communication methods convey messages clearly and unambiguously, capturing the attention of the target audience. Good communicators excel in selecting the appropriate medium for their specific purpose in mind. Communication can take various forms, including written, oral and visual. We often use a combination of all three forms.

- **Written:** An effective use of written communication is adding annotations to a learner's work before returning it and then following up with a dialogue. It is vital to build a two-way communication rather than a didactic communicative approach. Other methods include emails, newsletters, blogs or digital communication tools such as text messages or chats.
- **Oral:** An effective use of oral communication is speaking to a learner in person about behavioural concerns in class. An ineffective use would be giving a learner their final exam grade verbally without any written documentation or explanation. Other oral communication methods include the use of telephones, audio calls or meetings.
- **Visual:** An effective use of visual communication is creating a video about a topic to convey key information to learners. An ineffective use would be sending a photograph of their work after submission without any annotations. Video conferencing is also a commonly used method.

It's important to recognise that communication can occur face to face, remotely or through digital/online formats. Selecting the most suitable method depends on the message's nature. For instance, sensitive messages are often best delivered in person, while formal information might be more appropriately conveyed through a letter or email. Determine whether the communication is didactic – a message to be read, watched or listened to without immediate response – or intended to initiate a conversation, as this will influence the choice of communication method.

It is essential to consider the recipient's preferences as well. Some learners benefit from having the opportunity to read feedback at their own pace, while others may better understand through a face-to-face discussion. Tailoring your communication approach to the needs of the individual will enhance the effectiveness of your message.

Non-verbal communication is equally essential to effective communication. This includes body language such as facial expressions, eye contact, gestures, posture, movements, signals and appearance. Your personality is conveyed through your body language. It's important to be aware of your learners' body language. A key communication strategy is to pay attention to both what your learners are saying and what they aren't saying, such as their facial expressions when you explain something.

Active listening is a communication technique that involves fully focusing, understanding, responding and remembering what the speaker is saying. It requires the listener to give their full attention, avoid interrupting and engage with the speaker through verbal and non-verbal feedback (Rogers and Farson, 1957).

In addition to having specific learning preferences, learners and other professionals may have additional needs that you should be aware of and accommodate when communicating with them. For example, a learner with a visual impairment might require audio descriptions or commentaries for videos used in their learning. Similarly, a colleague with hearing difficulties might prefer email communication over phone calls. Numerous accessibility tools are available to help you adapt your communications to ensure they are received and understood by everyone. The key is to be aware of the additional needs of those you are communicating with so you can plan your communication appropriately.

In conclusion, effective communication in teaching requires a thoughtful selection of methods tailored to the message's nature and the recipient's preferences and needs. By integrating different forms of communication and utilising accessibility tools, educators can ensure their communications are clear, inclusive and impactful.

Summary

Planning for teaching and learning in the FES sector requires a holistic and inclusive approach. The process encompasses rigorous curriculum design, effective classroom management and diverse assessment strategies. Reflective practice and continuous professional development are essential for professionals in the FES sector to remain current with pedagogical advancements and subject-specific knowledge and practices. Through thoughtful planning and implementation, FES professionals can create supportive and engaging learning environments that meet the needs of all learners.

Check your understanding (level 5)

1. What are the key principles of rigorous curriculum thinking and inclusive practice?
2. How does the person-centred approach integrate principles from social learning theory, personal construct theory and positive psychology?
3. What strategies can be employed to manage positive classroom behaviour and maintain an inclusive learning environment?
4. Could you identify and explain different types of assessment methods and their purposes?
5. What are the essential steps in the six-step planning and delivery process for effective teaching?
6. How can Universal Design for Learning (UDL) be applied to create an inclusive curriculum?
7. Could you describe practical strategies for promoting self-advocacy and independence among learners?
8. What is the importance of reflective practice for continuous improvement in teaching, and what models can be used to facilitate it?
9. How can teachers develop inclusive resources that cater to the diverse backgrounds and abilities of learners?
10. Could you explain the role of effective communication in teaching and the different forms it can take to ensure inclusivity and clarity?

Developmental questions L6+7

1. How can the principles of UDL be integrated into both face-to-face and digital delivery methods to create a cohesive and inclusive learning environment? You need to provide specific examples.
2. How can initial and diagnostic assessments be effectively integrated into your curriculum to address diverse learner needs and improve educational outcomes?
3. How can you incorporate feedback and self-reflection to drive ongoing improvements in your practice?
4. What are the potential challenges and benefits of implementing a PBL approach in a diverse classroom setting? How can you balance the needs of various learners while maintaining the integrity and objectives of the curriculum?

Helpful websites and resources

- Blended learning models: www.blendedlearning.org/models
- Education and Training Foundation: https://learning.etfoundation.co.uk/courses/advancing-equality-in-further-education
- NHS England: www.hee.nhs.uk/our-work/person-centred-care
- Ofsted guidance: www.gov.uk/government/publications/whats-working-well-in-remote-education/whats-working-well-in-remote-education
- UDL guidelines: https://udlguidelines.cast.org

Further reading

- Cole, F (2024) *An Educator's Guide to Project-Based Learning: Turning Theory into Practice*. London: David Fulton Publishers.
- Hutchison, E D and Charlesworth, L W (eds) (2024) *Dimensions of Human Behavior: The Changing Life Course*. Thousand Oaks, CA: Sage.
- Nunan, D (1988) *The Learner-Centred Curriculum: A Study in Second Language Teaching*. Cambridge: Cambridge University Press.
- Spady, W G (1994) *Outcome-Based Education: Critical Issues and Answers*. Arlington, VA: American Association of School Administrators.
- Stoller, F L (2004) Content-Based Instruction: Perspectives on Curriculum Planning. *Annual Review of Applied Linguistics*, 24: 261–83.

References

Appleyard, K and Appleyard, N (2015) *Reflective Teaching and Learning in Further Education*. Northwich: Critical Publishing.

Armitage, A, Cogger, A, Evershed, J, Hayes, D, Lawes, S and Renwick, M (2016) *Teaching in Post-14 Education & Training*. 5th ed. Maidenhead: Open University Press.

Avis, J, Fisher, R and Thompson, R (2019) *Teaching in Lifelong Learning: A Guide to Theory and Practice*. Milton Keynes: Open University Press.

Bolton, G and Delderfield, R (2018) *Reflective Practice: Writing and Professional Development*. London: Sage.

Brookfield, S D (2017) *Becoming a Critically Reflective Teacher*. San Francisco, CA: Jossey-Bass.

CAST (2020) *Key Questions to Consider When Planning Lessons*. Wakefield, MA: CAST. (Reprinted from *Universal Design for Learning: Theory and Practice*, by Meyer, A, Rose, D H and Gordon, D (2014), Author). [online] Available at: https://www.cast.org/products-services/resources/2020/udl-guidelines-key-questions-planning-lessons (accessed 10 July 2024).

CAST (2024) *Universal Design for Learning Guidelines Version 3.0*. [online] Available at: http://udlguidelines.cast.org (accessed 14 August 2024).

Clarke, S (2008) *Active Learning Through Formative Assessment*. London: Hodder Education.

Cole, F (2024) *An Educator's Guide to Project-Based Learning: Turning Theory into Practice*. London: David Fulton Publishers.

Crenshaw, K (1989) Demarginalizing the Intersection of Race and Sex: A Black Feminist Critique of Antidiscrimination Doctrine, Feminist Theory and Antiracist Politics. *University of Chicago Legal Forum*, 1989(1): 139–67.

Crenshaw, K (1991) Mapping the Margins: Intersectionality, Identity Politics, and Violence Against Women of Color. *Stanford Law Review*, 43(6): 1241–99.

Department for Education (DfE) (2021) *What's Working Well in Remote Education*. [online] Available at: www.gov.uk/government/publications/whats-working-well-in-remote-education/whats-working-well-in-remote-education (accessed 29 September 2024).

Department for Education (DfE) (2024) Diploma in Teaching (Further Education and Skills) qualification framework. [online] Available at: www.gov.uk/government/publications/further-education-initial-teacher-education/diploma-in-teaching-further-education-and-skills-qualification-framework (accessed 8 October 2024).

Dewey, J (1916) *Democracy and Education: An Introduction to the Philosophy of Education*. New York: MacMillan.

Dewey, J (1933) *How We Think*. New York: D. C. Heath.

Dix, P (2017) *When the Adults Change, Everything Changes: Seismic Shifts in School Behaviour*. Bancyfelin: Independent Thinking Press.

Duckworth, S (2020) Intersectionality [infographic]. [online] Available at: www.instagram.com/p/CDrJDbHBdaw/ (accessed 8 October 2024).

Dweck, C (2006) *Mindset: The New Psychology of Success*. New York: Random House.

Education and Training Foundation (ETF) (2022) *Professional Standards for Teachers and Trainers*. [online] Available at: www.et-foundation.co.uk/professional-standards/teachers (accessed 29 September 2024).

Education and Training Foundation (ETF) (2023) *New Level 5 Full FE Teaching Qualification*. [online] Available at: www.et-foundation.co.uk/resources/teacher-education/qualifications-in-education-and-training (accessed 29 September 2024).

Esposito, R P, Mcadoo, H and Scher, L (1978) The Johari Window Test: A Research Note. *Journal of Humanistic Psychology*, 18(1): 79–81.

Flavell, J H (1976) Metacognitive Aspects of Problem Solving. *The Nature of Intelligence*, 12: 231–5.

Gibbs, G (1988) *Learning by Doing: A Guide to Teaching and Learning Methods*. Oxford: Further Education Unit, Oxford Polytechnic.

Hamer, J and Smith, J (2021) *Online and Blended Delivery in Further Education: A Literature Review into Pedagogy, Including Digital Forms of Assessment*. [online] Available at: www.gov.uk/government/publications/literature-review-into-online-and-blended-learning-in-fe (accessed 29 September 2024).

Hamilton, M and Hillier, Y (2006) *Changing Faces of Adult Literacy, Language and Numeracy: A Critical History*. Stoke-on-Trent: Trentham Books.

Hoole, G (2023) The Intersectionality of Theory of Mind in 21st-Century Education: Insights for Inclusion. [online] Available at: www.fenews.co.uk/fe-voices/the-intersectionality-of-theory-of-mind-in-21st-century-education-insights-for-inclusion (accessed 29 September 2024).

Hutchison, E D and Charlesworth, L W (eds) (2024) *Dimensions of Human Behavior: The Changing Life Course*. Thousand Oaks, CA: Sage.

Institute for Apprenticeships and Technical Education (IfATE) (2024) *Learning and Skills Teacher*. [online] Available at: www.instituteforapprenticeships.org/apprenticeship-standards/learning-and-skills-teacher (accessed 29 September 2024).

Kolb, D A (1984) *Experiential Learning: Experience as the Source of Learning and Development*. Englewood Cliffs, NJ: Prentice Hall.

Luft, J and Ingham, H (1955) The Johari Window, a Graphic Model of Interpersonal Awareness. *Proceedings of the Western Training Laboratory in Group Development*. Los Angeles: University of California, Los Angeles.

Moon, J A (2004) *A Handbook of Reflective and Experiential Learning: Theory and Practice*. Abingdon: RoutledgeFalmer.

Mycroft, L and Sidebottom, K (2022) *Creating Spaces to Think in Further Education*. [online] Available at: www.et-foundation.co.uk/professional-development/practitioner-led-development-research/advanced-practitioners/resources (accessed 29 September 2024).

Nunan, D (1988) *The Learner-Centred Curriculum: A Study in Second Language Teaching*. Cambridge: Cambridge University Press.

Open University (2020) Defining Management of Learning Space. [online] Available at: www.open.edu/openlearncreate/mod/page/view.php?id=146248 (accessed 29 September 2024).

Rogers, C (1961) *On Becoming a Person*. Boston, MA: Houghton Mifflin.

Rogers, C R and Farson, R E (1957) *Active Listening*. Chicago, IL: Martino Publishing.

Schön, D (1983) *The Reflective Practitioner*. London: Temple Smith.

Schön, D (1987) *Educating the Reflective Practitioner*. London: Jossey-Bass.

Seligman, M E P and Csikszentmihalyi, M (2000) Positive Psychology: An Introduction. *American Psychologist*, 55(1): 5–14.

Spady, W G (1994) *Outcome-Based Education: Critical Issues and Answers*. Arlington, VA: American Association of School Administrators.

Stoller, F L (2004) Content-Based Instruction: Perspectives on Curriculum Planning. *Annual Review of Applied Linguistics*, 24: 261–83.

Tummons, J (2012) *Curriculum Studies in the Lifelong Learning Sector*. London: Learning Matters.

Tummons, J (ed) (2020) *PCET: Learning and Teaching in the Post Compulsory Sector*. London: Learning Matters.

University of Cambridge (2024) Inclusive Curriculum Design. [online] Available at: www.cctl.cam.ac.uk/inclusive-teaching/guiding-principles (accessed 29 September 2024).

Vizard, D (2012) *How to Manage Behaviour in Further Education*. London: Sage.

8 Inclusive teaching

Professional links

This chapter contributes to the following professional links:

The Diploma in Teaching mandatory content (DfE, 2024)

- 2.4 Safeguarding or EDI.
- 2.8 Role and currency of research and evidence.

Learning and Skills Teacher Occupational Standards (IfATE, 2024)

- K5 Evidence-informed inclusive teaching, learning and assessment strategies.
- K10 How to promote and foster a safe and supportive learning environment.
- S6 Promote understanding of equality and diversity and sustainable development.
- S8 Design and use resources that are inclusive and add value to learners' development.
- B5 Act in a manner that is ethical, fair, consistent and impartial, valuing equality, diversity and champion British values within professional boundaries.

Professional Standards (ETF, 2022)

- 1 Critically reflect on and evaluate your practices, values, and beliefs to improve learner outcomes.
- 5 Value and champion diversity, equality of opportunity, inclusion and social equity.
- 6 Develop collaborative and respectful relationships with learners, colleagues and external stakeholders.
- 15 Plan and deliver learning programmes that are safe, inclusive, stretching and relevant to learners' needs.

Chapter objectives

At the end of this chapter you will be able to:

- explore the differences between equality and equity in education, and consider how you can work towards achieving equality and equity for your learners;
- identify practical strategies that you can use to help make your classroom an inclusive environment;
- consider how you can start to transform your curriculum, influenced by an understanding of ideas around intellectual decolonisation and decolonial praxis.

Introduction

This chapter takes the form of two distinct sections. The first looks at issues surrounding equality, diversity and inclusion in the classroom. The second introduces and discusses some of the recent scholarship on intellectual decolonisation and how you might take inspiration from this to start the process of transforming your curriculum.

Equality, diversity and inclusion

Further education is the most diverse of all the education sectors, and therefore it is important to consider how you can create an inclusive learning environment to work towards meeting the needs of all learners (Peart, 2014).

Taking a macro-level view of equality, diversity and inclusion, some of the key legal measures to address these issues, as highlighted by Choudry (2021), include the following.

- The United Nations Convention on the Rights of the Child (UNCRC): This came into force in the UK on 15 January 1992 for all young people aged 17 years and under (Choudry, 2021).
- The Equality Act 2010: The latest available revised version of the Act defines the protected characteristics of age; disability; gender reassignment; marriage and civil partnership; pregnancy and maternity; race; religion or belief; sex; and sexual orientation (legislation.gov.uk, 2024).
- Statutory safeguarding obligations: In England, the Department for Education's *Keeping Children Safe in Education* document is the statutory guidance for schools and colleges in England, and is updated every academic year (DfE, 2023).
- Ofsted's *Further Education and Skills Inspection Handbook*: This is updated regularly, and an Ofsted inspection assesses how a provider fulfils its duties under the Equality Act 2010 (Ofsted, 2024).
- The Professional Standards: The focus here will be on the Education and Training Foundation (ETF) Professional Standards for Teachers and Trainers. The key Professional Standards that trainees and teachers need to be aware of with regard to equality, diversity and inclusion are standards 1, 5, 6 and 15 (ETF, 2022).

Zooming in to the micro picture, sitting in your class will be learners from many different backgrounds (Choudry, 2021). National figures for England published by Gov.UK (2024a) on schools, pupils and their characteristics highlight that 24.6 per cent of pupils are eligible for free school meals, which is an increase from 23.8 per cent in 2023 (Gov.uk, 2024a). 37 per cent of students are from a minority ethnic background. 54,000 students were identified as being a young carer in 2023–4. The figures in this publication represent a national picture across England, with information combined from the school census, school-level annual school census, general hospital school census and alternative provision census (Gov.uk, 2024a). In the 2023–4 academic year, 4.8 per cent of students had an education, health and care plan, an increase from 4.3 per cent of students in 2022–23 (Gov.uk, 2024b). It is important to note that the government does not currently publish equivalent data for the FES sector. Therefore, while this data does not precisely reflect the diversity of the FES sector, many learners who enrol onto 16–19 learning programmes in the FES sector will have come from either secondary, alternative provision, special schools or non-maintained special schools. This information can therefore provide a useful starting point that gives you an overview of where your learners have come from, which will also inform part of the important foundations from which to understand the diversity in your classroom in the FES and lifelong learning sector.

Critical question ?

» Taking the above-mentioned statistics from the Department for Education into consideration, to what extent do they reflect the range of diversity in your teaching groups?

A vital consideration when thinking about issues around equality, diversity and inclusion is the difference between equality and equity. It is an important difference for you as a teacher to be aware of and it is also empowering for your learners to be aware of the difference (Kara, 2021). Equality teaches that everyone is the same, while equity acknowledges the different starting points of individuals (Kara, 2021, p 10). With this difference in mind, providing learners with *equality* of opportunity in a classroom may look like a teacher providing students with the same resources during the academic year. For example, an A level history teacher would provide all learners with the same resources (eg textbooks and revision materials), instruction and support regardless of the starting points of the individual learners. In contrast, providing *equity* of opportunity for learners in your classroom acknowledges that learners will come into your classroom with different starting points. In a classroom this would mean that the teacher strives to provide individual learners with the specific support and resources they need to be successful. For example, an A level history teacher would ensure they are aware of the learners who have exam arrangements in their class so that when completing timed assessments in class or during a mock exam, access arrangements and reasonable adjustments can be made for individuals in line with the Joint Council for Qualifications guidance (JCQ, 2024). These arrangements and adjustments will depend on individual needs. Examples of this include (but are not limited to) providing learners with 25 per cent extra time (common for learners with a diagnosis of dyslexia), an enlarged script if a learner has a visual impairment, or the use of a low-ratio room if a learner suffers from anxiety. In a day-to-day teaching context this may also include being able to remove barriers that individuals may face, for example by using adaptive teaching techniques, questioning, modelling, scaffolding and reshaping explanations or instructions for individuals where necessary. One of your key responsibilities as a teacher is to consider how you can create a learning environment and utilise learning resources to create successful futures and outcomes for your learners from their different starting points. This requires you to know your learners and consider a range of ways that you can support them appropriately.

Creating an inclusive classroom

Kara (2021) highlights the importance of language in creating diverse and inclusive classrooms and looks at some essential things that teachers can do when using language to support this. These recommendations include the following.

- The correct pronunciation of learner's names. If you are not sure or familiar with the pronunciation of a learner's name, it is important and respectful to ask them. This shows to the learner that you are willing to learn and understand and that you support the creation of a positive and respectful classroom environment. Repeatedly getting the name or pronunciation of a name wrong can be demoralising to a learner and will have an impact on the nature of the positive working relationship that you are able to build with them.
- Using learners' preferred pronouns. This is essential to support learners to feel safe and included in your classroom and the wider learning environment.
- Being aware of the negative connotations of using acronyms to describe different groups collectively that are not actually a standardised group. For example, 'minority ethnic' in the acronym BAME (Black, Asian and minority ethnic) fails to acknowledge that the 'minority ethic' form a global majority. Furthermore, it does not include those of Gypsy, Roma or Traveller heritage.
- Understanding the difference between race and ethnicity. Kara (2021) notes that:

  > *In sociological parlance, 'race' historically describes a set of biological markers; however, over time, the biological concept of race has been replaced with the idea of race as a social construct ... 'Ethnicity' is a term that is used to describe the cultural identity of groups of people. While 'race' has been seen as a fixed marker of identity in the past, 'ethnicity' is seen to encompass the culture, traditions and social identity of groups of people. It is seen as something learnable, less fixed, more mutable and inclusive of language and style of dress. It can be defined in sub-categories like ethno-linguistic (shared language), or ethno-religious (shared religion). Ethnic theory is predicated on race being a social construct and stems very much from post-Second World War sociological discourse.*
  >
  > (Kara, 2021, p 5)

- Putting people first over their disability. For those with a disability, it is important to think about the terms used. Many prefer terms that put the person first to show that their disability is not their defining feature. An example is saying a person who uses a wheelchair rather than a wheelchair user.
- Being aware of the varied terminology used to describe sexuality. The acronym LGBT[QIA]+ incorporates lesbian, gay, bisexual, transgender, queer/questioning, intersex, asexual, non-binary and pansexual. The + is a marker of inclusivity and therefore it is important to consider the huge spectrum of sexuality. The Human Rights Campaign website has a guide to the different flags that represent the LGBT[QIA]+ community (Human Rights Campaign, nd).

One of the most important things as a teacher is that if you are not sure about language and terminology, just ask. Ask the learner, ask colleagues. Language shifts and changes. Keeping up to date with these changes will help to ensure that you support an understanding and awareness of diversity that is as current as possible.

CASE STUDY

It is the start of a new academic year and Joe, a tutor of business and hospitality, is familiarising himself with the names on the register of one of the level 3 classes he is teaching for the first period of the day. This is Joe's first lesson with the group, and he wants to ensure that he pronounces the names of the learners correctly. At the start of the lesson, Joe projects the register on the board and calls out the names of the learners in the group. Joe notices that when he calls one name, Hannah, no one answers, so he moves on to the next learner. Joe also sees that there is one extra learner in the lesson than he has marked on the register. At the end of the lesson, one learner stays behind. The learner explains to Joe that when he called the register, his dead name was displayed on the board. The learner explains that he is transgender, and his name is George (dead name Hannah), and his pronouns are he/him. George's gender is different to the sex assigned to him at birth. George explains to Joe that he did not want to answer when the register was called due to the use of his dead name. George also explains that he felt uncomfortable with his dead name being displayed on the board for others in the class to see.

Critical questions

Having read the case study above:

» Why is it a problem that Joe displayed the register on the board for the whole class to see?

» When George explains the situation to Joe at the end of the lesson, what do you think is the best way for Joe to support and talk to George about calling out and displaying his dead name at the start of the lesson?

It is essential that tutors create an inclusive and supportive environment for learning. Coe et al (2020, p 6) highlight four priorities tutors can focus on to support this.

1. Basing relationships with all learners on mutual respect, care, warmth and empathy. Ensure that negative emotions and interactions with learners are avoided and the individual needs, emotions, culture and beliefs of learners are sensitively considered.
2. Promote a positive climate of peer-to-peer relationships based on respect, care, co-operation and trust.
3. Nurture learner motivation through developing their feelings of competence, autonomy and relatedness.
4. Build a learning environment focused on high expectations, challenge and trust, where learners feel confident to complete tasks and work. Encourage them to credit their success and failures to things they can change.

Critical questions ?

Discuss the following questions with a range of people such as your mentors, peers on your programme and subject-specialist teachers. Do they agree or have different ideas to this?

» How do you create an inclusive learning environment for your learners?

» Do you agree with Coe et al about what they identify as the essential features of creating a supportive learning environment – is there anything else you would add?

Adult learners

One of the key differences in the FES sector compared to secondary education is the adult learning programmes offered at all levels. While the ideas and strategies in this chapter are appropriate to use with all levels and ages of learner, adult learners also have a distinct set of needs. The term 'adult learner' (mature student) is used to describe any person socially accepted as an adult who is involved in a systematic learning process, either formal or informal, and normally over 19 years of age. Adult learners may be returning to education after an extended break, may have had no or minimal contact with mainstream education, or may have no or limited formal qualifications. Adult learners may also have to balance competing priorities to education, including work, family responsibilities or caring responsibilities (Peart, 2014; Busher and James, 2019). Peart (2014) suggests the following strategies that tutors can use to support an inclusive learning environment for adult learners.

- Show respect to all adult learners and build a relationship based on mutual respect and trust. How you do this will depend on your individual learners and your learning context, but creating space where adult learners feel safe to express their opinions and respect the opinions of others is vital to creating an inclusive classroom.

- Wherever possible, be flexible in accommodating the competing priorities of adult learners outside of education, such as work, family and caring commitments. Attendance is clearly a key factor in giving any learner the best opportunity to be successful. However, being flexible within reasonable boundaries can support adult learners to balance their external priorities and feel supported while completing their qualification. It is also important to understand the specific stance that your institution takes on attendance and take this, as well as any attendance policies, into consideration when seeing where and if flexibility with attendance is possible, if necessary. A UK government report published in 2022 highlights the link between absence and attainment in two key stages, including Key Stage 4 (students in Year 10 and 11 in England and Wales). It is highlighted in this report that the more sessions missed in Key Stage 4, the lower the level of attainment at the end of the GCSE year as an overall trend (Gov.UK, 2022). The report *Missing Children, Missing Grades* (2023) by the Children's Commissioner also reinforces the findings of the link between Key Stage 4 attendance and attainment, highlighting that students with persistent or severe levels of absence were less likely to perform well in their GCSEs compared to peers who were rarely absent. While these reports concern younger age groups, the link between attendance and attainment is relevant for all ages of learner. The chances of making progress and successfully completing a course are enhanced when attendance and engagement in lessons with a tutor and other learners is high.
- Provide regular feedback to support learners in understanding what they are doing well and how they can continue to improve and make progress. The Education Endowment Foundation (EEF) guidance report on feedback stresses the importance of teachers providing opportunities for learners to use feedback to close the feedback loop, enabling them to make progress (Education Endowment Foundation, 2021).
- Support learners to use digital technologies. It can be easy to assume (especially in a world where technology is so commonplace in many people's everyday life in the Global North) that learners will arrive at the start of their study programme with an understanding of and competence in using digital technology, platforms and software. However, this may not be the case, and it is important not to assume prior knowledge. In your classroom, create opportunities to model how to use software and internal systems for uploading and accessing work. This will support learners to increase their fluency in using digital technologies where appropriate. This many include core digital skills that we expect of learners, including how to save files on a cloud-based storage system, how to use and navigate a virtual learning environment (VLE), how to file documents in a logical way and how to use word processing software effectively to maximise efficiency.
- Create a community of learners where they feel like they belong. Creating an environment where learners are inspired and feel safe to share ideas will support

the creation of group cohesion and belonging. Also consider the physical space that adult learners have access to. Do they have a separate study and social space for 16–19 year-old learners if they are enrolled in a general or specialist FES college?

CASE STUDY

Leanne is 19 years-old and did not complete her A levels due to complex mental health needs. She is academically very able but lacks self-confidence in her ability to achieve academically after having started but being unable to finish an A level programme of study at two different colleges. Leanne enrols onto a level 3 Access to Higher Education course at her local FES college. In the first half term she is highly motivated inside and outside of class and produces some excellent written work. During the second half of the first term, Leanne's attendance suddenly drops, and she explains that her mental health has deteriorated and she doesn't feel able to complete the access course.

Critical question

Taking the case study into consideration:

» How can you support Leanne to re-enter the classroom and help her increase her self-esteem?

CASE STUDY

Low attendance from a group of adult learners enrolled onto a level 3 Access to Higher Education course in a large general FES college is affecting their ability to make progress academically and complete the assessments required for the course. When their tutor asks why their attendance is low, they say that they are not motivated to come into college as there are no separate study or social spaces for adult learners, and they do not enjoy having to find space among large social groups of 16–19 year-olds to try and learn when they are not in timetabled lessons.

Critical questions

Taking the case study into consideration:

» What could the college do to support the adult learners to have a separate social and study space mid-way through the academic year?

» Why is it important to create this separate space for adult learners?

Inspired by intellectual decolonisation

Two things must be made clear. Firstly, the complex nature and long history of scholars calling for and working on intellectual decolonisation from the Global South that pre-date the traction that this has gained in the Global North in the last decade, galvanised by the student led movements of *Rhodes Must Fall* and *'Why Is My Curriculum White?'* (Moosavi, 2020). Secondly, my positionality as an author must be made clear. As a white woman working in the Global North, I worked for nine years in an English FES college whose learner and staff body are predominantly white British. I acknowledge that I work and have worked in a position where white privilege has led to potential tacit power advantages across my career. Furthermore, I have previously worked in partnership with a HE institution to deliver a validated initial teacher education programme. Therefore, there is a tension present from studying and being inspired by the process of intellectual decolonisation from this academic background. Historically, universities were institutional settings that enclosed and separated knowledge, which created environments where knowledge outside of the university was invalidated, leading to epistemicide – the destruction of other knowledge systems (Hall and Tandon, 2017).

It may seem contradictory in this section titled 'inspired by intellectual decolonisation' to say that intellectual decolonisation is a challenging task and may not even be possible. However, it is essential to acknowledge this so that we avoid tokenistic decolonisation, exclusion and appropriation of the Global South (Moosavi, 2020). Therefore, this chapter does not claim to know how to or say that we can achieve intellectual decolonisation of the curriculum. However, it highlights some important things to begin the process of curriculum transformation, inspired by ideas that have grown and originated from authors who reflect on and have started the process of initiating decolonial praxis in their work. We must look to teach in culturally sensitive ways that ensure tokenism is avoided.

While there is no one fixed definition of decoloniality, Mignolo and Walsh (2018) offer a thought-provoking one:

> *Decoloniality ... is not a static condition, an individual attribute, or a lineal point of arrival or enlightenment. Instead, decoloniality seeks to make visible, open up, and advance radically distinct perspectives and positionalities that displace Western rationality as the only framework and possibility of existence, analysis and thought.*
>
> (Mignolo and Walsh, 2018, pp 17–18)

Critical question ⓘ

» Reflecting on Mignolo and Walsh's definition, how Western centric or Eurocentric is the subject-specific curriculum that you teach? What could be done to recognise and value other knowledge? How achievable is this in the context of your educational setting, considering practical considerations such as time constraints in planning and delivery?

Understanding the plural nature of decolonising is also important in developing an understanding of intellectual decolonisation and decolonial praxis. The historical process of decolonisation refers to the removal of political, military and governmental rule of a colonised land by its invaders (London Metropolitan University, nd). Mbembe (2016) centres the importance of Ngugi wa Thiong'o's concept of decolonising the mind, where 'decolonising' involves an ongoing process of '*seeing ourselves clearly*' and coming out of a state of '*blindness or dizziness*' (Ngugi wa Thiong'o, cited in Mbembe, 2016, p 34). To consider concepts around intellectual decolonisation and decolonisation of the curriculum, it is first necessary to decolonise ourselves. Decolonial praxis involves a process of thought, action, reflection and action, which gives meaning and shape to decoloniality (Mignolo and Walsh, 2018). As educators, when we see people using the phrase '*decolonising the curriculum*', it is most commonly the process of initiating decolonial praxis into our teaching – both in what we teach and in how we teach.

Moosavi (2020) identifies intellectual decolonisation as the want to undo the legacy of colonialism in academia because of the belief that how academia is experienced – what is researched, published, cited and taught – is impacted by coloniality. It is also grounded in the principle of consciously departing from the disposition that '*events, developments and questions only matter when they manifest in the Global North*' (Moosavi, 2020, pp 332–4). There cannot be one blueprint for decoloniality, as this is too universal and too Eurocentric (Mignolo, 2017). Moosavi makes us aware that scholars from the Global North have arrived late to intellectual decolonisation, which was a process started decades ago by scholars in the Global South (Moosavi, 2020). It is important that scholars from the Global South are not silenced when looking at where and how it may be possible to initiate intellectual decolonisation, in order to avoid '*decolonisation without decolonising*' (Moosavi, 2020, p 334). Hassan reflects on the role that Southern theory can hold in supporting trainee teachers to gain a deeper understanding of educational theory and practice, highlighting that Northern theory originating from the central colonial territory is '*provincial in nature*' and therefore cannot give us a complete picture of educational theory and practice (Hassan, cited in Race et al, 2022, p 5). Within this introduction to Southern theory and its potential to enrich our understanding of educational theory and practice, Hassan (in Race et al, 2022) considers the work of Rabindranath Tagore's Southern theory of inclusive education in the late nineteenth and early twentieth centuries. Hassan (cited in Race et al, 2022) makes us aware that Tagore advocated that the child's social and cultural environment should be connected to their learning, and that teacher training should include approaches to stimulating critical thinking and creative imagination in children. Tagore believed that education had an emancipatory power on the mind from the chains of colonialism, and his inclusive educational philosophy strived to build a holistic model of education for every child according to their needs and abilities based on a multilevel curriculum (Mukherjee, 2018). Tagore called for a decolonised model of education in India that was influenced by a pedagogy of experiential learning (Hassan, cited in Race et al, 2022). This was in stark contrast to what he described as the 'factory model' of schools that did not consider the individual learning needs of a child (Mukherjee, 2018). This is one example where authors have introduced a voice from the Global South, encouraging us to critically reflect on what we can learn from this to enrich our understanding of educational theory and practice. While only one example, it offers a way in to start the process of critically evaluating our teaching and learning practices, as well as the curricula and the foundations of knowledge that these are based on, with a consideration of how we can introduce other important voices and ideas.

Abyssal thinking reinforces a hierarchical division between the visible and invisible, where certain people, cultures and knowledge are marginalised from mainstream discourse and power structures (de Sousa Santos, 2007). Western epistemologies often ignore or devalue alternative ways of being or knowing, which in turn perpetuate inequalities and injustices; de Sousa Santos (2007) argues that this is as prevalent in modern Western thinking as it was in the colonial period. To move towards post-abyssal thinking it is imperative that we recognise and value diverse perspectives to create more inclusive and equitable societies, where diverse systems of knowledge production and dissemination are present, where multiple ways of understanding the world are recognised and valued, and that support us to see and understand beyond dominant Western paradigms (de Sousa Santos, 2007).

Critical question

» To what extent is abyssal thinking present in your subject-specific curriculum? What can be done to move towards a curriculum that is centred around post-abyssal thinking?

The concept of visibility and invisibility is also looked at by Carol Azumah Dennis (2018), who advocates a decolonised pedagogy as one that thinks '*alongside, from and within knowledges that have been rendered invisible*' (Azumah Dennis, 2018, p 199).

Activity

» Read the following ideas about pedagogical approaches to decolonisation, summarised from a longer list of ten thought-provoking suggestions made by Carol Azumah Dennis (2018, p 202). Think critically about these suggestions and consider to what extent it is possible to incorporate elements of these approaches into your own teaching.

1. Create a space where you can speak about decolonial praxis – with colleagues and learners.
2. Reflect on the subject-specific curriculum you teach. Is there a monopoly of European knowledge, assumptions and methodologies in your curriculum? If the curriculum is monopolised or dominated by European knowledge, why is this? Is it due to the legacy of colonialism in education?
3. Is there a singular, authoritative voice, perspective or approach in your curriculum? How can you challenge this?
4. Put the knowledge of the founding fathers of philosophy and social sciences in their place – acknowledge that they emerged from a specific time and place and are not universal.

→

> **5.** How can you locate, illuminate and amplify silenced or trivialised voices in your subject specialism and place them meaningfully alongside orthodox voices to offer a meaningful critique?

One of the major challenges faced by educators in the FES sector is time. Time to think, time to plan and time to reflect. Many FES curricula that have end point assessments or exams must teach a specific body of knowledge already pre-set by an exam board or awarding body within a pressurised timetable. This means that while you may agree with the concept and theory of taking action to transform your curriculum, inspired by some of the core ideas of decolonial praxis, having the time and space to do this in the context of FES courses can be incredibly challenging practically, and may not even be possible. Kemmis et al (2014) advocate that to develop and have new practices, it is crucial that the practice architecture is in place to allow them to survive. Practice architectures are made up of three interconnected elements. The culturally discursive arrangements involve the semantic space such as shared languages. The material economic arrangements involve the physical space that enable and restrict how we do things in work, such as the room, workplace, building, town and local region we are in. The socio-political arrangements involve the social space that defines how we connect through the relationships built between people, such as teachers who work in the same college or a department within a college; physical sites, such as a college, are crucial in holding practices in place (Kemmis et al, 2014). For example, if no one speaks the language of decolonial praxis in a college, then the process of decolonial praxis (or processes inspired by it) will not take hold in the college. If there are no material resources (books, websites, times, places, training) to support an understanding of decolonial praxis, then decolonial praxis will not take hold there. If there are not appropriate social arrangements for decolonial praxis to take place – the relationship between teachers, learners and communities, then it cannot take place.

While it certainly cannot be considered decolonising the curriculum, asking your learners the question 'where are the silences in our curriculum?' can be a powerful question to encourage them to start thinking about the visible, invisible and silenced voices in the curriculum that they are taught. Encourage them to consider what power structures and hierarchies have led to decisions about whose voices and whose knowledge is prioritised and seen as valued.

Critical question ⑦

» Where are the silences in your curriculum? What can you meaningfully do to address these silences?

Summary

The first section of this chapter considered the importance of creating an inclusive learning environment which supports equality and equity of opportunity for learners, with some practical suggestions and reflections on how this can be implemented in your classroom.

The second section of this chapter introduced some of the context surrounding intellectual decolonisation and decolonial praxis, providing some initial ideas for how you can start to transform your curriculum. This will take time and will not be a linear process. It may also be challenging, but it is important work.

Check your understanding (level 5)

1. What are the key legal measures in place in the UK to address issues of equality, diversity and inclusion in education?
2. What are three key strategies you could use in your classroom to create an inclusive environment for learning?
3. What is the difference between equality of opportunity and equity of opportunity?
4. Why is it important for teachers to understand the difference between equality of opportunity and equity of opportunity?
5. What would providing learners with equality of opportunity look like in your classroom or learning environment?
6. What would providing learners with equity of opportunity look like in your classroom or learning environment?
7. What does the difference look like in your classroom/learning environment between providing learners with equality of opportunity and equity of opportunity?
8. What is epistemicide?
9. What is decolonisation, decolonial thinking and decolonial praxis?
10. How has intellectual decolonisation been defined?
11. Why is it not possible to have a singular definition of decoloniality?
12. What is abyssal and post-abyssal thinking?
13. How does the physical site affect your ability to hold practices in place?

Developmental questions (L6+7)

1. Read your institution's equality, diversity and inclusion policy. Consider what the policy requires staff to do in their teaching to create a supportive and inclusive learning environment for students. Is anything missing or does anything need adding to this policy in relation to issues surrounding equality, diversity and inclusion?
2. Look up the 54 articles of the United Nations Convention on the Rights of the Child (UNCRC). Which articles do you think are the most significant in relation to the groups of learners that you teach and why?
3. The Equality Act 2010 provides protection against four types of behaviour: direct discrimination, indirect discrimination, harassment and victimisation.
    a. How does the Equality Act define each of these kinds of behaviour?
    b. How can you create a learning environment that protects students from these four behaviours?
    c. How would you support a student who was being subjected to one of these four behaviours? What other colleagues would you ask to support you with this?

Further reading

- Azumah Dennis, C (2018) Decolonising Education: A Pedagogic Intervention. In Bhambra, G K, Gebrial, D and Nişancıoğlu, K (eds) *Decolonising the University* (pp 190–207). London: Pluto Press.
- Choudry, S (2021) *Equitable Education: What Everyone Working in Education Should Know About Closing the Attainment Gap for All Pupils*. St Albans: Critical Publishing.
- Moosavi, L (2020) The Decolonial Bandwagon and the Dangers of Intellectual Decolonisation. *International Review of Sociology*, 30(2): 332–54.
- Mukherjee, M (2018) Decolonizing Pedagogy for Inclusive Education: Tagorean Analysis of a Case Study. In Kennedy, K J and Chi-kin Le, J (eds) *Routledge International Handbook of Schools and Schooling* in Asia (pp 709–21). London: Routledge.
- Thomas, A (2022) *Representation Matters: Becoming an Anti-racist Educator.* London: Bloomsbury.

References

Azumah Dennis, C (2018) Decolonising Education: A Pedagogic Intervention. In Bhambra, G K, Gebrial, D and Nişancıoğlu, K (eds) *Decolonising the University* (pp 190–207). London: Pluto Press.

Busher, H and James, N (2019) Struggling to Become Successful Learners: Mature Students' Early Experiences of Access to Higher Education Courses. *Studies in the Education of Adults*, 51(1), 74–88.

Children's Commissioner (2023) *Missing Children, Missing Grades*. [online] Available at: https://assets.childrenscommissioner.gov.uk/wpuploads/2023/11/CC-REPORT-_-Attendance-and-Attainment-_-Oct-23.pdf (accessed 29 September 2024).

Coe, R, Rauch, R, Kime, S and Singleton, D (2020) *Great Teaching Toolkit: Evidence Review*. Cambridge: Evidence Based Education and Cambridge Assessment International Education. [online] Available at: www.cambridgeinternational.org/Images/584543-great-teaching-toolkit-evidence-review.pdf (accessed 29 September 2024).

Choudry, S (2021) *Equitable Education: What Everyone Working in Education Should Know About Closing the Attainment Gap for All Pupils*. St Albans: Critical Publishing.

Department for Education (DfE) (2023) *Keeping Children Safe in Education 2023: Statutory Guidance for Schools and Colleges*. [online] Available at: https://assets.publishing.service.gov.uk/media/64f0a68ea78c5f000dc6f3b2/Keeping_children_safe_in_education_2023.pdf (accessed 29 September 2024).

Department for Education (DfE) (2024) Diploma in Teaching (Further Education and Skills) Education Framework. [online] Available at: www.gov.uk/government/publications/further-education-initial-teacher-education/diploma-in-teaching-further-education-and-skills-qualification-framework (accessed 15 November 2024).

de Sousa Santos, B (2007) Beyond Abyssal Thinking: From Global Lines to Ecologies of Knowledges. *Review – Fernand Braudel Centre for the Study of Economies, Historical Systems, and Civilizations*, 30(1): 5–89.

Education Endowment Foundation (EEF) (2021) *Teacher Feedback to Improve Pupil Learning Guidance Report*. [online] Available at: https://d2tic4wvo1iusb.cloudfront.net/production/eef-guidance-reports/feedback/Teacher_Feedback_to_Improve_Pupil_Learning.pdf?v=1713045386 (accessed 29 September 2024).

Education and Training Foundation (ETF) (2022) *Professional Standards for Teachers and Trainers*. [online] Available at: www.et-foundation.co.uk/professional-standards/teachers (accessed 29 September 2024).

Equality Act 2010 [online] Available at: www.legislation.gov.uk/ukpga/2010/15/part/2/chapter/1 (accessed 29 September 2024).

Gov.UK (2022) *The Link between Absence and Attainment at KS2 and KS4*. [online] Available at: https://explore-education-statistics.service.gov.uk/find-statistics/the-link-between-absence-and-attainment-at-ks2-and-ks4 (accessed 29 September 2024).

Gov.UK (2024a) *Schools, Pupils and Their Characteristics*. [online] Available at: https://explore-education-statistics.service.gov.uk/find-statistics/school-pupils-and-their-characteristics (accessed 29 September 2024).

Gov.UK (2024b) *Special Educational Needs in England*. [online] Available at: https://explore-education-statistics.service.gov.uk/find-statistics/special-educational-needs-in-england (accessed 29 September 2024).

Hall, B L and Tandon, R (2017) Decolonization of Knowledge, Epistemicide, Participatory Research and Higher Education. *Research for All*, 1(1): 6–19.

Human Rights Campaign (nd) LGBTQ+ Pride Flags. [online] Available at: www.hrc.org/resources/lgbtq-pride-flags (accessed 29 September 2024).

Institute for Apprenticeships and Technical Education (IfATE) (2024) *Learning and Skills Teacher*. [online] Available at: www.instituteforapprenticeships.org/apprenticeship-standards/learning-and-skills-teacher (accessed 28 September 2024).

Joint Council for Qualifications (2024) Access Arrangements, Reasonable Adjustments and Special Consideration. [online] Available at: www.jcq.org.uk/exams-office/access-arrangements-and-special-consideration (accessed 29 September 2024).

Kara, B (2021) *A Little Guide for Teachers: Diversity in Schools*. London: Corwin.

Kemmis, S, McTaggart, R and Nixon, R (2014) *The Action Research Planner: Doing Critical Participatory Action Research*. Singapore: Springer.

London Metropolitan University (nd) What Does Decolonising Mean? [online] Available at: www.londonmet.ac.uk/about/centre-for-equity-and-inclusion/race/decolonising-academia/what-does-decolonising-mean (accessed 29 September 2024).

Mbembe, J A (2016) Decolonizing the University: New Directions. *Arts and Humanities in Higher Education*, 15(1): 29–45.

Mignolo, W D (2017) Coloniality Is Far from Over, and So Must Be Decoloniality. *Afterall*, 43(1): 38–45.

Mignolo, W and Walsh, C E (2018) *On Decoloniality: Concepts, Analytics, Praxis*. London: Duke University Press.

Moosavi, L (2020) The Decolonial Bandwagon and the Dangers of Intellectual Decolonisation. *International Review of Sociology*, 30(2): 332–54.

Mukherjee, M (2018) Decolonizing Pedagogy for Inclusive Education: Tagorean Analysis of a Case Study. In Kennedy, K J and Chi-kin Le, J (eds) *Routledge International Handbook of Schools and Schooling in Asia* (pp 709–21). London: Routledge.

Ofsted (2024) *Further Education and Skills Inspection Handbook*. [online] Available at: www.gov.uk/government/publications/further-education-and-skills-inspection-handbook-eif/further-education-and-skills-handbook-for-september-2023 (accessed 29 September 2024).

Peart, S (2014) *Equality and Diversity in Further Education*. St Albans: Critical Publishing.

Race, R, Ayling, P, Chetty, D, Hassan, N, McKinney, S J, Boath, L, Riaz, N and Salehjee, S (2022) Decolonising Curriculum in Education: Continuing Proclamations and Provocations. *London Review of Education*, 20(1): 1–15.

9 Effective digital and online pedagogies

MICHELE FULLER

Professional links

This chapter contributes to the following professional links:

The Diploma in Teaching mandatory context (DfE, 2024)

- 2.3 Range of support needs.
- 2.7 Contemporary learning theory, neuroscience.
- 2.9 Application of theory to practice.
- 3.11 Face to face and remote delivery.
- 4.10 Application of evidence-based methods.
- 4.23 Government policy.
- 5.1 Personal digital skills.
- 5.2 Range of educational technology.
- 5.3 Artificial intelligence, augmented reality, virtual reality and similar technologies.
- 5.4 Managing digital delivery.

Learning and Skills Teacher Occupational Standards (IfATE, 2024)

- K1 The pedagogical theory and how to apply this theory to practice.
- K5 Evidence-informed inclusive teaching, learning and assessment strategies.
- K6 Strategies to engage and challenge all learners.
- K11 Barriers to learning, and ways to overcome them and adapt teaching, learning and assessment.

→

- K20 Advances in digital, online, and emerging technologies and their application in the teaching environment and principles of digital and online safety.
- S2 Identify, consider and take steps to minimise the impact of barriers to learning.
- S4 Use a variety of teaching and assessment methods depending on the learning environment and learners' needs.
- S9 Engage and inspire all learners.
- S16 Prepare learners for their transition through education, further training, and into employment.
- S21 Continually update and maintain their own knowledge and skills as a teaching professional and a subject specialist as part of managing their own continual professional development (CPD).
- S25 Use innovative and up to date digital and online technologies in a way that is safe to improve teaching, learning and assessment.

Professional Standards (ETF, 2022b)

- 1 Critically reflect on and evaluate your practices, values, and beliefs to improve learner outcomes.
- 3 Inspire, motivate, and raise aspirations of learners by communicating high expectations and a passion for learning.
- 5 Value and champion diversity, equality of opportunity, inclusion and social equity.
- 9 Critically review and apply your knowledge of educational research, pedagogy, and assessment to develop evidence-informed practice.
- 16 Select and use digital technologies safely and effectively to promote learning.

Chapter objectives

At the end of the chapter you will be able to:

- explore and evaluate a diverse range of educational technologies and learning management systems (LMS) suitable for online and blended learning environments in FES contexts;
- demonstrate understanding of key principles in online classroom management, including effective content organisation, clear communication strategies and setting appropriate expectations for learners;

- design and implement engaging, interactive online lessons that incorporate sound digital pedagogical strategies and accommodate diverse learning needs;
- critically assess various online teaching models (such as synchronous, asynchronous, blended, flipped) and their applicability to different subjects and learner groups within FES settings;
- develop and apply effective online assessment methods, adapting them to specific learning contexts and subject areas;
- analyse the ethical implications of integrating AI and other emerging technologies into online education, considering both opportunities and challenges;
- formulate strategies to create inclusive and accessible online learning environments that accommodate learners with diverse needs, backgrounds and abilities;
- synthesise current research and best practices to create professional development plans for continuous improvement of online teaching skills and methodologies;
- evaluate the impact of digital and online pedagogies on learner engagement, achievement and progression, using data-driven approaches to inform practice;
- collaborate with colleagues and students to share insights, resources and innovative approaches to online and blended learning in FES contexts.

Introduction

The landscape of education is undergoing a profound transformation, driven by the rapid evolution of digital technologies and the increasing prevalence of online and blended learning modalities (Doucet et al, 2020; Selwyn, 2021). The FES lecturer/teacher is at the forefront of this change as they educate and prepare students for the workplace as they first enter employment or when they are considering a career change or further academic study (Jisc, 2023, 2024). This shift has been accelerated by recent global events, including the Covid-19 pandemic which started in the UK in March 2020 with the first official government 'lock-down', and recent infrastructural challenges associated with the use of unsuitable building materials (Doucet et al, 2020; Coleman, 2021; Duckworth et al, 2021). The use of technology in education (TEL) (Scott, 2021), commonly referred to as educational technology (EdTech), has become increasingly important for both policymakers and educators. This importance is shown by the Department for Education's 2019 national EdTech strategy. Since then, educational institutions have quickly adopted new technologies for two main reasons: to better meet the changing needs of students (Jisc, 2021a) and to help prepare students for jobs in today's technology-driven workplaces (DfE, 2019; Hamer and Smith, 2021; Jisc, 2023).

Furthermore, the emergence of AI and its subfield, generative AI (GenAI), has introduced new possibilities and challenges in education (Mollick and Mollick, 2023a; Sharples, 2023; Luckin et al, 2024). The field of AI in Education (AIEd) is rapidly evolving, offering potential for personalised learning experiences, automated assessment and intelligent tutoring systems (Holmes et al, 2019; Sharples, 2023; Mollick and Mollick, 2023b; Mollick, 2024). The use of AI is becoming increasingly common in the secondary education sector and the workplace, so it would be remiss of the modern FES lecturer not to include and embrace this in their session planning, delivery and assessment to mirror this. As these powerful tools become more accessible and widely adopted, it is crucial to critically examine the motivations behind their integration and the implications they hold for teaching, learning and assessment (TLA) in diverse educational settings. The advent of GenAI has the potential to dramatically transform the educational landscape (Giannini, 2023). As powerful models like ChatGPT, Claude2, Gemini and Copilot become increasingly widespread, educators and researchers must critically examine the opportunities and risks these technologies present for online teaching, learning and assessment (TLA) (Luckin et al, 2024; Jisc, 2024; Open Innovation Team and Department of Education, 2024; Webb, 2024).

As the educational landscape continues to evolve, it is crucial for FES educators and policymakers to critically engage with these technological advancements, ensuring that their implementation aligns with sound pedagogical principles and promotes inclusive, equitable learning environments (Bond et al, 2024; Jisc, 2024). This transformation necessitates a fundamental rethinking of traditional FES educational approaches to prepare learners for the complexities of the twenty-first-century workplace and society (Doucet et al, 2020; Webb, 2024).

The emergence of what Doucet et al (2018) term the Fourth Industrial Revolution, characterised by AI, global interconnectedness and disruptive technologies, necessitates a fundamental rethinking of FES educational approaches. 'Traditional' methods are increasingly viewed as inadequate in preparing students for the complexities of the twenty-first century workplace. Consequently, there is a growing emphasis on personalised, collaborative learning experiences that foster critical skills for the digital age (Sharples, 2023; Mollick, 2024).

In the FES context, the integration of information and communication technology (ICT) skills into teacher training programmes has become paramount (Ilomäki et al, 2016; Coleman, 2021; Jisc, 2023). This integration extends beyond mere technical proficiency in classroom-related technology such as interactive whiteboards and needs to encompass the functional application of digital knowledge and skills in pedagogical contexts (Fernández-Batanero et al, 2022). Online teaching, while presenting unique challenges, affords significant opportunities for enhancing student engagement and improving learning outcomes (Anderson, 2017; Sun and Chen, 2016). The shift towards online and hybrid models of delivery, accelerated by recent events such as Covid-19, underscores the need for flexibility and adaptability in modern education (Lemov, 2020; Coleman, 2021).

This chapter introduces the knowledge and skills necessary to navigate the digital learning environment effectively. It explores key concepts in online pedagogy, examines best practices in digital teaching, and addresses the challenges and opportunities presented by technology-enhanced learning (TEL) and the increasing impact of AI and GenAI on education in the lifelong learning sector.

By engaging with these concepts and developing digital competencies, student teachers can position themselves as innovative educators capable of creating inclusive, engaging and effective learning experiences in diverse educational settings. This proactive approach not only enhances teaching effectiveness but also promotes equity and accessibility in education, supporting the achievement of all learners in the digital age.

Range of educational technologies

In the rapidly evolving landscape of education, a diverse array of digital tools and platforms has emerged to enhance teaching, learning and assessment practices (Selwyn, 2021). The 2022–3 Jisc UK FES learner digital experience insights survey identified Microsoft Teams, Showbie and Quizlet as the most popular tools among learners, with other commonly used platforms including YouTube, Microsoft Word and Moodle (JISC, 2023). However, it is important to consider emerging technologies such as AI, augmented reality (AR), virtual reality (VR) and various online delivery platforms, which present distinct advantages and challenges in educational settings (Luckin et al, 2016; Sharples, 2023).

Each of these technologies requires lecturers to develop a comprehensive understanding of their capabilities and limitations to effectively leverage them within educational contexts (Mishra and Koehler, 2006). This understanding is particularly important given the rapid pace of technological change and the need for educators to continually adapt their practices (Laurillard et al, 2018; Dabbous and Emms, 2020; Hamer and Smith, 2021).

The effective integration of these technologies necessitates a careful consideration of pedagogical principles, a range of accessibility issues and the diverse needs of learners in the FES sector (Coleman, 2021; Jisc, 2023, 2024). This section aims to help lecturers learn how to evaluate and use digital technologies in their specific subject areas. It's important to remember that different subjects may have different technological needs. The main goal is to ensure that technology is used to improve teaching, learning and assessment. Technology, as described below in Table 9.1, should not be used just because it's available but because it helps students learn better with an awareness of the associated affordances, challenges and considerations (Selwyn, 2021; Luckin et al, 2024).

Table 9.1 *Benefits and challenges of a range of technologies*

Technology	Description	Affordances	Challenges and considerations
Virtual learning environments (VLEs) and learning management systems (LMS)	VLE or LMS platforms provide centralised hubs for course content, assessments and communication. They support both synchronous (real-time) and asynchronous (self-paced) learning. VLEs like Moodle, Canvas and Blackboard offer a centralised platform for course management and delivery. Integrate game like elements within VLE: completion badges, use gamified quizzes, interactive exercises, create virtual classroom with avatars and rewards.	Flexible learning, collaboration and communication, diverse content delivery	Digital literacy, engagement and motivation

→

Table 9.1 *(Cont.)*

Technology	Description	Affordances	Challenges and considerations
Interactive applications	Tools like Kahoot! and Padlet can significantly enhance student engagement. Use Kahoot! for quick formative assessments or revision activities. Employ Padlet for collaborative brainstorming or peer feedback sessions. Create gamified challenges, interactive story telling activities.	Enhanced engagement, collaborative learning, anonymous contributions	Student participation, effective use
Video feedback	Incorporating video feedback can personalise the learning experience. Provide detailed, multi-modal feedback on assignments. Create short instructional videos to supplement written materials with embedded quizzes or challenges. Use avatars or animated characters to deliver feedback. Use screen recording to demonstrate practical skills or software use.	Personalised feedback, multi-modal explanations, visual and auditory support	Technical skills, time investment
Artificial intelligence (AI) and Generative AI (GenAI)	AI and GenAI are capable of tasks requiring human-like cognition and generating new content. Makes it possible to develop GenAI-powered games and simulations and provide personalised learning experiences and adaptive challenges. Use to create interactive stories or scenarios. Allow learners to explore different choices and consequences. Implement GenAI-driven feedback systems. Provide personalised guidance and support.	Personalised learning pathways, adaptive assessment, intelligent tutoring, content creation	Data privacy and bias, over-reliance on technology
Augmented reality (AR) and virtual reality (VR)	Make learning more interactive and engaging. Develop VR simulations for hands-on experience: allow learners to practise skills in a safe environment. Use AR/VR to gamify problem-solving activities: challenge learners to find solutions in an immersive environment. Create AR scavenger hunts or virtual field trips.	Immersive learning experiences, virtual field trips, interactive 3D models	Cost and accessibility, technical expertise

Table 9.1 (Cont.)

Technology	Description	Affordances	Challenges and considerations
Learning analytics	Use learning analytics to personalise gamification; tailor challenges and rewards to individual needs and progress. Provide learners with gamified dashboards to track their own progress; encourage self-reflection and goal setting. Use data to identify areas where gamification can be most effective; optimise the learning experience for all learners.	Early identification of struggling learners, personalised feedback	Data privacy and ethics, interpretation of data

Best practices for managing an online classroom

To effectively manage an online classroom, several key practices are recommended, as shown in Table 9.2 (adapted from Tanis, 2020).

Table 9.2 Practice descriptions

Key practice	Description
Teacher presence and integration	The physical distance in online learning requires teachers to reimagine their presence. It's crucial to establish clear communication channels, provide timely support and foster student interaction. Unlike traditional settings where teacher presence is implicit, online educators must actively cultivate their presence through consistent communication and engagement (Hamer and Smith, 2021).
Designing engaging activities	Online pedagogy should not simply replicate traditional classroom activities (Petrie et al, 2021). Activities should be designed to be explicit, structured and engaging (Tanis, 2020). This might involve incorporating interactive elements, multimedia resources, gamification and collaborative tasks that leverage the affordances of the online environment (Hamer and Smith, 2021; Beetham and McNeill, 2023; Bond et al, 2023; Arnold, 2024; Emin-Martinez and Ney, 2013; Christopoulos and Mystakidis, 2023).
Addressing digital inequities	Effective online pedagogy acknowledges that students have varying levels of digital literacy and access to technology. Providing adequate technical support and designing learning experiences that are inclusive and accessible is crucial (Hamer and Smith, 2021; Beetham and McNeill, 2023; Arnold, 2014; Christopoulos and Mystakidis, 2023).

→

Table 9.2 *(Cont.)*

Key practice	Description
Learner choice and flexibility	While online learning inherently offers flexibility, pedagogical approaches should provide learners with choices regarding the pace, place and mode of learning. This empowers students to tailor their learning experiences and fosters a sense of ownership. However, curriculum design should balance flexibility with structure to ensure students benefit from cohort support and a well-sequenced curriculum (Beetham and McNeill, 2023).
Assessment strategies	Online assessments should align with the learning objectives and the chosen pedagogical approach. Exploring various assessment formats like e-portfolios, digital projects, gamification and online proctoring can provide creative, authentic and relevant evaluation methods (Beetham and McNeill, 2023; Bond et al, 2023; Arnold, 2014; Christoploulos and Mystakidis, 2023). A variety of assessment methods also increases the interest and accessibility of the assessment to the student (Bond et al, 2023; Emin-Martinez and Ney, 2013).

Remember that successful FES online classroom management requires ongoing adaptation and a student-centred approach (Beetham and McNeill, 2023; DfE, 2023; Jisc, 2024). Regularly seek feedback from students regarding their online learning experience and be willing to adjust strategies based on their needs and preferences (Lemov, 2020).

Successful online pedagogy requires a thoughtful integration of technology, sound pedagogical principles, and an understanding of the unique affordances and limitations of online learning environments (Doucet et al, 2018; Lemov, 2020). It's not simply about replicating the traditional classroom experience but about leveraging technology to create engaging, inclusive and effective learning experiences that cater to the diverse needs of learners (Lemov; 2020; Hamer and Smith, 2021; DfE, 2023; Mollick and Mollick, 2023b).

Critical question ?

» Critically reflect on what technologies you currently routinely use within your subject-specialist sessions and what are the benefits and limitations? (Consider researching the internet, journals and books to see how colleagues embed technologies into their subject specialist teaching, learning and assessment.)

Discussion

Incorporating new technologies into teaching can greatly enhance the learning experience. Here are a few examples, along with their benefits and limitations in specific subject contexts.

Virtual reality (VR) – subject context: history

- Benefits: VR can bring historical events to life, allowing students to experience different eras immersively. This can increase engagement and retention of information.
- Limitations: The cost of VR equipment can be high, and there may be technical issues or a learning curve for both teachers and students.

AI-powered adaptive learning systems – subject context: mathematics

- Benefits: AI can provide personalised learning experiences by adjusting difficulty levels based on student performance. This offers tailored instruction and immediate feedback.
- Limitations: Ensuring equitable access to technology for all students can be challenging, and teachers may need training to effectively integrate these systems.

Augmented reality (AR) – subject context: science

- Benefits: AR can overlay digital information onto the real world, making abstract concepts more tangible. For example, students can explore the human body in 3D.
- Limitations: Similar to VR, AR can be costly and may require significant technical support.

Online pedagogical principles and theories

Grounding online learning in evidence-based pedagogical principles is vital. Social constructivism emphasises the importance of social interactions and collaboration in learning, suggesting that students construct knowledge through their interactions with others (Siemens, 2005; Harasim, 2017; Lemov, 2020). Connectivism focuses on the role of technology in learning, highlighting the importance of networked connections and information flow. Self-regulated learning encourages students to take control of their learning process, fostering independence and lifelong learning skills (Anderson, 2013; Harasim, 2017). It encourages students to take ownership of their learning by setting goals, monitoring progress and adjusting strategies. Tools like learning journals and self-assessment rubrics can support this (Zimmerman, 2002; Lemov, 2020).

It is important to recognise that the core principles of effective teaching remain constant, regardless of the delivery mode (see Table 9.3). As Hamer and Smith (2021) emphasise, fundamental pedagogical principles, reflected in the 20 Professional Standards for England (ETF, 2022) and the Ofsted Inspection Framework (Ofsted, 2024), continue to be crucial in online and blended learning environments. These principles include:

- carefully planned and structured teaching;
- strong subject knowledge and understanding of curriculum;
- responsiveness to learner needs;
- constructive use of assessment data.

Table 9.3 *Online teaching models*

Model	Flexibility	Student engagement	Technology requirements	Suitable courses
Synchronous instruction	Low	High	High	Interactive courses involve real-time interaction, such as debates or group discussions.
Asynchronous instruction	High	Medium	Low to medium	Self-paced courses with access to content whenever it suits learners, such as discussion forums and online communities.
Blended learning	Medium	High	Medium to high	Comprehensive courses combine in-person sessions (such as workshops) with online components.
Flipped classroom	Medium	High	Medium to high	Focus on pre-learning online (videos, readings) and in-depth discussions during class.

Several theoretical frameworks provide valuable insights into effective online pedagogy.

Community of Inquiry (CoI) Model: Originally developed by Randy Garrison, Terry Anderson and Walter Archer (2001). The CoI model focuses on three interconnected elements essential for successful online learning experiences: social presence, cognitive presence and teaching presence (Garrison et al, 2001; Hamer and Smith, 2021).

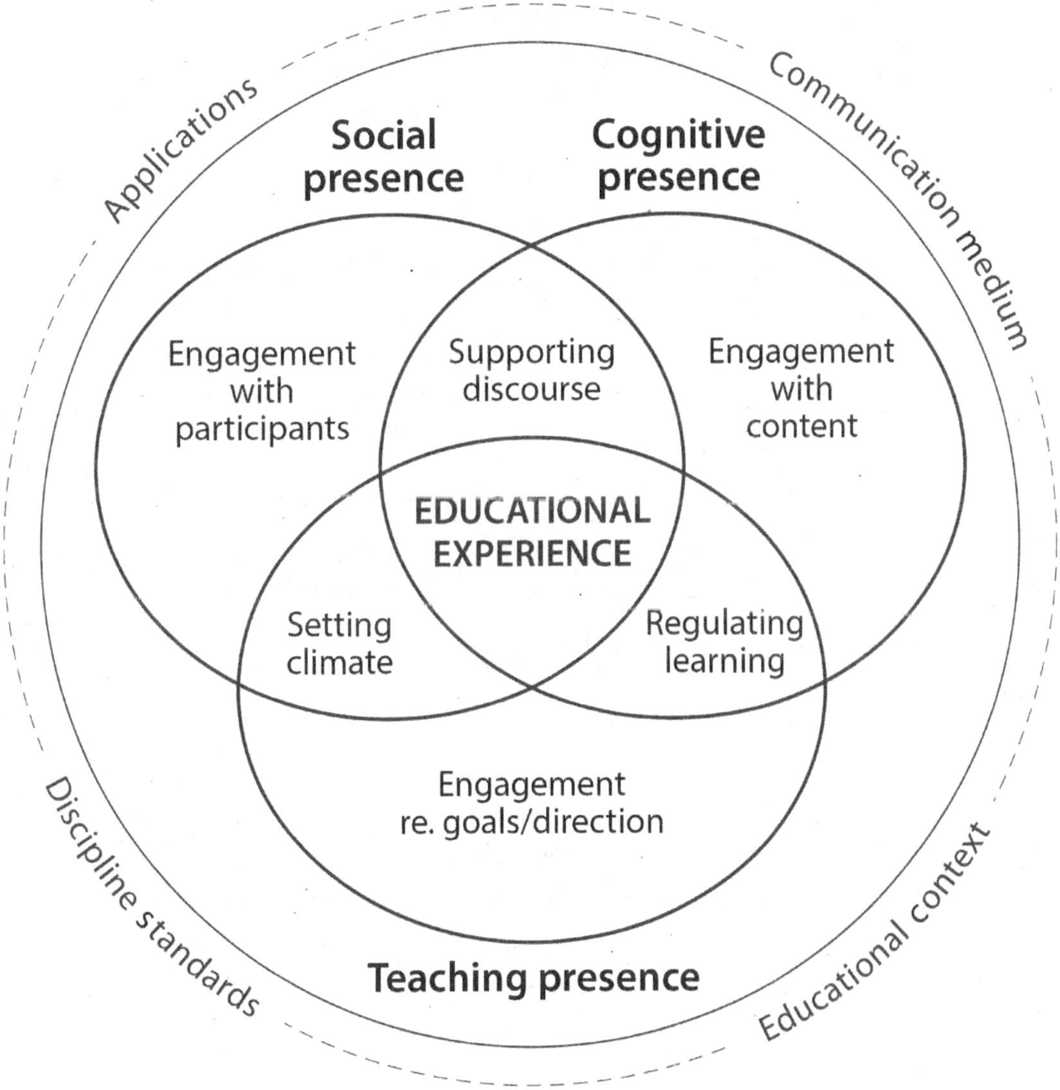

Figure 9.1 *Community of Inquiry (CoI) model*

(Image used with permission from the Community of Inquiry website and licensed under the CC-BY-SA International 4.0 license (https://creativecommons.org/licenses/by-sa/4.0/). The original image is located at www.thecommunityofinquiry.org/framework)

Technological Pedagogical Content Knowledge (TPACK) Model: The TPACK model (Mishra and Koehler, 2006) emphasises the integration of three knowledge domains: content knowledge (CK), pedagogical knowledge (PK) and technological knowledge (TK).

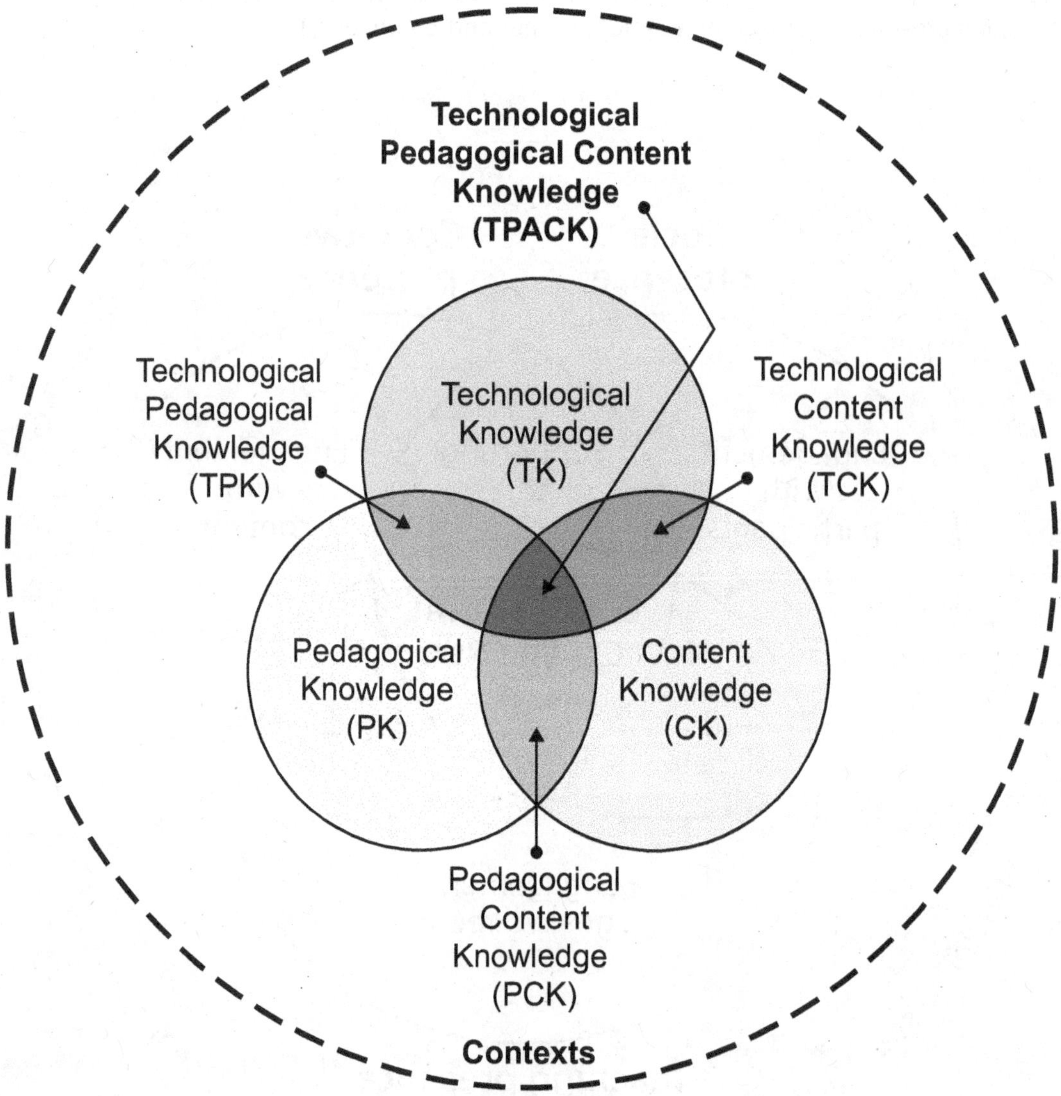

***Figure 9.2** TPACK model*

(Reproduced by permission of the publisher, © 2012 tpack.org)

Activity-Centred Analysis and Design (ACAD) Framework: Developed by Goodyear and Carvalho (2014), this framework views learning as an emergent activity shaped by three designable components: epistemic design (tasks), physical design (set) and social design.

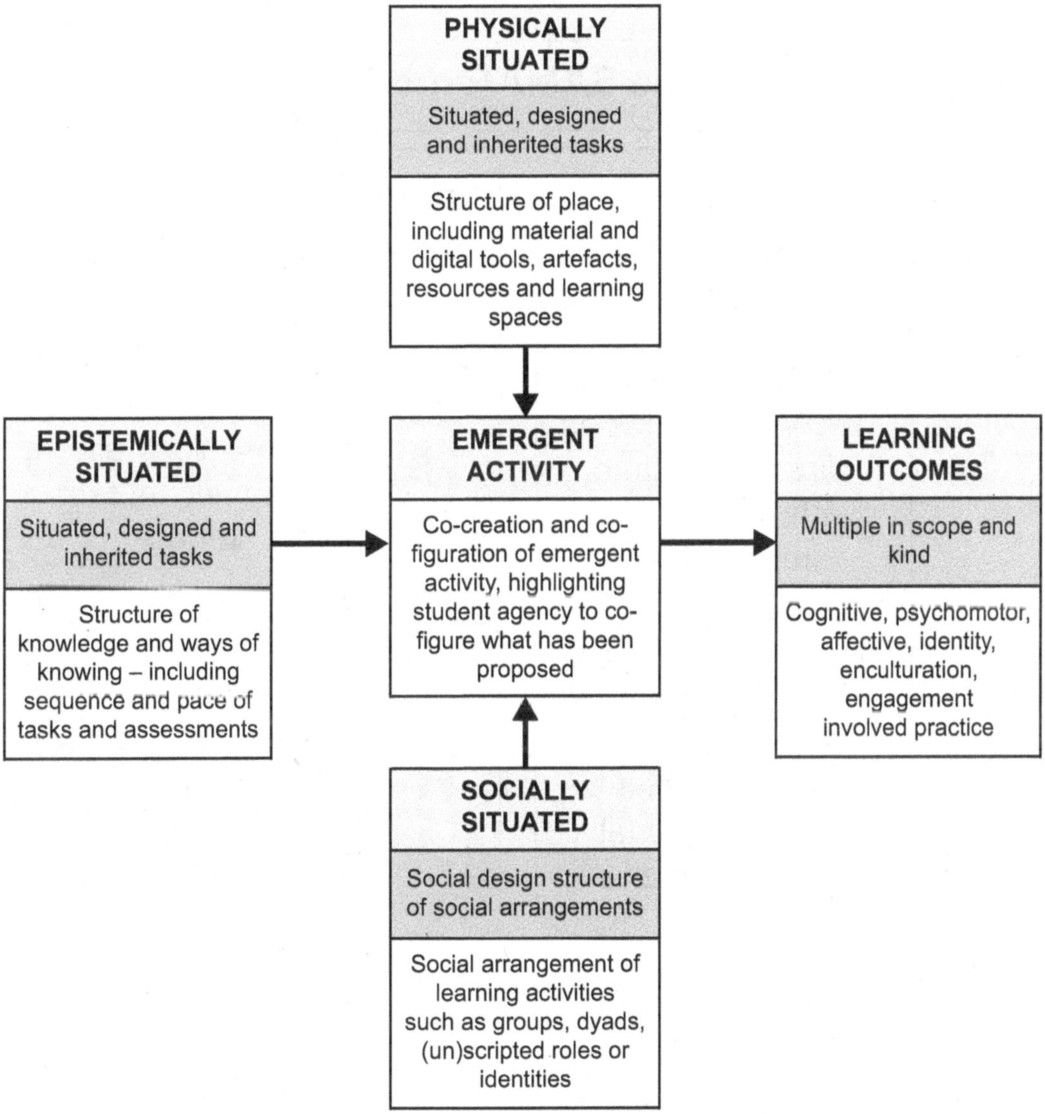

***Figure 9.3** Adapted from the ACAD model*

Substitution, Augmentation, Modification and Redefinition (SAMR) Model: Puentedura's (2006) (as cited in Blundell et al, 2022) SAMR model categorises technology use in teaching and learning into two levels: enhancement (substitution and augmentation) and transformation (modification and redefinition).

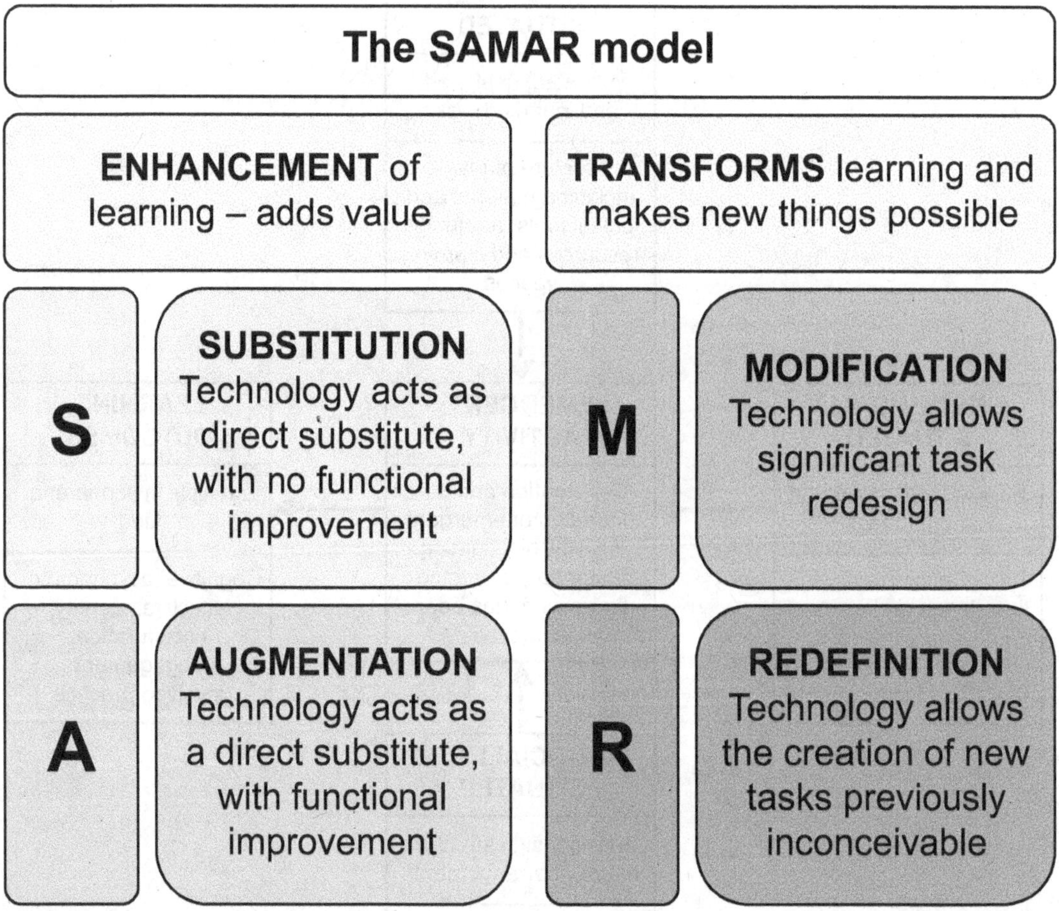

Figure 9.4 *SAMR model (adapted from Puentedura, 2006)*

Laurillard's Conversational Framework (Laurillard et al, 2018): This framework focuses on a conversational framework informing the design of learning experiences that incorporate six types of learning: acquisition, inquiry, practice, discussion, collaboration and production (Laurillard et al, 2018).

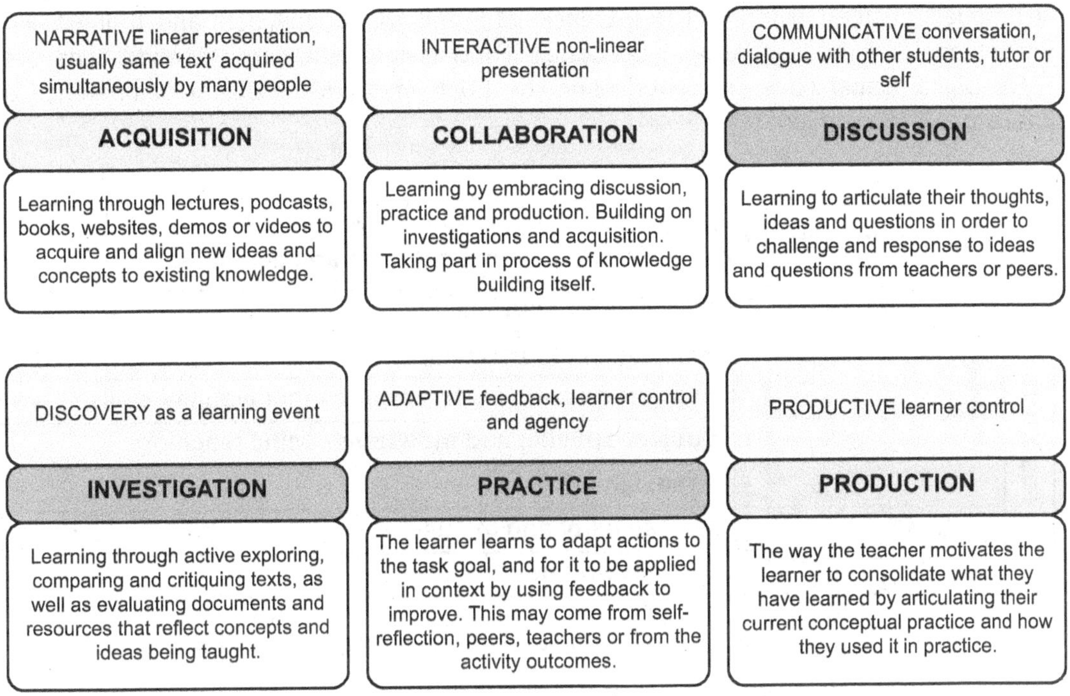

Figure 9.5 *Laurillard's Conversational Framework and learning types*

Embedding effective assessment with digital technology

Digital technologies offer significant opportunities to enhance assessment and feedback processes. However, as Hamer and Smith (2021) note, how teachers use assessment information and how learners respond to feedback are more crucial than the format of delivery. Key considerations include:

- integrating digital technologies with traditional assessment strategies;
- using a range of digital assessment formats and feedback tools;
- providing timely feedback on learners' progress;
- adapting teaching based on digital data;
- addressing challenges such as the digital divide and ensuring accessibility.

The Digital Teaching Professional Framework (DTPF)

Developed by the Education and Training Foundation (ETF) in collaboration with Jisc, the DTPF provides a comprehensive framework for digital competence in the FES sector. It outlines three competency levels (Exploring, Adopting and Leading) and cross-references five key models (instead of three): ETF Professional Standards for Teachers and Trainers, ETF Professional Standards for Aspiring Leaders, ETF Professional Standards for Middle Leaders, ETF's Digital Capabilities Framework, and the EU Framework for Digital Competence of Educators (DigCompEdu) (ETF, 2024).

Competency level		Seven elements to the framework which cover different teaching contexts and activities:	
Teachers	Stage 1: Exploring	A	Planning for your teaching
		B	Approaches to teaching
		C	Supporting learners to develop employability skills
	Stage 2: Adopting	D	Subject-specific and industry-specific teaching
		E	Assessment
	Stage 3: Leading	F	Accessibility and inclusion
		G	Self-development

Figure 9.6 *Digital Teaching Professional Framework (adapted from ETF, 2024)*

For student teachers in FES, understanding and applying these pedagogical principles and theories is crucial for developing effective online teaching practices. By critically evaluating and integrating these frameworks into your planning and delivery, you can create engaging, inclusive and effective learning experiences that meet the diverse needs of FES learners in the digital age.

CASE STUDY

Building community in a fully online Master's programme

Context: An online master's programme in education struggled to foster a sense of community among its geographically dispersed students.

Implementation: The programme introduced virtual coffee hours, online discussion forums and collaborative projects to encourage interaction and connection.

Outcomes: Students reported feeling more connected to their peers and instructors, leading to increased satisfaction with the programme and higher retention rates.

CASE STUDY

Ways of engaging: project designed to support disaffected young people

Context: The Ways of Engaging project, initiated by the East Anglia Learning and Skills Research Network (LSRN), was designed to support disaffected young people in FES and alternative provision settings (Duckett, 2021). The project drew on extensive research and practical experience in engaging NEET (not in education, employment or training) cohorts.

Pedagogical approach: The project's approach aligns with several key pedagogical theories and principles discussed in online and blended learning contexts:

- Personalised learning: Echoing the principles of the TPACK model (Mishra and Koehler, 2006), the project emphasised a learner-focused approach, tailoring content and delivery to individual needs.
- Social constructivism: Activities such as group discussions and teamwork exercises reflect the Community of Inquiry (CoI) model's emphasis on social presence and collaborative learning (Hamer and Smith, 2021).
- Authentic learning: The project's focus on real-world applications and employability skills aligns with Laurillard's Conversational Framework, particularly the aspects of practice and production (Laurillard et al, 2018).
- Flexible learning design: The adaptation to online delivery during the pandemic demonstrates principles from the SAMR model (Puentedura, 2006), showing how technology can be used to modify and redefine learning activities.

Implementation: The curriculum focused on three main components: leadership, employability and volunteering. Key activities included:

- introductory skills sessions focusing on teamwork, target setting and problem-solving;
- self-reflection exercises using various media (writing, images, objects);
- research projects on topics of personal interest;
- discussions on leadership and teamwork skills;
- mind mapping exercises on abstract concepts like respect.

These activities were adapted for online delivery during the Covid-19 pandemic, demonstrating flexibility and resilience in the face of changing circumstances.

Outcomes: The project found that:

- personalised learning approaches were crucial for maintaining student engagement and motivation;

→

- linking learning to real-world contexts increased student interest and motivation;
- flexible, customised learning, including distance learning elements, was effective in meeting individual learner needs.

The approach allowed for greater learner autonomy and teacher flexibility in terms of time management and resource allocation.

Recommendations: The project recommended that teachers:

- focus on moving learners from their current position to their potential, aligning with the fundamental pedagogical principles emphasised by Hamer and Smith (2021);
- adapt session planning to accommodate diverse learning preferences, reflecting the ACAD framework's emphasis on epistemic, physical and social design elements (Goodyear and Carvalho, 2021);
- embrace flexible approaches to time allocation, independent learning and resource-based learning.

This case study demonstrates how pedagogical theories and principles can be effectively embedded in practice, even in challenging contexts and with diverse learner groups. It highlights the importance of personalisation, flexibility and real-world relevance in engaging learners, principles that are equally applicable in online and blended learning environments (Duckett, 2021).

Digital technologies: legal and regulatory responsibility

In the rapidly evolving landscape of online education within the post-16 FES sector in England, lecturers must navigate a complex web of legal and ethical responsibilities (Gov.UK, 2021a, 2021b; ICO, 2021; Jisc, 2021a, b, c; Aiken and Epstein, 2022; DfE, 2023) (see Table 9.4 for an overview of these responsibilities and possible ways of working with them). This section provides a comprehensive overview of key areas of concern, including accessibility, student privacy, data protection, intellectual property and academic integrity (DfE, 2023).

Table 9.4 *Legal and ethical considerations*

Legal and ethical considerations	Key legislation/ guidelines	Challenges in online education	Implementation strategies for educators	Case study example
Accessibility and equity	Equality Act 2010 (Gov.UK, 2021a)	Lack of suitable devices, unreliable Wi-Fi, limited private workspaces (Jisc, 2023).	Use accessible formats, adhere to WCAG guidelines, conduct regular audits, offer training and advocate for resources.	A college provides laptops to students in need, offers digital literacy workshops and ensures online materials are compatible with screen readers.
Student privacy and data protection	GDPR and Data Protection Act 2018 (ICO, 2021)	Misuse of data, unauthorised access and potential bias in learning analytics.	Develop clear data policies, use secure storage, collect only necessary data, anonymise for research, obtain informed consent and provide opt-out options.	LearnWell Online Academy informs students about data collection and usage, allowing them to opt out of certain data tracking features while still benefiting from personalised learning paths.
Intellectual property	Copyright Designs and Patents Act 1988)	Unauthorised use of copyrighted materials in online courses.	Respect copyright, obtain necessary permissions or licences, properly attribute sources, and utilise open educational resources (OER) with proper attribution.	The Open Learning Institute partners with a publisher to provide licensed e-textbooks at a discounted rate for students, ensuring legal access to quality materials.
Academic integrity	Quality Assurance Agency (QAA) guidelines (QAA, 2021)	Increased opportunities for plagiarism and cheating in online environments.	Establish clear academic integrity policies, use plagiarism detection tools and design assessments that promote critical thinking and original work.	A college incorporates diverse assessment methods like project-based assignments, presentations and peer reviews to encourage authentic work and deter academic dishonesty.

Summary

This chapter has examined various effective digital technologies and online teaching methods that can improve education in vocational settings. We've looked at how these tools and approaches can enhance teaching, support learning and refine assessment practices. Now, let's review the main points from each section and think about how to apply them in real-world teaching situations. This summary will help you reflect on what you've learned and consider ways to incorporate these ideas into your own teaching practice.

At the beginning of the chapter, we discussed the affordances and applications of various educational technologies such as AI, AR, VR and online delivery platforms. We also touched on the potential impact of GenAI and LLMs on education. These technologies have the potential to revolutionise the way we create educational content, assess student learning and provide personalised support (Selwyn, 2021). However, it is important for educators to critically evaluate the ethical implications and limitations of these tools and to use them in ways that complement rather than replace human interaction and expertise (Aiken and Epstein, 2022; Mollick and Mollick, 2023b; Luckin et al, 2024).

Then we focused on best practices for managing digital technologies in the classroom, including strategies for selecting appropriate tools, structuring online lessons, facilitating interaction and collaboration, assessing learning outcomes and troubleshooting technical issues (Harasim, 2017; Lemov, 2020; Fernández-Batanero et al, 2022; Mollick, 2024). By following these guidelines and adapting them to their specific contexts, educators can create effective and inclusive online learning experiences for their students.

We briefly introduced key pedagogical principles and theories relevant to online learning, such as social constructivism, connectivism and self-regulated learning (Harasim, 2017; Lemov, 2020; Hamer and Smith, 2021). We also discussed research-backed online teaching methods such as blended learning, flipped classroom and gamification. By aligning your practice with these principles and strategies, you can design and deliver online vocational courses that are grounded in evidence-based pedagogy relevant for your subject specialism within a specific educational context.

Finally, we highlighted the legal and ethical responsibilities that come with using digital technologies in education, particularly in relation to accessibility, student privacy, data protection, intellectual property and academic integrity. With the increasing use of GenAIs and LLMs in education, it is crucial for you to be aware of the potential risks and challenges associated with these technologies, such as the potential for biased or inaccurate outputs, the need to protect student data privacy and the importance of promoting academic integrity (Aiken and Epstein, 2022).

To embed these takeaways in practice, vocational educators should start by critically reflecting on their current teaching, learning and assessment strategies and identifying areas where digital technologies and online pedagogies could add value. They should also seek out professional development opportunities to build their digital competencies and stay up to date with emerging trends and best practices in online education, including the use of GenAIs and LLMs.

As the landscape of education continues to evolve in response to technological advancements and societal changes, it is imperative that vocational educators are equipped with the knowledge, skills and dispositions needed to effectively leverage digital technologies and online pedagogies to support student learning and success. By critically engaging with the concepts and strategies discussed in this chapter and committing to ongoing professional development and reflection, educators can position themselves as leaders and innovators in the field of online vocational education.

Check your understanding (level 5)

1. What is meant by the terms online learning, blended learning, synchronous learning, asynchronous learning and flipped classroom?
2. What are the seven stages of the Jisc Digital Teaching Professional Framework?

Developmental questions L6+7

1. How might you review and change your approach to using technology in teaching if you considered practices from other subject areas?
2. Evaluate a recent session you have taught, and then engage with colleagues from different specialisms about the digital tools they use in both planning and delivery. What new technologies could you potentially incorporate into your future sessions, and what might be their benefits and limitations in your specific subject context?
3. Having read about the various strategies to help you teach online, how could you adapt your module/curriculum/programme?
4. Identify which colleagues are using digital technology and online learning opportunities, observe their practice and consider what you could change to further embrace digital and online teaching, learning and assessment strategies.
5. Create an action plan to help you develop your technological knowledge and abilities.
6. Continue to research the affordances and challenges of digital and online tools used by communities of lecturers in their sessions. Pick one you have not used before to adapt for use in one of your future sessions. Video or audio record your teaching and after the session critically reflect on how well it was received. You may wish to obtain feedback from your learners to co-create and collaborate on integrating digital and online learning opportunities.

Further reading

- Archambault, L, Leary, H and Rice, K (2022) Pillars of Online Pedagogy: A Framework for Teaching in Online Learning Environments. *Educational Psychologist*, 57(3): 178–91.
- Association for Learning Technology (ALT) (nd) [online] Available at: www.alt.ac.uk (accessed 22 September 2024).
- Beetham, H and Sharpe, R (eds) (2020) *Rethinking Pedagogy for a Digital Age: Principles and Practices of Design*. 3rd ed. Abingdon: Routledge.
- EDUCAUSE Learning Initiative (2024) *7 Things You Should Know About Best Practices in Online Teaching.* [online] Available at: www.educause.edu/research-and-publications/7-things-you-should-know-about (accessed 22 September 2024).
- Education and Training Foundation (ETF) (2020) *Taking Learning to the Next Level: Digital Teaching Professional Framework. Full Reference Guide.* [online] Available at: www.et-foundation.co.uk/wp-content/uploads/2023/06/ETF-DTPF-Full.pdf (accessed 22 September 2024).
- Jisc (nd) Shaping the Digital Future of FE and Skills. [online] Available at: www.jisc.ac.uk/shaping-the-digital-future-of-fe-and-skills (accessed 22 September 2024).
- Lemov, D (2020) *Teaching in the Online Classroom. Surviving and Thriving in the New Normal.* New York: Jossey-Bass.
- Mollick, E (2024) *Co-Intelligence. Living and Working with AI.* New York: Penguin Portfolio.
- OpenLearn (nd) Assistive Technologies and Online Learning. [online] Available at: www.open.edu/openlearn/education-development/assistive-technologies-and-online-learning/content-section-0?active-tab=description-tab (accessed 29 November 2024).

References

Aiken, M and Epstein, R (2022) Ethical Guidelines for AI in Education: A Review and Commentary. *International Journal of Artificial Intelligence in Education*, 32(4): 967–94.

Anderson, A, Barham, N and Northcote, M (2013) Using the TPACK Framework to Unite Disciplines in Online Learning. *Australasian Journal of Educational Technology*, 29(4). https://doi.org/10.14742/ajet.24.

Anderson, T (2017) How Communities of Inquiry Drive Teaching and Learning in the Digital Age. TeachOnline, Contact Nord. [online] Available at: https://teachonline.ca/fr/node/92055 (accessed 8 October 2024).

Archambault, L, Leary, H and Rice, K (2022) Pillars of Online Pedagogy: A Framework for Teaching in Online Learning Environments. *Educational Psychologist*, 57(3): 178–91.

Arnold, J (2024) *Gamification in Education*. San Diego: National University.

Beetham, H and Sharpe, R (eds) (2020) *Rethinking Pedagogy for a Digital Age: Principles and Practices of Design*. 3rd ed. Abingdon: Routledge.

Beetham, H and MacNeill, S (2023) *Beyond Blended. Post-pandemic Curriculum and Learning Design: Lessons from the Higher Education (HE) Sector.* Jisc. [online] Available at: https://repository.jisc.ac.uk/9227/1/beyond-blended-post-pandemic-curriculum-and-learning-design-report.pdf (accessed 22 September 2024).

Blundell, R, Costa Dias, M, Cribb, J, Joyce, R, Waters, T, Wernham, T and Xu, X (2022) Inequality and the COVID-19 Crisis in the United Kingdom. *Annual Review of Economics*, 14(1): 607–36.

Bond, M, Khosravi, H, De Laat, M, Bergdahl, N, Negrea, V, Oxley, E, Pham, P, Chong, S W and Siemens, G (2023) A Meta Systematic Review of Artificial Intelligence in Higher Education: A Call for Increased Ethics, Collaboration, and Rigour. *International Journal of Educational Technology in Higher Education*, 21: Article 4.

Bond, S, Hanson, M, Arvind, M and Margiotta, J (2022) Can Gamification Enhance Motivation in FE Maths Learners? Leeds City College CfEM Action Research Report 2021–22. [online] Available at: www.et-foundation.co.uk/wp-content/uploads/2023/02/Can-gamification-enhance-motivation-in-FE-maths-learners_Leeds-City-College-CfEM-action-research-report-2021-22.pdf (accessed 8 October 2024).

Carvalho, L and Goodyear, P (2014) *The Architecture of Productive Learning Networks*. 1st ed. Abingdon: Routledge. https://doi.org/10.4324/9780203591093

Christopoulos, A and Mystakidis, S (2023) Gamification in Education. *Encyclopaedia* 2023(3): 1223–43. https://doi.org/10.3390/encyclopedia3040089.

Coleman, V (2021) *Digital Divide in UK Education During COVID-19 Pandemic: Literature Review*. Cambridge Assessment research report. Cambridge: Cambridge Assessment.

Dabbous,, D and Emms, K (2020) Education Technology in Further Education Colleges: How Are Colleges Integrating Digital Technologies into Their Practice? Edge Foundation. [online] Available at: www.edge.co.uk/research/projects/research-reports/education-technology-further-education-colleges-how-are-colleges-integrating-digital-technologies-their-practice-2020/ (accessed 8 October 2024).

Department for Education (DfE) (2019) *Realising the Potential of Technology in Education: A Strategy for Education Providers and the Technology Industry*. [online] Available at: www.gov.uk/government/publications/realising-the-potential-of-technology-in-education (accessed 28 September 2024).

Department for Education (DfE) (2023) Online Education Accreditation Scheme: Guidance on Meeting the Online Education Standards. [online] Available at: https://assets.publishing.service.gov.uk/media/63d8ed588fa8f518884ceb67/Online_education_accreditation_scheme_guidance_-_online_education_standards.pdf (accessed 22 September 2024).

Department for Education (DfE) (2024) Diploma in Teaching (Further Education and Skills) qualification framework. [online] Available at: www.gov.uk/government/publications/further-education-initial-teacher-education/diploma-in-teaching-further-education-and-skills-qualification-framework (accessed 8 October 2024).

Doucet, A, Evers, J, Guerra, E, Lopez, N, Soskil, M and Timmers, K (2018) *Teaching in the Fourth Industrial Revolution: Standing at the Precipice*. Abingdon: Routledge.

Doucet, A, Netolicky, D, Timmers, K and Tuscano, F J (2020) Thinking about Pedagogy in an Unfolding Pandemic: An Independent Report on Approaches to Distance Learning During COVID19 School Closures. Education International. [online] Available at: https://issuu.com/educationinternational/docs/2020_research_covid-19_eng?fr=sYTY3OTEwMzc2ODU (accessed 22 September 2024).

Duckett, I (2021) Ways of Engaging: Some Approaches to Developing Learning Skills. In Duckworth, V, Harrison, B, Petrie, J and Singh, A (eds) *Future FE Pedagogies, Volume 1*. The Education and Training Consortium. [online] Available at: www.et-foundation.co.uk/wp-content/uploads/2021/09/Future-FE-Pedagogies-FINAL-FOR-PUBLICATION.pdf (accessed 22 September 2024).

Duckworth, V, Harrison, B, Petrie, J and Singh, A (eds) (2021) *Future FE Pedagogies, Volume 1*. [online] Available at: www.et-foundation.co.uk/wp-content/uploads/2021/09/Future-FE-Pedagogies-FINAL-FOR-PUBLICATION.pdf (accessed 22 September 2024).

Education and Training Foundation (ETF) (2022a) Occupational Standards for Learning and Skills Tutors [online] Available at: www.et-foundation.co.uk/news/new-framework-guidance-for-diploma-in-teaching-fe-and-skills-availabl/ (accessed 3 May 2024).

Education and Training Foundation (ETF) (2022b) Professional Standards for Teachers and Trainers. [online] Available at: www.et-foundation.co.uk/professionalstandards (accessed 29 September 2024).

Education and Training Foundation (ETF) (2024) Empowering Excellence in Further Education: Introducing the Updated Digital Teaching Professional Framework. [online] Available at: www.et-foundation.co.uk/professional-development/edtech-support/digital-skills-competency-framework (accessed 22 September 2024).

Emin-Martinez, V and Ney, M (2013) Supporting Tutors in the Process of Adoption of Game Based Learning Pedagogy. In Escudeiro, P and Vaz de Carvalho, C (eds) *Proceedings of the European Conference on Games Based Learning (ECGBL 2013), Porto, Portugal, 3–4 October 2013* (pp 156–62). Reading: Academic Conferences and Publishing International Limited. [online] Available at: https://core.ac.uk/download/pdf/51962975.pdf#:~:text=Abstract:%20In%20an%20attempt%20to%20address%20the%20difficulty%20to (accessed 8 October 2024).

Fernández-Batanero, J M, Montenegro-Rueda, M, Fernández-Cerero, J and García-Martínez, I (2022) Digital Competences for Teacher Professional Development: Systematic Review. *European Journal of Teacher Education*, 45(4), 513–31.

Garrison, D R (2016) *E-learning in the 21st Century: A Community of Inquiry Framework for Research and Practice*. 3rd ed. London: Routledge.

Garrison, D R and Kanuka, H (2004) Blended Learning: Uncovering Its Transformative Potential in Higher Education. *The Internet and Higher Education*, 7(2), 95–105.

Garrison, D R, Anderson, T and Archer, W (2001) Critical Thinking, Cognitive Presence, and Computer Conferencing in Distance Education. *American Journal of Distance Education*, 1: 7–23.

Giannini, S (2023) *Generative AI and the Future of Education*. Geneva: UNESCO. [online] Available at: https://unesdoc.unesco.org/ark:/48223/pf0000385877 (accessed 22 September 2024).

Goodyear, P, and Carvalho, L (2014) *The Architecture of Productive Learning Networks*. 1st ed. Abingdon: Routledge. https://doi.org/10.4324/9780203591093

Goodyear, P, Carvalho, L and Yeoman, P (2021) Activity-Centred Analysis and Design (ACAD): Core Purposes, Distinctive Qualities and Current Developments. *Education Technology Research and Development,* 69: 445–64. https://doi.org/10.1007/s11423-020-09926-7

Gov.UK (2021a) Equality Act 2010: Guidance. [online] Available at: www.gov.uk/guidance/equality-act-2010-guidance (accessed 22 September 2024).

Gov.UK (2021b) Intellectual Property and Copyright. [online] Available at: www.gov.uk/topic/intellectual-property/copyright (accessed 22 September 2024).

Hamer, J and Smith, J (2021) *Online and Blended Delivery in Further Education: A Literature Review into Pedagogy Including Digital Forms of Assessment*. London: Department of Education.

Harasim, L (2017) *Learning Theory and Online Technologies*. Abingdon: Routledge.

Hendrick, C and Macpherson, R (2017) *What Does This Look Like in the Classroom: Bridging the Gap Between Research and Practice*. Woodbridge: John Catt Educational Ltd.

Holmes, W, Bialik, M and Fadel, C (2019) *Artificial Intelligence in Education: Promises and Implications for Teaching and Learning*. Boston, MA: Center for Curriculum Redesign.

ICO (2021) *Guide to the UK General Data Protection Regulation (UK GDPR)*. [online] Available at: https://ico.org.uk/for-organisations/guide-to-data-protection/guide-to-the-general-data-protection-regulation-gdpr (accessed 22 September 2024).

Ilomäki, L, Paavola, S, Lakkala, M and Kantosalo, A (2016) Digital Competence: An Emergent Boundary Concept for Policy and Educational Research. *Education and Information Technology*, 21: 655–79. https://doi.org/10.1007/s10639-014-9346-4

Institute for Apprenticeships and Technical Education (IfATE) (2024) *Learning and Skills Teacher*. [online] Available at: www.instituteforapprenticeships.org/apprenticeship-standards/learning-and-skills-teacher-v1-3 (accessed 29 September 2024).

Jisc (2021a) Meeting Accessibility Regulations. [online] Available at: www.jisc.ac.uk/accessibility (accessed 22 September 2024).

Jisc (2021b) *Intellectual Property Rights in a Digital World*. [online] Available at: www.jisc.ac.uk/guides/intellectual-property-rights-in-a-digital-world (accessed 22 September 2024).

Jisc (2021c) *Privacy and Data Protection*. [online] Available at: www.jisc.ac.uk/guides/privacy-and-data-protection (accessed 22 September 2024).

Jisc (2023) *Learner Digital Experience Insights Survey 2022/2023: UK Further Education (FE) Survey Findings*. Jisc data analytics. [online] Available at: https://repository.jisc.ac.uk/9223/1/DEI-2023-learner-fe-report.pdf (accessed 22 September 2024).

Jisc (2024) *Principles for the Use of AI in FE Colleges: Artificial Intelligence Is Already Transforming Education, the Workplace, and Society*. [online] Available at: www.jisc.ac.uk/further-education-and-skills/principles-for-the-use-of-ai-in-fe-colleges (accessed 13 September 2024).

Laurillard, D, Kennedy, E, Charlton, P, Wild, J and Dimakopoulos, D (2018) Using Technology to Develop Teachers as Designers of TEL: Evaluating the Learning Designer. *British Journal of Educational Technology*, 49(6): 1044–58. https://doi.org/10.1111/bjet.12697

Lemov, D (2020) *Teaching in the Online Classroom: Surviving and Thriving in the New Normal*. New York: Jossey-Bass.

Luckin, R, Holmes, W, Griffiths, M and Forcier, L B (2016) *Intelligence Unleashed: An Argument for AI in Education*. London: Pearson.

Luckin, R, Rudolph, J, Grünert, M and Tan, S (2024) Exploring the Future of Learning and the Relationship between Human Intelligence and AI: An Interview with Professor Rose Luckin. *Journal of Applied Learning & Teaching*, 7(1): 1–18.

Mishra, P and Koehler, M J (2006) Technological Pedagogical Content Knowledge: A Framework for Teacher Knowledge. *Teachers College Record*, 108(6): 1017–54. https://doi.org/10.1111/j.1467-9620.2006.00684.x

Mollick, E (2024) *Co-Intelligence: Living and Working with AI*. New York: Penguin Portfolio.

Mollick, E and Mollick, L (2023a) *Assigning AI: Seven Approaches for Students with Prompts*. The Wharton School Research Paper. [online] Available at: https://dx.doi.org/10.2139/ssrn.4475995 (accessed 22 September 2024).

Mollick, E R and Mollick, L (2023b) *Using AI to Implement Effective Teaching Strategies in Classrooms: Five Strategies, Including Prompts*. The Wharton School Research Paper. [online] Available at: https://papers.ssrn.com/sol3/papers.cfm?abstract_id=4391243 (accessed 22 September 2024).

Muñoz-Cristóbal, J A, Hernández-Leo, D, Carvalho, L, Martinez-Maldonado, R, Thompson, K, Wardak, D and Goodyear, P (2018) 4FAD: A Framework for Mapping the Evolution of Artefacts in the Learning Design Process. *Australasian Journal of Educational Technology*, 34(2).

Ofsted (2024) Guidance: Further Education and Skills Inspection Handbook (updated September 2024). [online] Available at: www.gov.uk/government/publications/further-education-and-skills-inspection-handbook-eif/further-education-and-skills-handbook-for-september-2023 (accessed 8 October 2024).

Petrie, J, Singh, A, Duckworth, V, and Harrison, B (eds) (2021) Future FE Pedagogies. *Volume 1: The Education and Training Consortium*. [online] Available at: www.et-foundation.co.uk/wp-content/uploads/2021/09/Future-FE-Pedagogies-FINAL-FOR-PUBLICATION.pdf (accessed 8 October 2024).

Puentendura, R R (2006) Transformation, Technology, and Education in the State of Maine. [online] Available at: www.hippasus.com/rrpweblog/archives/2006_11.html (accessed 8 October 2024).

The Open Innovation Team and Department for Education (2024) *Generative AI in Education: Educator and Expert Views*. London: Department for Education. [online] Available at: https://assets.publishing.service.gov.uk/media/65b8cd41b5cb6e000d8bb74e/DfE_GenAI_in_education_-_Educator_and_expert_views_report.pdf (accessed 29 September 2024).

Quality Assurance Agency for Higher Education (QAA) (2021) *Contracting to Cheat in Higher Education: How to Address Contract Cheating, the Use of Third-Party Services and Essay Mills*. [online] Available at: www.qaa.ac.uk/docs/qaa/guidance/contracting-to-cheat-in-higher-education-2nd-edition.pdf (accessed 22 September 2024).

Scott, H (2021) The Proverbs of TEL. In Duckworth, V, Harrison, B, Petrie, J and Singh, A (eds) *Future FE Pedagogies, Volume 1*. The Education and Training Consortium. [online] Available at: www.et-foundation.co.uk/wp-content/uploads/2021/09/Future-FE-Pedagogies-FINAL-FOR-PUBLICATION.pdf (accessed 22 September 2024).

Selwyn, N (2021) Ed-Tech within Limits: Anticipating Educational Technology in Times of Environmental Crisis. *E-Learning and Digital Media*, 18(5): 496–510.

Sharples, M (2023) Towards Social Generative AI for Education: Theory, Practices, and Ethics. Cornell University. [online] Available at: http://arxiv.org/abs/2306.10063 (accessed 22 September 2024).

Siemens, G (2005) Connectivism: A Learning Theory for the Digital Age. *International Journal of Instructional Technology and Distance Learning*, 2(1): 3–10.

Sun, A, and Chen, X (2016) Online Education and its Effective Practice: A Research Review. *Journal of Information Technology Education: Research*, 15: 157–90. https://doi.org/10.28945/3502

Tanis, J C (2020) The Seven Principles of Online Learning: Feedback from Faculty and Alumni on its Importance for Teaching and Learning. Research in Learning Technology, 28. [online] Available at: https://files.eric.ed.gov/fulltext/EJ1257615.pdf (accessed 8 October 2024).

Vygotsky, L S (1978) *Mind in Society: The Development of Higher Psychological Processes*. Cambridge, MA: Harvard University Press.

Webb, M (2024) AI 2030 – Navigating the Future of Artificial Intelligence. *Jisc blog*. [online] Available at: www.jisc.ac.uk/blog/ai-2030-navigating-the-future-of-artificial-intelligence (accessed 29 September 2024).

Zimmerman, B J (2002) Becoming a Self-regulated Learner: An Overview. *Theory Into Practice*, 41(2): 64–70.

Part 4 Professional practice for the teacher

10 Teaching practice requirements

Professional links

This chapter contributes to the following professional links:

The Diploma in Teaching mandatory content (DfE, 2024)

- 1.1 Curriculum development.
- 2.8 Role and currency of research and evidence.
- 2.9 Application of theory to practice.
- 3.5 Rigorous curriculum thinking.
- 3.7 Planning and delivering sessions.
- 3.10 Teacher expectations of learners including classroom management.
- 3.12 Assessment and feedback.
- 4.2 Preparation for placement.
- 4.4 Team and solo teaching.
- 4.5 Curriculum planning and review.
- 4.6 Lesson planning and adaptations.
- 4.7 Planning and conducting assessment.
- 4.9 Assessment feedback and advice or guidance.
- 4.11 Management and supporting learners, including behaviour.
- 4.16 Professional responsibilities.
- 4.17 Working with colleagues.

Learning and Skills Teacher Occupational Standards (IfATE, 2024)

- K1 The pedagogical theory and how to apply this theory to practice.
- K3 The principles of designing, planning, and organising curriculum.

→

- K5 Evidence-informed inclusive teaching, learning and assessment strategies.
- K9 Principles and practices of assessment and feedback.
- K10 How to promote and foster a safe and supportive learning environment.
- S4 Use a variety of teaching and assessment methods depending on the learning environment and learners' needs.
- S11 Provide ongoing learner feedback.
- S19 Engage learners to establish standards of behaviour, mutual respect and safe working.
- S20 Challenge learners to address inappropriate behaviour or viewpoints.
- B4 Act in a professional manner, and in a way that builds and maintains positive relationships with colleagues, students and stakeholders.

Professional Standards (ETF, 2022)

- 6 Develop collaborative and respectful relationships with learners, colleagues and external stakeholders.
- 7 Engage with and promote a culture of continuous learning and quality improvement.
- 9 Critically review and apply your knowledge of educational research, pedagogy, and assessment to develop evidence-informed practice.
- 13 Promote and support positive learner behaviour, attitudes and well-being.
- 19 Apply appropriate and fair methods of assessment and provide constructive and timely feedback to support learning and achievement.

Chapter objectives ◎

At the end of this chapter you will be able to:

- have an increased understanding of the practical and academic considerations in preparation for placement;
- consider different approaches to and key considerations regarding curriculum planning;
- identify some key approaches to lesson planning;
- explain what adaptive teaching is;
- develop your awareness of different approaches to marking, assessment and feedback;

- critically evaluate issues around putting theory into practice;
- identify some core approaches for managing and supporting learners, including behaviour management techniques.

Introduction

There is a wealth of existing research on all areas covered in this chapter. While it is not possible to offer a comprehensive overview of all research and thinking on these areas, this chapter aims to draw your attention to some of the recent thinking from influential educators on these issues, as well as contextualise key ideas in a historical educational context where appropriate. It is recommended that you use this chapter as a starting point to introduce yourself to each of these issues, and then follow up each area with additional reading and research.

Preparation for placement

Preparation for your teaching placements comprises several elements – practical and logistical considerations, and academic considerations. These may vary slightly depending on whether you are a pre-service or an in-service trainee, but there will also be some crossover. For example, if you are an in-service trainee doing your teaching qualification at the very beginning of your career in teaching, some of the following pre-service considerations may also be appropriate. If you are a pre-service trainee, you will have a voluntary teaching placement while studying as a student. If you are an in-service trainee, you will be employed as a teacher in the sector and will be working towards your teaching qualification on a part-time basis at the same time.

Pre-service trainees

If you are a pre-service trainee, here are some important practical and logistical considerations for your placement.

- Make sure you have the contact details of a key member of staff or your mentor before your placement starts. They will be a key point of contact and can answer any questions you have about your placement.
- Ensure you are familiar with the travel route that you will use to commute to your placement and the timings for how long it will take to get there. This is hopefully an obvious point, but however you plan to commute to your placement, it is good to know your route and have a backup option in case of disruption to transport links or road routes if you are planning to drive.
- Know what time you need to arrive for and ensure that you are on time. Make sure you communicate with your placement provider if you are going to be late. Punctuality and attendance are an essential part of professionalism and will be taken into consideration for future reference requests. The IfATE Learning and

Skills Teacher apprenticeship requires trainees to meet a range of knowledge, skills and behaviour outcomes including B4: '*act in a professional manner and in a way that builds and maintains positive relationships with colleagues, students and stakeholders*' (IfATE, 2024). Standard 6 of the ETF Professional Standards for teachers and trainers requires tutors to '*develop collaborative and respectful relationships with learners, colleagues and external stakeholders*' (ETF, 2022). From these standards you can see the importance of professionalism in the workplace.

- Be aware of the dress code of your placement provider. Again, this is an important part of your professionalism as a tutor.
- Check the routine for signing in and out of the building. Check whether you are required to sign in and out of the building each day you are on placement. This is essential for safeguarding reasons and in the event where an evacuation or lockdown of the building is necessary.
- Identify the groups you are working with and what your timetable will be. What days will you be expected to be on placement, and what is the duration of your placement? This may change throughout placement, so where possible be aware of any upcoming changes to groups you are working with/courses you are teaching or supporting to deliver.
- Know when you will start teaching. Most placements for pre-service trainees will start with an observation period where you will shadow a member or multiple members of teaching staff. This is hugely valuable for you to see a range of different approaches to teaching. After any initial observation period, make sure that you understand what you will be taking over. You may start with team teaching some lessons before building up to taking over whole lessons.
- Know what the expectations are of whether you are required to be in the building when you are not teaching. For example, a placement provider may be happy for you to work from home if you are not timetabled to be teaching for a certain part of the day/week. Alternatively, they may expect you to be in the building to work/plan/prepare when you are not teaching.
- Ensure that you contact your mentor or other named key member of staff if you are unable to attend placement, for example due to illness or caring commitments. Communicate the reason for absence as early as possible. Communicating before 8am is useful for staff because it allows them enough time to put alternative arrangements in place if necessary. Providers may have their own timings to communicate absence by, and it will be important to ensure you communicate by this time. Also know what the expectation will be if you are unable to make it in terms of setting work for any classes/groups you are teaching. Some providers will expect you to set work for a class/group if you are able to, as a tutor or teacher would have to. If you are not able to communicate your absence to your placement provider, for example due to a serious emergency, then make sure wherever possible that there is someone else who can do this for you – for example, a friend, family member or fellow trainee who knows what your placement provider and placement days are.

- An early part of your pre-service training may be to complete safeguarding and Prevent training. You will need to check whether your placement provider requires you to complete any further mandatory training or whether they will accept the safeguarding and Prevent training that you may have already completed as part of your teaching qualification.
- If you have any social media accounts, consider very carefully what your privacy settings are. It is strongly recommended that all privacy settings on any social media platform are as high as they can be. Consider using an alias where appropriate. Future employers may check social media accounts as part of a background screening process before any formal vetting (Rosser, 2017). 21 per cent of recruiters admitted to rejecting a candidate after looking them up on Facebook (Fennell, 2023). Consider your digital footprint carefully – think before posting content and make sure that you understand what is viewable to the public on your social media account(s). Ask yourself if you would be happy for a future employer to read, watch or see what you post.

While these may be obvious and logical considerations when preparing for your placements, it is worthwhile reiterating them here as they will all contribute to your professionalism. It may be that post qualification, the provider you are training with has a job opportunity that you want to apply for, or alternatively you apply for a job elsewhere which requires a reference from your main placement. The professional image that you maintain will play an important role in any future reference regardless of whether you are completing your qualification on a pre-service or in-service route.

In terms of academic considerations, it is important to take the following into account where the information is available to you. As with the practical considerations above, your mentor or other key contact from your placement will be able to support you in establishing what, from the following considerations, you are able to access before or shortly after your placement starts. The following considerations are also relevant to in-service trainees who have started their employment shortly before or at the same time as completing their teaching qualification.

- A copy of the scheme of learning/work or lesson overview for the group(s) that you are working with. Some departments may have this complete for the year, and others may have this complete for a certain number of weeks in the academic year and add to it as the year progresses. Having access to a document such as a scheme of learning will help you to understand the sequencing of the curriculum and lessons on the course that you are delivering and what is required of you in terms of planning and preparation.
- If the course(s) you are teaching on has key resources such as a textbook, training handbook or regulation handbook, ensure that you have a copy of these to support with your own subject knowledge and planning. If the course you teach on has key physical resources you will need, ensure that you will have access to these. For example, a tutor of hospitality may need their own set of professional kitchen

knives, or a tutor of hairdressing/barbering may need their own set of hairdressing/barbering equipment.

- Consider whether you need to carry out any CPD/subject knowledge enhancement. It may be that despite being a specialist in the subject, you have not studied a particular area of that subject for a while, or at all. For example, it is quite common for a history graduate to teach subjects as part of an A level in history that they did not study during their degree. In a situation where your subject knowledge needs developing, it will be essential for you to identify any gaps in knowledge or skills that you will be required to teach and ensure that you work to acquire this knowledge and/or these skills. Ask your mentor or other staff in the department what you can do to support this. For example, they may recommend a key book to read or have access to some online training that will support you. For subjects where there is a practical element of teaching, ensure that you communicate clearly what you are and are not qualified to teach.

Curriculum planning and review

There are many different models of curriculum that have been used over time, and there is not one centrally agreed definition of what curriculum is. Chapter 11, 'Teaching my subject', also gives you some information on curriculum and curriculum models. Some of the different curriculum models that have been influential and may still be used by different settings or educators include the following.

Curriculum as product: Also known as the objectives model. This focuses on behavioural targets for learning and is most closely associated with the work of Ralph Tyler. It is associated with behaviourist approaches where students play a largely passive role in learning (Armitage et al, 2016). It focuses on four key questions:

- *What are your curriculum aims and objectives?*
- *Which learning experiences meet these aims and objectives?*
- *How can these learning experiences be organised into a curriculum programme?*
- *How can the curriculum be evaluated?*

(Armitage et al, 2016, p 202)

Critical question ⑦

» While considered as one of the most influential curriculum models of the twentieth century, to what extent do you think this model is now outdated or obsolete?

Curriculum as process: This model focuses on the 'how' of learning – the process and products – so that a learner can use and develop the content rather than receive it passively. Developed by Stenhouse in the 1970s, it requires the teacher to define the content of a course, teaching procedures used for the specific subject and the criteria to judge the students' work (Armitage et al, 2016).

Critical questions

- » How is the curriculum as process model different to the curriculum as product model?
- » To what extent do you think this curriculum model still has relevance in a modern educational context?

Hidden curriculum: This model was formulated by Jackson (1968) in his work *Life in Classrooms*. Jackson emphasises that education should be seen as a process of socialisation, asserting that institutional expectations are just as significant as academic expectations when evaluating the demands of school life. These may include but are not limited to the transmission of values or attitudes such as punctuality, professionalism, work ethic, organisation, critical thinking, civic responsibility, tolerance and inclusivity. For example, if a teacher uses group work and collaborative learning in their teaching, they are conveying a message to students about the importance of collaboration and communication.

Critical question

- » What values and attitudes are you transmitting to your learners through your teaching as part of a hidden curriculum?

There are many more curriculum models that you may or will come across in different books on teaching and learning, including the ones summarised above. Definitions and models of curriculum will differ depending on the year that the book was published and the context that the author is writing in. As you conduct wider reading for your training programme and CPD, be mindful of what is emphasised as important in different curriculum models. Some critical questions you can ask to think about wider factors that may have influenced the author's definitions and ways of thinking about curriculum models could include the following.

- What key educational policies or reviews were influential at the time the work was published, and how might these have influenced their ideas or agendas about curriculum design and thinking?

- Is the author(s) taking a generic or subject-specific approach to curriculum thinking and design?
- What government was in power at the time the author was writing and what were their key educational policies and reforms? Could this have influenced the author's views and interpretations of curriculum?

Both Tom Sherrington and Ruth Ashbee argue that subject-specific curriculum thinking should be the key consideration in curriculum design (Sherrington and Caviglioli, 2017; Ashbee, 2021). Ashbee (2021) also stresses the importance of curriculum design as a moral issue, arguing that creating a democratic curriculum is crucial as it allows learners from diverse starting points to achieve and gain the knowledge and skills to enable them to engage in a democratic society with meaning, purpose and understanding.

Another logistical consideration when thinking about curriculum design is that for many Key Stage 4 and Key Stage 5 courses (level 2 and level 3), curricula are determined by specifications for exams such as GCSE or A levels (Sherrington and Caviglioli, 2017). How this specification is interpreted by those who design the curriculum at course level will therefore look different in different educational settings and contexts. It is also important to highlight the differences and connections between curriculum and pedagogy. Simply put, curriculum is about what we teach, and pedagogy is about how we teach it (Sherrington and Caviglioli, 2020).

Activity ⑦

» Sherrington and Caviglioli (2020) highlight the follow eight considerations as important for curriculum planning in their first *Teaching WALKTHRUs* book. These are:

1. designing a curriculum that is knowledge rich;
2. using small steps to sequence concepts;
3. mapping the curriculum coherently;
4. blending knowledge and experience;
5. pitching up the curriculum to make it appropriately challenging;
6. planning your curriculum to incorporate reading as a core feature;
7. tiering questions and problems;
8. delivering core content and signposting hinterland knowledge. Hinterland knowledge is the knowledge that teachers will only make brief reference to but is still important as it helps to provide background and context to the core knowledge.

» Identify what each step would look like in your subject-specific curriculum. You could do this independently or with your mentor or other member of staff who teaches the same curriculum.

There are multiple ways to approach curriculum planning, and your setting will have its own policies and priorities for curriculum planning that you will need to familiarise yourself with.

CASE STUDY

Arden is a pre-service trainee completing a PGCE in Lifelong Learning (FES and Skills), with a subject-specialist placement teaching A level economics. On the first day of their placement, Arden meets with their mentor and asks if it is possible to have a copy of the scheme of learning and any core texts/resources used to teach the course. Arden's mentor explains that the scheme of learning covers up to October half term, and that Arden will take over teaching the Year 12 economics group after October half term. Arden looks through the scheme of work but starts to feel anxious that they will not know what to plan or how to sequence the lessons after October half term when they are due to start teaching. Arden also wants to know whose responsibility it will be to complete the scheme of learning after October half term – will it be their responsibility or the responsibility of the group's main class tutor? They can access the exam board scheme of work on the exam board's website but are not sure how to interpret this into the college version.

Critical questions

» What questions could Arden ask their mentor to help them establish what they need to teach and whose responsibility it is to complete the scheme of learning after October half term?

» Who else could Arden talk to about this issue and how might they be able to support them?

» How might using the appropriate exam board specification help Arden to understand what needs to come next in the scheme of work? Who would Arden need further support from to interpret this to ensure that they are planning and sequencing the series of lessons appropriately?

Ofsted and curriculum

Ofsted outlines its working definition of curriculum as follows:

> *Our working definition of curriculum is that it is a framework for setting out the aims of a programme of education, including the knowledge and skills to be gained at each stage (intent); for translating that framework over time into a structure and narrative, within an institutional context (implementation); and for evaluating what knowledge and understanding students have gained against expectations (impact).*

> *The curriculum lies at the heart of education. It determines what learners will know and be able to go on to do by the time they have finished that stage of their education. Curriculum matters, as it defines the knowledge and experiences that learners will receive beyond their home environment. To this extent, what is taught and how, and who is included, appear to be key principles of curriculum design.*
>
> (Ofsted, 2019, pp 4–5)

Under the current *Further Education and Skills Inspection Handbook* (Ofsted, 2024), one of the four key judgements is on the quality of education. As part of this, the curriculum is evaluated. This includes the knowledge, skills and behaviours learners need to be aspirational in their learning, and to gain employment and independence. Ofsted will also look at the way teachers teach and assess to support learners to build and apply knowledge and skills, as well as the outcomes that learners achieve from their education (Ofsted, 2024). The intent, implementation and impact of the curriculum is also evaluated by Ofsted. The intent of the curriculum is primarily evaluated through consideration of curriculum leadership provided by senior and subject leaders, with a focus on factors that contribute to learners having access to an education that allows them to achieve highly. The implementation of the curriculum is evaluated by inspectors through a focus on how the curriculum is taught at subject, class, lecture or workshop level. The impact of the education provided is evaluated through a focus on what learners have learned and the skills they have gained and can apply (Ofsted, 2024).

Activity ?

» Look up the most recent version of Ofsted's *Further Education and Skills Inspection Handbook.* This can be found on the Gov.UK website. Read through the subsection titled *The Quality of Education.* Identify what elements of intent, implementation and impact you will have responsibility for as a trainee or employed tutor. It may be useful to do this with your mentor or a fellow subject tutor. What do these elements look like in your curriculum planning currently?

Lesson planning and adaptive teaching

As with curriculum design, there are multiple approaches to lesson planning. Peps Mccrea (2015, p 27) highlights four important questions that teachers can ask before planning a lesson. These are the following.

- *Where are your learners starting from?*
- *Where do you want them to go?*
- *How will you know when they are there?*
- *How can you best help them get there?'*

Learning objectives are essential to support teachers in planning and supporting the learner to understand what they will be able to do. As a tutor, it is important that you are clear about what the learning objectives are and how the tasks in the lesson will support learners to be able to meet the objectives set (Sherrington and Caviglioli, 2021). It is also important not to confuse task completion with learning, and be aware that for learning to take place, learners need to be able to connect ideas to prior knowledge, establish secure links and consolidate new learning (Nuttall, 2007). Sherrington and Caviglioli (2021, pp 64–5) recommend the following five considerations when thinking about learning objectives.

- Plan learning objectives to span a series of lessons. Effective learning objectives include the facts, concepts or procedures learners should know, building on prior knowledge. They should also include the skills learners should be able to carry out independently or with greater fluency.
- Ensure that short-term and long-term learning objectives are explicit. This will allow the tutor to assess how far learners are towards meeting these objectives, enabling them to plan accordingly.
- Learners need to understand the learning objectives, which will enable them to assess their own progress and contextualise ideas they come across.
- Design tasks that support the learning objectives. Tasks should be designed to support learners to gain the knowledge they need. Explaining and modelling a task or parts of it will support learners to have clear expectations of how to complete it. Support learners to understand new ideas in relation to prior knowledge and include generative learning activities where possible. Eight key generative learning activities include: summarising, drawing, mapping, imagining, self-testing, self-explanation, teaching and enacting. These are explained in full detail in Fiorella and Mayer's article 'Eight Ways to Promote Generative Learning' (2016).
- Focus on whether learners have learnt something rather than whether they have completed a task. Support learners to use self-assessment techniques to check their own learning.

Activity ?

» Identify a topic that you have taught or will teach with your mentor or other subject-specialist tutor. Review the learning objectives and planning using Sherrington and Caviglioli's (2021) five points on learning objectives above. Are they focused on what you want your learners to learn over what tasks you want them to complete? Are the lesson activities planned focused on task completion or working towards meeting learning objectives? Do you need to adapt your planning because of this review?

Adaptive teaching

While not a new educational idea, the terminology of adaptive teaching has replaced differentiation in current discourse on lesson planning and delivery (Quigley, 2023). It is about making adaptations in the lesson that respond to the needs of learners and whether they are managing in the lesson. Micro-adaptations involve the tutor making real-time adjustments to their teaching in the lesson to support all students to reach the same appropriately challenging goal. Pre-teaching ideas before starting a topic, using flexible grouping and checking for understanding are all strategies tutors can use to support micro-adaptations. Flexible grouping may mean moving learners in a lesson who all need to go over a misconception to sit together, or supporting peer learning by sitting learners in pairs who have different levels of understanding (Clark, 2024). Learners with a learning difficulty or disability may need significant adaptations to make sure reasonable adjustments are made (Quigley, 2023).

Activity ⑦

» Look up Jon Eaton's 2022 guest blog *EEF Blog: Moving from 'Differentiation' to 'Adaptive Teaching'* on the Education Endowment Foundation's website (see the reference list at the end of this chapter for the link). From the PDF poster 'understanding adaptive teaching', identify what adaptive teaching strategies you can use before and during teaching and what this would look like in your subject-specific context.

Assessment, marking and feedback

It is important to familiarise yourself with the marking and feedback policy of your specific setting, as there will be an expectation that you work in line with this to mark and assess work. Exam boards and awarding bodies will also have mark schemes/assessment criteria that you will need to familiarise yourself with, as it may be a requirement of your placement or employment that you use these to carry out assessments of learners' work. This is a short section on assessment and feedback and cannot begin to look in full detail at the vast range of research and practice that there is on this topic. Further recommended reading can be found in the further reading section.

Table 10.1 provides some definitions of different methods of assessment.

Table 10.1 Different types of assessment methods

Type of assessment	Summary
Formative	Ongoing assessment used throughout a lesson/course to form judgements about whether and to what extent learning has been successful. For assessment to be truly formative, it must be used by the learner to make improvements.
Summative	Final assessments used to grade learners/sum up their achievements/grade their attainment. Most used at the end of a module, course or academic year.
Diagnostic/initial assessment	Carried out at the beginning of a course to establish prior understanding and ascertain a base line/starting point of each learner.
Norm-referenced assessment	Assessment which compares learners to each other – the mark an individual learner achieves shows how they have done compared to the norm/average of all candidates. Statistically this method is only effective for exams with at least a few hundred candidates.
Criterion-referenced assessment	Measures what a learner can do against a set of criteria (eg from a checklist, list of competences or a mark scheme) – awarding a pass if they meet the criteria and a fail if they cannot.
Peer assessment	Learners mark a peer's work against either a model answer(s), worked solutions, mark scheme or assessment criteria. If marking against assessment criteria, learners can either create their own assessment criteria or you can provide them with a set of criteria that they will mark their work against.
Self-assessment	Learners mark their own work against either a model answer(s), worked solutions, mark scheme or assessment criteria. If marking against assessment criteria, learners can either create their own assessment criteria or you can provide them with a set of criteria that they will mark their work against.
Spoof assessment	Involves the teacher creating a final piece of work for learners to mark – either by doing it themselves, eg writing an essay or using a piece of work a student completed from a previous year with their permission. Learners mark the piece of work against either a model answer(s), worked solutions, mark scheme or assessment criteria.

Source: Adapted from Petty (2015)

Marking and feedback are different things but are often confused. Traditionally, marking might look like a set of written comments at the end of a piece of work submitted by a learner. It may comment on what a learner has done well and what they need to do to improve, and it will often be far more work for the tutor than the learner. While it is still vital that learners understand where they have made misconceptions and spelling and grammatical errors, it is a time-consuming task and there are different strategies that can be used to ensure that learners engage with and learn from feedback (Hendrick and Macpherson, 2017). Research shows that giving learners numerical scores or grades has an adverse effect on learning because learners ignore the comments when marks are given alongside them (Black et al, 2004). Feedback, according to Dylan Wiliam, should be '*more work for the recipient than the donor*' and should focus on what students need to do to improve future performance (Wiliam, cited in Hendrick and Macpherson, 2017, p 29).

Black et al (2004) define Assessment for Learning as:

> *... any assessment for which the first priority in its design and practice is to serve the purpose of students' learning. It thus differs from assessment designed primarily to serve the purpose of accountability, or of ranking, or of certifying competence. An assessment activity can help learning if it provides information that teachers and their students can use as feedback in assessing themselves and one another and in modifying the teaching and learning activities in which they are engaged. Such assessment becomes 'formative assessment' when the evidence is actually used to adapt the teaching work to meet learning needs.*
>
> (Black et al, 2004, p 10)

Wiliam and Christodoulou (cited in Hendrick and Macpherson, 2017, pp 28–29, 34–35) offer a range of suggestions for supporting learners to engage with and learn from feedback. They recommend that teachers ensure that learners are responding to feedback by being set a direct and completable task, and that they complete this task in front of you in lesson time. Make sure that learners understand the feedback you give them. Giving questions as feedback can support learners in understanding what they need to do to improve and it needs to be precise. There is also a lot of power in giving whole-class feedback. Rather than a tutor marking every individual piece of work, the tutor reads through every response in the class and takes notes, identifying common misconceptions and going through these with the whole class. The work and research of Collin and Quigley in their guidance report on feedback for the Education Endowment Foundation also reinforces this, highlighting that tutors must ensure learners are given opportunities to use feedback to close the feedback loop so that learning can progress (Collin and Quigley, 2021).

Activity ?

» Discuss with your mentor what strategies you both use to formatively assess learners in your classroom. Are the strategies you use similar or different to those used by your mentor?

» Are there any strategies that your mentor uses that you could try in your classroom?

» What would using these strategies look like in your classroom?

Sherrington and Caviglioli (2021) look at the role of selective marking as a valuable form of feedback. In the process of selective marking, the tutor marks one section of the learner's work and gives detailed feedback on this that learners can respond to specifically. This may include (but is not limited to) adding in more precise details, developing an argument or correcting errors. Once learners have this feedback, they respond to it in the lesson so the tutor can monitor the responses. The ideal outcome is that learners can produce an improved version of the section of work through using the feedback to redraft. Learners can then use this to self-assess the rest of their work.

Using success criteria can also be a powerful method for teachers and learners to support the scaffolding process when completing a task. Before you ask students to complete a task or piece of work, show them examples of work that is of an excellent standard. This may be a piece that a previous learner has written/created (with their permission to use anonymously) or an example that a teacher has produced. Ask students to identify what makes the piece excellent and use this to form part of the success criteria that learners use to scaffold their own responses. It can also be useful to share examples of work that is not as good as the excellent examples and ask learners to compare them and identify what makes one better than the other. When defining a list of success criteria for a piece of work, it important that the tutor identifies and includes any absolute features that the learner must include in the work. It is important to check that all students understand the success criteria and what they mean. Finished work can be assessed by the tutor or self-assessed/peer assessed against the criteria. It is important to ensure that learners respond to the feedback given. For example, using a whole-class feedback approach, the tutor could identify a common success criterion that students did not or only partially met. The tutor could model an example of what this would look like in the assessment live in class or give different examples of what this would look like in a completed assessment, and then ask students to go back and add this criterion in or add to it more fully (Sherrington and Caviglioli, 2021, pp 112–13). It is important that if you are asking students to add something in to improve a piece of work, you show them what this looks like. For example, if a tutor is giving feedback to a learner about a history essay that focused on source analysis and evaluation, they should avoid saying to a learner in their feedback '*you need to add in more developed inferences*'. Instead, the tutor would show the learner what examples of excellent, well-developed inferences from the source they were focusing on looked like. After showing these examples, the tutor would phrase the feedback as a question such as: '*can you go back to the quote you used from the source and make a developed inference from it?*' If the learner knew how to make a well-developed inference from the source, then they would have done this as part of the essay to begin with, so it is important that the learner knows what this looks like and can respond to the feedback (William and Christodoulou, cited in Hendrick and Macpherson, 2017).

Application of evidence-based methods

Pearce (2022) offers a summary of the difference between evidence-informed teaching and evidence-based teaching. Evidence-informed teaching combines research alongside the professional judgement and experience of teachers, as well as taking the context of the institution and class into consideration. There is an important acknowledgement that while research can identify practices that are most likely to be effective, this must be in combination with teachers' judgement and experience of what is effective and needs to be adapted to suit different institutions and classes. Evidence-based teaching is more prescriptive, with an emphasis on findings from research taking precedence over teachers' experience or context.

The Department for Education's (2017) research report on evaluating evidence-informed teaching in England highlights that teachers commonly drew on research evidence that had been identified or translated by school leaders to apply to their own practice, rather than directly applying research findings. The report found that many teachers (except for those completing higher-level academic study) relied on organisations such as the Education Endowment Foundation (EEF) or senior leaders to summarise research. Commonly, teachers did not trust research evidence on its own, and wanted to observe the impact in a classroom setting or hear colleagues that they trust talk about how it had improved their teaching and outcomes for learners. At an organisational level, the report found that in effective research-engaged educational settings, research evidence was integrated into every aspect of their work and contributed to a culture of continuous improvement and reflection (DfE, 2017).

Part of the process of reflecting on what you have taught is thinking about how you might teach the same lesson with a different group or in the next academic year. In his work *The Hidden Lives of Learners*, Nuthall (2007) makes the crucial point that teaching requires you to make adaptations. If you teach the same lesson to two different groups, you are unlikely to teach it the same way twice. You will have to adapt your teaching, questioning and explanations to the different learners in the different groups. Something that worked with one group may not work with the next. It is important to understand what adaptations you need to make, and for this to be effective you need to know why they are needed.

Cognitive science is used widely to inform teaching practice and policy (EEF, 2021). A seminal piece of research based on research in cognitive science, focusing on master teachers and research on cognitive supports, is Barak Rosenshine's *Principles of Instruction* (2012). Rosenshine's work has influenced many educators since its publication and presents ten research-based principles of instruction alongside suggestions for classroom practice. It is recommended as essential further reading.

Critical question ?

One of the findings from the Department for Education's 2017 report was that where there was a strong whole-school evidence culture, senior leaders filtered research evidence to support staff to engage with research critically (DfE, 2017). The EEF report *Cognitive Science Approaches in the Classroom: A Review of the Evidence* (2021) advises caution when implementing the principles of cognitive science approaches to '*make sure that principles are successfully implemented, avoiding "lethal mutations" when a practice becomes disconnected from the theory*' (EEF, 2021, p 8).

» To what extent do you think senior leaders, or other practitioners filtering and summarising research evidence could lead to 'lethal mutations', and what might the dangers of this be when applying theory to practice?

Activity ⑦

» Reflect on a lesson that you either observed or delivered that was taught to the same group twice. What adaptations did you or the observed tutor have to make between teaching the two groups?

Managing and supporting learners, including behaviour

Knowing your learners is one of the most important things you can do as a teacher to support them (Strickland, 2022). This will help you to use adaptive teaching methods to ensure all learners can be supported to make progress. For learners progressing from school to FES and sixth form colleges, there is currently no mandatory requirement for schools to pass on any information, both general information or with regard to any learning support requirements about learners. The only exception to this is that schools must pass on information about learners with an EHC plan as a legal requirement. Learners who attend the different types of FES colleges often come from much wider catchments compared to schools and therefore from a wide range of secondary settings. This means it is important to get to know your learners at the beginning of the academic year and ensure that they are aware of the support that is available to them if they require it, as well as the processes they need to follow if they need to apply for exam arrangements. Learners who had exam arrangements in place at school will need to reapply once they start in an FES college, and if learners have not had exam arrangements in place previously, they can apply for an assessment to determine whether they are eligible for exam arrangements to be put into place.

Many new teachers and trainee teachers understandably express anxiety about how to manage behaviour, and Dix (2017) highlights that many teachers say that managing behaviour is a key area they feel they have gaps in regarding their training. You can use both proactive strategies to support effective behaviour management and strategies to deal with disruptive behaviour if it occurs during a lesson. It will also be important to familiarise yourself and work within the behaviour policy of your institution.

Paul Dix highlights the importance of creating the right culture across a setting to support behaviour management, arguing that '*culture eats strategy for breakfast*', and that this is determined by the way that adults in the setting behave (Dix, 2017, p 2). Dix emphasises that visible consistency and visible kindness across an organisation are key to supporting positive behaviour. What consistency looks like may differ between different educational settings, but Dix reinforces that it is crucial that there is visible, positive consistency across a setting that all staff follow to support positive behaviour and improvements in behaviour. He emphasises that behaviour management is a '*team sport*' that requires discipline (Dix, 2017, p 10). Dix explores many strategies to support the creation of a positive behavioural culture within a school or college. One of these is considering what would happen if all staff greeted learners at the beginning of the lesson at the classroom door with a smile and enthusiasm. What positive impact do you think this would have on behaviour and culture in your setting?

Critical question ⓘ

» Do staff in your setting approach behaviour management with visible consistency and kindness? What are the challenges with achieving this, and how could they be overcome?

Sam Strickland (2022) highlights many different proactive strategies to support positive behaviour. These include, but by no means are limited to, the following.

- **Classroom culture:** It is important that you teach and model the behaviour that you want to see in your classroom. Tactically ignore misbehaviour where appropriate when it occurs, but always find an appropriate point to address it afterwards. It is important to always address poor behaviour and rudeness, otherwise it will signal to other learners that it is acceptable behaviour.
- **Planning for positive behaviour:** Define positive behaviour and what you want the social norm to be in your classroom. Ensure you have clear expectations for learners to follow when they enter and leave the classroom. Decide where you want learners to sit and how you want your classroom laid out. In FES it may seem less common for a tutor to ask learners where to sit and instead to allow learners to sit where they choose. However, if you feel that it would have a positive impact on behaviour then using a seating plan could be trialled and the effects on behaviour monitored and evaluated.
- **Building positive relationships:** Building positive relationships based on mutual respect, professional boundaries and positivity can have a crucial impact on creating a positive classroom culture and minimise situations where learners are likely to display disruptive behaviour. If learners feel safe, valued and positively challenged in your classroom, then opportunities for positive behaviour are maximised and opportunities for disruptive behaviour will lessen. Establishing clear routines, communicating with kindness, knowing learners' names, being firm but fair and always being the adult are underpinning factors that promote the building of positive, professional relationships based on mutual respect.
- **Knowing your students:** Ensure you know which of your students have learning support profiles and EHC plans, and what their individual needs are. If permission to contact parents has been given (for 16–19 learners), communicating with parents and carers can be a vital way to support learners.
- **Understanding cognitive load:** Plan lessons tailored to the existing knowledge and skills base of students and use problem-solving and independent approaches

to learning when learners are already very skilled with knowledge. Using worked examples and modelling success will support learners in knowing what they are aiming to achieve.

Even using proactive behaviour management techniques will not necessarily eliminate a situation where you may need to use de-escalation strategies to manage behaviour. Strickland (2022, p 254), signposts the following signals that suggest a learner may become aggressive or lose control:

- high levels of agitation;
- fidgeting;
- shaking;
- jaw clenching;
- fist clenching;
- high-pitched and challenging tone of voice;
- borderline irrational behaviour.

If you do encounter these behaviours and need to de-escalate a situation, Stickland (2022, pp 254–5) advises that you should:

- keep your tone of voice measured, calm and clear;
- ensure the language you use is respectful and polite;
- avoid invading a learner's personal space;
- have a facial expression that is neutral;
- keep your own breathing calm;
- distract the learner's thinking by asking a random and neutral question, such as about the weather;
- give the learner a range of choices rather than a set of closed choices when redirecting behaviour;
- don't get drawn into secondary behaviours, eg arguing back;
- acknowledge the learner's feelings;
- recognise that the situation must be very difficult for the learner.

Phrases you could use could include '*let's try...*', '*maybe we can...*', '*it seems as if...*' (Strickland, 2022, p 255). It is important not to engage in an argument with the learner. For example, you could say, '*I need you to return to your seat. Thank you*'. Rather than '*Why aren't you doing what I've said?*' give the learner time to act on your request. Do not threaten a learner with sanctions and avoid sarcasm and humour as this is easily misinterpreted and may cause the situation to become inflamed rather than calmer (Stickland, 2022). Even if you follow this advice, you may still face a behavioural situation that reaches crisis point. If this is the case, it is important to alert another member of staff, when possible, to come and support you. This may be by email, phone or by asking another learner to leave the room and get a member of staff to come and support you. If a learner or learners lose control or become violent, remove the rest of the class and yourself from the room and get help from another member of staff. It is important that any sanctions applied after the disruptive behaviour has occurred are appropriate and proportionate. Arranging a follow-up meeting with the learner to review what happened, supported by another member of staff, will enable you to review the situation and learn from any mistakes made (Stickland, 2022). Strickland offers an important reminder which is often forgotten when disruptive behaviour occurs: '*It is important to remember that when pupils misbehave it is often not the teacher's fault*' (Strickland, 2022, p 286).

Activity

» Discuss a time in your teaching or teaching placement when you have encountered disruptive behaviour. Did you use any strategies from those suggested above? If so, how effective were they?

» Did you use any different strategies to manage the behaviour? How effective were they?

» Would you approach the situation differently next time? If so, in what ways would you approach it differently and why?

Summary

This chapter has covered many different areas that are crucial for your teaching practice. While they have been considered separately, they all interlink. Ensuring you are well prepared for your placement or role, both practically and academically, will ensure you are able to engage with all other areas effectively throughout your placement or job. Having a clear understanding of curriculum planning and what this looks like in your subject-specific context will enable you to think about planning effective lessons that are robustly contextualised within the wider curriculum. This will allow you to have an understanding of what you are assessing your learners for and how to do this in the most appropriate way, assessing learning and progress against key objectives. This will all be informed by your understanding and critical application of theory to practice. Managing and supporting learners, including behaviour management, all takes place in the context of delivering the lessons that you have planned and will deliver.

Check your understanding (level 5)

1. What are the key practical considerations you will need to be aware of when preparing for your teaching placement or role?

2. What are the key academic considerations you will need to be aware of when preparing for your teaching placement or role?
3. How much control (if any) will you have over curriculum design?
4. How might you use Sherrington and Caviglioli's eight considerations within curriculum design to inform your own planning?
5. How much control do the tutors in your subject area have over curriculum design?
6. What factors influence curriculum design in your specific setting? Is curriculum design driven by generic or subject-specific curriculum thinking?
7. Why is it important to set clear learning objectives when you are planning lessons and to share these with learners?
8. What is formative assessment?
9. What strategies can you use in your assessment to support learners to make progress?
10. What is evidence-informed teaching?
11. What proactive strategies can you use to manage behaviour in your classroom?
12. What would you do if a learner displayed aggressive behaviour?

Developmental questions L6+7

1. Consider Ashbee's (2021) argument about the importance of designing a curriculum that supports students to be able to participate meaningfully in a democratic society.
    a. How does your subject-specific curriculum support students to be able to do this?
    b. Is there anything further the curriculum could do to support this?
    c. How would you implement this?
2. How does curriculum design and lesson planning support positive behaviour management?

Further reading

Curriculum and lesson planning

- Ashbee, R (2021) *Curriculum: Theory, Culture and the Subject Specialisms*. London: Routledge.
- Mccrea, P (2015) *Lean Lesson Planning: A Practical Approach to Doing Less and Achieving More in the Classroom.* Bedford: Teacherly.co.
- Sherrington, T and Caviglioli, O (2020) *Teaching WALKTHRUs: Five-Step Guides to Instructional Coaching* (pp 48–65). Woodbridge: John Catt Educational Ltd.

Assessment and feedback

- Collin, J and Quigley, A (2021) *Teacher Feedback to Improve Pupil Learning: Six Recommendations for Using Teacher Feedback to Improve Pupil Learning*. Education Endowment Foundation. [online] Available at: https://educationendowmentfoundation.org.uk/education-evidence/guidance-reports/feedback (accessed 23 September 2024).
- Wiliam, D (2018) *Embedded Formative Assessment*. 2nd ed. Bloomington, IN: Solution Tree Press.

Behaviour

- Bennett, T (2020) *Running the Room: The Teacher's Guide to Behaviour*. Woodbridge: John Catt Educational Ltd.
- Education Endowment Foundation (EEF) (2021) *Improving Behaviour in Schools*. [online] Available at: https://educationendowmentfoundation.org.uk/education-evidence/guidance-reports/behaviour (accessed 23 September 2024).
- Rogers, B (2015) *Classroom Behaviour: A Practical Guide to Effective Teaching, Behaviour Management and Colleague Support*. 4th ed. London: Sage.
- Strickland, S (2022) *The Behaviour Manual: An Educator's Guidebook*. Woodbridge: John Catt Educational Ltd.

Evidence-informed teaching

- Nuthall, G (2007) *The Hidden Lives of Learners.* Wellington: NZCER.
- Rosenshine, B (2012) Principles of Instruction: Research-Based Strategies That All Teachers Should Know. *American Educator*, Spring: 12–39.
- Sherrington, T and Caviglioli, O (2017) *The Learning Rainforest: Great Teaching in Real Classrooms*. Woodbridge: John Catt Educational Ltd.

References

Armitage, A, Cogger, A, Evershed, A, Hayes, D, Lawes, S and Renwick, M (2016) *Teaching in Post-14 Education and Training*. 5th ed. Maidenhead: Open University Press.

Ashbee, R (2021) *Curriculum: Theory, Culture and the Subject Specialisms*. London: Routledge.

Black, P, Harrison, C, Lee, C, Marshall, B and Wiliam, D (2004) Working Inside the Black Box: Assessment for Learning in the Classroom. *Phi Delta Kappan*, 86(1): 8–21.

Clark, J (2024) *Teaching One Pagers: Adaptive Teaching: Remove the Ceiling and Focus Support for All Learners*. [online] Available at: https://static1.squarespace.com/static/5c47c0b3e17ba324ad0c9d7f/t/661cb43dddd51e635e2f52ed/1713157181852/Adaptive+Teaching.pdf (accessed 29 September 2024).

Collin, J and Quigley, A (2021) *Teacher Feedback to Improve Pupil Learning: Six Recommendations for Using Teacher Feedback to Improve Pupil Learning*. Education Endowment Foundation. [online] Available at: https://educationendowmentfoundation.org.uk/education-evidence/guidance-reports/feedback (accessed 29 September 2024).

Department for Education (DfE) (2017) *Evidence-Informed Teaching: An Evaluation of Progress in England. Research Report*. [online] Available at: https://assets.publishing.service.gov.uk/media/5a749aca40f0b61938c7ece0/Evidence-informed_teaching_-_an_evaluation_of_progress_in_England.pdf (accessed 29 September 2024).

Department for Education (DfE) (2024) Diploma in Teaching (Further Education and Skills) Education Framework. [online] Available at: www.gov.uk/government/publications/further-education-initial-teacher-education/diploma-in-teaching-further-education-and-skills-qualification-framework (accessed 15 November 2024).

Dix, P (2017) *When the Adults Change, Everything Changes: Seismic Shifts in School Behaviour*. Bancyfelin: Independent Thinking Press.

Eaton, J (2022) Moving from 'Differentiation' to 'Adaptive Teaching'. *Education Endowment Foundation Blog*, 19 October. [online] Available at: https://educationendowmentfoundation.org.uk/news/moving-from-differentiation-to-adaptive-teaching (accessed 29 September 2024).

Education Endowment Foundation (EEF) (2021) *Cognitive Approaches in the Classroom: A Review of the Evidence*. [online] Available at: https://educationendowmentfoundation.org.uk/education-evidence/evidence-reviews/cognitive-science-approaches-in-the-classroom (accessed 29 September 2024).

Education and Training Foundation (ETF) (2022) *Professional Standards for Teachers and Trainers*. [online] Available at: www.et-foundation.co.uk/professional-standards/teachers (accessed 29 September 2024).

Fennell, A (2023) Social Media Recruitment Statistics. [online] Available at: https://standout-cv.com/social-media-recruitment-statistics (accessed 29 September 2024).

Fiorella, L and Mayer, R E (2016) Eight Ways to Promote Generative Learning. *Educational Psychology Review*, 28(4): 717–41.

Hendrick, C and Macpherson, R (2017) *What Does This Look Like in the Classroom? Bridging the Gap Between Research and Practice*. Woodbridge: John Catt Educational Ltd.

Institute for Apprenticeships and Technical Education (IfATE) (2024) *Learning and Skills Teacher*. [online] Available at: www.instituteforapprenticeships.org/apprenticeship-standards/learning-and-skills-teacher (accessed 29 September 2024).

Jackson, P (1968) *Life in Classrooms*. London: Holt, Rinehart and Winston.

Mccrea, P (2015) *Lean Lesson Planning: A Practical Approach to Doing Less and Achieving More in the Classroom*. Bedford: Teacherly.co.

Nuthall, G (2007) *The Hidden Lives of Learners*. Wellington: NZCER.

Ofsted (2019) *Education Inspection Framework: Overview of Research*. [online] Available at: https://assets.publishing.service.gov.uk/media/6034be17d3bf7f265dbbe2ef/Research_for_EIF_framework_updated_references_22_Feb_2021.pdf (accessed 29 September 2024).

Ofsted (2024) *Further Education and Skills Inspection Handbook*. [online] Available at: www.gov.uk/government/publications/further-education-and-skills-inspection-handbook-eif/further-education-and-skills-handbook-for-september-2023 (accessed 29 September 2024).

Pearce, J (2022) *What Every Teacher Needs to Know: How to Embed Evidence-Informed Teaching and Learning into Your School*. London: Bloomsbury Publishing Plc.

Petty, G (2015) *Teaching Today: A Practical Guide*. 5th ed. Oxford: Oxford University Press.

Quigley, A (2023) Adaptive Teaching: What Is It Anyway? *Alex Quigley*, 9 December. [online] Available at: https://alexquigley.co.uk/adaptive-teaching-what-is-it-anyway (accessed 29 September 2024).

Rosenshine, B (2012) Principles of Instruction: Research-Based Strategies That All Teachers Should Know. *American Educator*, Spring: 12–39.

Rosser, K (2017) What Is Social Media Screening? [online] Available at: www.reed.com/articles/what-is-social-media-screening (accessed 29 September 2024).

Sherrington, T and Caviglioli, O (2017) *The Learning Rainforest: Great Teaching in Real Classrooms*. Woodbridge: John Catt Educational Ltd.

Sherrington, T and Caviglioli, O (2020) *Teaching WALKTHRUs: Five-Step Guides to Instructional Coaching*. Woodbridge: John Catt Educational Ltd.

Sherrington, T and Caviglioli, O (2021) *Teaching WALKTHRUs 2: Five-Step Guides to Instructional Coaching*. Woodbridge: John Catt Educational Ltd.

Strickland, S (2022) *The Behaviour Manual: An Educator's Guidebook*. Woodbridge: John Catt Educational Ltd.

11 Teaching my subject

Professional links

This chapter contributes to the following professional links:

The Diploma in Teaching mandatory content (DfE, 2024)

- 1.1 Curriculum development.
- 1.2 Pedagogic content knowledge.
- 1.3 Threshold concepts and troublesome knowledge.
- 1.4 Required wider or prerequisite knowledge.
- 1.5 Embedding maths and English.
- 1.6 Ensuring and maintaining subject expertise.
- 2.8 Role and currency of research and evidence.
- 4.13 The Occupational Standards
- 4.14 Developing expertise

Learning and Skills Teacher Occupational Standards (IfATE, 2024)

- K1 The pedagogical theory and how to apply this theory to practice.
- K2 How to support contextualised opportunities to develop English and maths.
- K3 The principles of designing, planning, and organising curriculum.
- S1 Integrate subject and pedagogic research into teaching activity to enhance teaching and support changes of practice.
- S3 Contextualise English and mathematics in a way that promotes understanding of key topics.
- S21 Continually update and maintain their own knowledge and skills as a teaching professional and a subject specialist as part of managing their own continual professional development (CPD).

→

- B2 Underpin their practice by reference to professional standards and evidence-based teaching and learning.
- B3 Committed to continuous professional development.

Professional Standards (ETF, 2022)

- 8 Develop and update knowledge of your subject specialism, taking account of new practices, research and/or industry requirements.
- 9 Critically review and apply your knowledge of educational research, pedagogy, and assessment to develop evidence-informed practice.
- 15 Plan and deliver learning programmes that are safe, inclusive, stretching and relevant to learners' needs.

Chapter objectives

At the end of this chapter you will be able to:

- discuss the troublesome knowledge and threshold concepts as aligned to your subject area;
- apply subject-specific pedagogy to your teaching;
- identify subject-specific groups to inform your practice;
- define the principles of effective curriculum planning in your subject area;
- describe effective ways of embedding maths and English in your subject area.

Introduction

The learning and skills practitioner is often referred to as a dual professional: they have good subject knowledge or experience of working in the sector, and often they embark on teaching programmes to develop their teaching skills and the craft of teaching. However, the new framework for the sector places huge importance on subject knowledge enhancement and development, as well as the specificity of teaching the subject. In other words, the focus is not just on the craft of teaching but the specific craft of teaching your subject. This can be quite challenging in a sector that is so broad in the subjects it offers and where for the most part the teaching qualifications are generic and not subject based in comparison to the schools sector, which offers subject-based qualifications. In addition, the new qualifications framework and the then government requirements that learners achieve Grade 4 or above in English and maths (not to mention the previous governments' discussion that learners must study English and maths up to the age of 18) requires FES teachers to be able to support their learners to develop these skills. This chapter provides you with advice on developing your subject and the teaching of it, together with information on how you can embed English and maths into your curriculum.

Subject specialism

The Department for Education (2022) state that teachers must, as subject specialists and subject leaders, have a clear understanding of the intent, implementation and impact of their specialist curriculum. In addition, they should have expert pedagogical subject knowledge of the curriculum content of the subjects that they teach. Furthermore the education inspection framework guidance (Ofsted, 2019) for the sector examines whether:

- teachers present subject matter clearly, promoting appropriate discussion about the subject matter they are teaching;
- leaders focus on improving staff's subject, pedagogical and pedagogical content knowledge to enhance the teaching of the curriculum and the appropriate use of assessment. The practice and subject knowledge of staff are built up and improve over time.

Critical questions ?

» Do subject specialist teachers matter?

» What role does subject knowledge play in how 'good' a teacher is? Does it matter whether a chemistry teacher has a chemistry degree or a teacher in construction has actually worked in the industry?

Discussion

It can be argued that teachers' subject knowledge plays a crucial role in effective teaching. The following provides you with some reasons why.

- **Student outcomes:** Although not specific to the FES sector, research published by Teach First suggests that if teachers have a deep understanding of their subject matter, they can effectively convey concepts, address misconceptions and inspire students. This in turn provides better outcomes, whether that be progression into employment or further study.
- **Motivation:** Having secure subject knowledge allows teachers to motivate students. When teachers are enthusiastic and knowledgeable about their subject, it sparks interest and engagement in the classroom.
- **Identifying misunderstandings:** Teachers with strong subject knowledge can anticipate common misconceptions within specific subjects. This helps them identify and address misunderstandings promptly, ensuring better learning outcomes.

→

- **Effective curriculum planning:** Subject knowledge is essential for well-structured lesson planning. Teachers need to know how to sequence content over time, understand progression and recognise potential pitfalls for students.
- **Meeting standards:** Without good knowledge of what they are teaching, it's impossible for teachers to meet the Occupational Standards, Diploma in Teaching content and the Professional Standards effectively.

In summary, subject knowledge is as important as pedagogy and will help you identify the progress of your students.

Activity ⑦

» Take a look at the standards highlighted above. How would you currently compare your practice against the standards? Which areas do you feel you need to develop further?

Signature pedagogies in teaching

The following section will consider subject pedagogy and its importance in teaching.

Schulman (2005, p 52) defines signature pedagogies as '*the types of teaching that are used to educate members of a particular professions*'. He goes on to identify three dimensions of a signature pedagogy: surface, deep and implicit. Surface pedagogy refers to the concrete, operational acts of teaching and learning. Deep pedagogy is based on a set of assumptions around how best to impart a body of learning, while implicit pedagogy is based on the moral dimensions that comprise a set of beliefs around professional values attitudes and dispositions. So how can you develop signature pedagogies in your practice? We would suggest that your workplace mentor would be a good person to work with to help support you in promoting learning in your subject specialism. The following is a list of activities that your mentor should be able to support you with:

- helping you identify the signature pedagogies in your subject;
- connecting the taught parts of your course to subject practice;
- supporting your specialist pedagogies, including signature assessment and feedback practices (Pitt and Quinlan, 2021);
- discussing '*the choice of one pedagogy over another*' (Parker et al, 2016, p 141);
- providing connections with subject-specialist teams and staff.

Activity ⓘ

» To stimulate your thinking around subject-specialist teaching and learning, go to the following website: www.improvingtechnicaleducation.org.uk/teacher-education.

Activity ⓘ

» As a business studies specialist, some of the signature pedagogies include work-based learning and placements, simulations or real-world projects and the use of case studies. Consider your subject. What do you believe may be signature pedagogies in the discipline?

The four-stage typology of teacher development

According to the Department of Education in Northern Ireland, there are four key stages of a teacher's professional development:

> *initial teacher education (ITE) (which equips aspiring student teachers with the necessary qualifications to become professional educators); induction (which normally takes one school year to complete); early professional development (EPD) (which normally takes two school years to complete); and continued teacher professional learning (TPL) (where teachers routinely reflect on their professional practices and identify opportunities for improvement throughout their careers.*
>
> (Department of Education (NI), 2024)

However, this model does not map onto the requirements of the FES sector, as currently there is no requirement for an EPD or early careers teacher transition prior to full qualification. Our route, as discussed in Chapter 1, is to follow a process of professional formation to gain QTLS following qualification. Therefore, for our sector we would suggest considering the four-stage model of becoming a teacher that McDonald et al (2013) identified, and explore how your subject knowledge and subject pedagogy should develop within each stage. Table 11.1 highlights McDonald et al's four stages of teacher development, along with our suggestions for your personal aim at each stage and some of the activities to help you develop your subject knowledge that you may wish to consider in each of the stages. You may wish to add in other activities that you feel would be beneficial at each stage.

Table 11.1 *The process of becoming a teacher*

Stage	Aim	Activity
Representation and survival	Learning from subject specialist – knowledge, skills and competencies	Gap analysis. Exploration of CPD available. Observing specialist tutors.
Approximation	Expertise development	Starting to use signature pedagogies in the classroom. Accessing subject associations and networks to support and develop knowledge.
Enactment	Application of expertise	Drawing further on evidence-informed research to support subject delivery and feedback to learners.
Investigation and consolidation	Reflect and refine	Critically reflecting on the signature pedagogies. Exploring research groups within your field.

(Adapted from McDonald et al, 2013)

Other developmental models for our sector could include Fuller's model from 1969, which was one of the first theories of teacher development and comprises three stages: concerns with self, concern with tasks and concerns with the impact on student learning. It is our opinion that this model starts to consider the teacher's role and relationships with their students at the beginning of their teaching journey, only moving on to teaching methods and teacher capability towards the end of the stages. We would argue that while still in development, subject knowledge and pedagogy should be embedded in all stages.

Critical questions ⑦

» As a trainee or new teacher, how do you feel you have developed your craft? What areas do you feel are still a concern?

» Looking at Fuller (1969) the three stages are sometimes identified as self-survival (self-adequacy and acceptance), task improvement (student performance and teacher duty) and impact (social and educational impact). How does subject development fit into these three areas?

Discussion

You may have come up with ideas such as: Do they like me? I need to be liked and respected. How will I manage to control a class if the behaviour is poor? How will I know they are enjoying my lesson and do I have enough material for an hour for stage 1? Are my learners achieving the goals I set them? Am I covering the right stuff at the right level? Have I made my teaching inclusive for stage 2? Have the group developed their soft skills? How have I managed to improve performance and outcomes for stage 3?

Regardless of what thoughts you have had, and these will be different for different teachers, the art of subject pedagogy lies at the heart of all of the answers.

CASE STUDY

Enhancing subject knowledge in early childhood studies

Nabeela is an early childhood lecturer with over ten years of experience of teaching level 3 BTEC courses. Despite her extensive experience, Nabeela felt the need to update her knowledge on the latest educational theories and practices to better support her students' learning as she had noticed that she was struggling to engage her students with new and innovative approaches. Having completed some research on new pedagogies, she decided to focus on enhancing her understanding of play-based learning and the concept of the 'capable child', which emphasises viewing children as active participants in their learning.

Nabeela, with the support of her line manager, enrolled in several online courses and workshops focused on early childhood education. These courses covered topics such as play-based learning, inclusive education and the latest research on child development. She joined a local educators' network where she could share experiences and learn from her peers. This network provided a platform for discussing challenges and exchanging ideas on effective teaching strategies. In addition, she began a reflective journal to document her teaching experiences, challenges and insights gained from her professional development activities. This practice helped her critically analyse her teaching methods and identify areas for improvement.

Within the classroom, Nabeela redesigned her lesson plans to include more play-based activities and encouraged her students to take an active role in their learning. She also used open-ended questions to stimulate critical thinking and problem-solving skills. After several months of implementing these changes, Nabeela observed significant improvements in her students' engagement and learning outcomes. They were more enthusiastic about participating in class activities, and their problem-solving skills had noticeably improved. Nabeela also felt more confident and motivated in her teaching role.

Nabeela's journey highlights the importance of CPD for all educators, regardless of their length of experience in the classroom. Through updating subject knowledge and embracing new teaching strategies, all teachers can create a more dynamic and inclusive learning environment for their students.

Threshold concepts and troublesome knowledge

Threshold concepts were first defined by Meyer and Land in 2003. They are concepts that are fundamental to a particular subject area and discipline with several distinctive features.

- They are transformative in that they have the ability to change the way in which a learner perceives and therefore understands a subject.
- They are integrative, connecting different elements of knowledge.
- They are irreversible, and once a learner has assimilated them they become an essential part of the learning process.

As concepts they represent a deeper level of understanding and can create significant leaps in a learner's intellectual ability. Within education, threshold concepts have been used to provide information on the best ways to teach and assess a particular subject and to give insights on how we best learn a particular discipline, ergo what are the signature pedagogies as discussed previously. So how do we identify the threshold concepts of our subject? They are often the areas that students struggle with but are the knots in the fishing net that hold your subject together.

Let us take English as a subject, as we know all learners need to continue to develop their English skills. While English may not be your specialist subject, you will be expected to support your learner and embed English within your classes.

Some of the threshold concepts might include:

- understanding the relationship between grammar and meaning;
- understanding the effect of context, both on writers and readers;
- understanding the need to use supporting evidence for ideas;
- an awareness of the ways in which language can affect readers;
- understanding how different ways of structuring text can produce different effects;
- understanding that language can be analysed to reveal a variety meanings.

While as a subject specialist you could argue that there are others that could be included, it is my opinion that these six areas are key to a learner's ability to perform well in the subject. As an educator, it is now your role to take these concepts and create the curriculum, including appropriate subject and generic pedagogies that will enable you and your learners to achieve the desired outcomes.

Troublesome knowledge

Troublesome knowledge is a term coined by Perkins (1999) and refers to threshold concepts that are difficult, counter-intuitive and sometime alien to the learner. These concepts are often ones that the learner struggles to understand, and as such they require a shift in a learner's thinking. For educators, the troublesome knowledge requires us to prioritise certain elements when designing curricula to ensure that we reinforce and support learning, developing pedagogical strategies to facilitate learning and assessments.

Critical question ?

» If you consider some of the English threshold concepts identified above, what might be the troublesome knowledge area?

Discussion

Table 11.2 provides some potential troublesome knowledge of English threshold concepts.

Table 11.2 *Threshold concepts and troublesome knowledge*

Concept	Troublesome knowledge
An awareness of the ways in which language can affect readers.	Acknowledging that language varies across contexts, regions and social groups.
Understanding the effect of context, both on writers and readers.	Students may struggle with the idea that multiple valid interpretations exist for a single text.
Understanding the need to use supporting evidence for ideas.	The shift from viewing literature as mere entertainment to understanding it as a reflection of cultural, historical and social contexts.
Understanding the relationship between grammar and meaning.	Students may need to unlearn prescriptive grammar rules and appreciate linguistic diversity.
Understand how different ways of structuring text can produce different effects.	Grasping how allusions, intertextual references and adaptations contribute to meaning.
Understanding that language can be analysed to reveal a variety of meanings.	Understanding the different lenses through which literature can be analysed can be challenging.

Professional bodies and subject associations

Subject associations are membership organisations whose members are subject experts. Subject associations are independent of government, often charities, and their mission is to further teaching and learning in a specific subject in schools, colleges and ITE in universities. Membership provides:

- affordable, relevant, high-quality professional development;
- expert advice and information, eg The Law Society;
- low-cost, high-quality teaching resources;
- access to a community interested in subject teaching and learning;
- access to courses and conferences;
- up-to-date subject knowledge and pedagogy.

According to Dame Alison Peacock, Chief Executive of the Chartered College of Teaching:

> *Subject Associations are a vital part of our education landscape. Teachers across all phases benefit from the high quality professional learning provided by individual associations whether this is via web resources, journals or through opportunities to engage in study. It is vitally important that teachers are inspired to build their own subject knowledge, moving beyond the generic towards the specific. To teach is to engage in lifelong learning.*
>
> (CfSA, 2024)

For trainee teachers, James Noble Rogers, Chair of the University Council for the Education of Teachers (UCET), states:

> *Subject Associations are an invaluable source of curriculum materials, research findings and advice for teachers working across all phase and subject areas. We would recommend that all teachers, from those still in the process of qualifying right up to experienced practitioners and leaders, think about joining their relevant association. The resources they provide are research informed, relevant, independent and of the highest quality. By becoming a member of a subject association teachers become part of a professional community with excellent networking opportunities.*
>
> (CfSA, 2024)

Within education a specific council exists that is the voice for subjects. The Council for Subject Associations (CfSA) is a co-ordinating membership organisation, speaking with one consistent voice on behalf of different member subject associations. The CfSA is the national voice for education. It was set up in 2007 with the support of the then Department of Children, Schools and Families (DCSF).

This organisation has links to over 32 subject associations and other support organisations and is aimed at teachers, leaders and other professionals within education. Its main aim is to:

keep school leaders and teachers up-to-date and at the cutting edge of transforming education, to provide the best outcomes for children and young people. Therefore, we work to research every concept to a depth where we can develop, write, design and ensure that we resource, support and train teachers with the latest thinking and responses, so that they can teach their pupils effectively.

(CfSA, 2024)

The CfSA supports a range of other education associations, which represent a professional sector membership comprising teachers and educators across all subjects and age phases in the UK. Together CfSA members provide subject expertise, research-informed advice and resources in curriculum, pedagogy, teacher training and teacher development, gathering and building on the knowledge and expertise of serving teachers, headteachers, governors, leaders, academics, students and governments.

Activity ?

Have a look at the Council for Subject Associations website: www.subjectassociations.org.uk

» What subject bodies are there in your subject area?

» How could you link into these specific organisations to support your development?

» Are there any other organisations in your subject area that you feel would be useful in supporting your development?

Curriculum design, curriculum development and subject specialism

Curriculum design and curriculum development are often used interchangeably. However, as processes they have very different definitions and functions in an organisation. Curriculum design refers to the structure of the overall curriculum, whereas curriculum development is the planning and structuring of content. Curriculum development is content; curriculum design is how students will learn the content.

As a teacher, you will undoubtedly be involved in curriculum design at some point in your career. Ensuring that you integrate subject specificity and threshold concepts into your design is crucial to the success of your subject and the learner outcomes.

Curriculum design involves creating a structured plan for what students will learn, how they will learn it and the goals they should achieve. Here are some key considerations for effective curriculum design.

- Learning goals: Clearly define learning objectives or goals. What do you want students to know, understand and be able to do?

- Content selection: Choose relevant and meaningful content that aligns with the learning goals.
- Sequencing: Organise the content logically. Consider the order in which topics are introduced.
- Assessment: Plan how you'll assess student understanding and progress.
- Flexibility: Be open to adapting the curriculum based on student needs and feedback.

Within the design you also need to consider the pedagogical approaches, both the generic pedagogy (the art and science of teaching) and the subject-specific or signature pedagogies previously discussed. Effective pedagogy, whether generic or subject specific, involves using research-based strategies to enhance student learning. For example, you may wish to consider the following.

- Scaffolding: Provide support and guidance as students learn. Gradually remove support as they gain confidence.
- Variety of techniques: Use a mix of teaching approaches, including whole-class instruction, group work and individual activities.
- Higher-order thinking: Encourage critical thinking, problem-solving and metacognition.

Remember that both curriculum design and pedagogy should be learner centred, considering the 'why', 'how' and 'what' of education. In addition, the Education Endowment Foundation suggests that it is important that all educators consider the teaching approaches that ensure long-term retention as this is crucial to the development of our young people. They continue by advising that understanding prior knowledge and building upon this is important in supporting learning. The government has also produced a comprehensive guide to effective practice in curriculum planning – the information on where to find this is in the further reading section at the end of the chapter. This guide situates the design of curriculum in the wider remit of the FES sector and offers various case studies on practice within the sector, including delivery structures and accountability.

While this chapter does not intend to go into curriculum models in any great depth, it is useful to be aware of a few of the main models that exist. The chapter provides a brief overview of them so that you can consider what works best with your discipline.

Product model

The product model focuses on the end result and is based upon the work of Tyler (1949) and Bloom (1956). As a model it can be motivational for a student in that they know their end goal and how to get there. However, it can be results driven and not always linked to actual learning.

Process model

In comparison, the process model based on work by Stenhouse (1975) is more concerned with student progress and is less concerned about the final outcome.

Spiral model

In a spiral curriculum, the learner revisits topics on occasions, building on previous learning and moving the learning to a deeper and more complex level. It is based upon the work by Bruner (1960) and is featured throughout the different education phases. As a student moves from primary school to secondary school and then into FES, the same topics are covered repeatedly, each time in greater levels of depth, further challenging students while building upon and reinforcing their existing knowledge.

While these three models can be standalone, it is also fair to say that you can use elements of each within your discipline. Indeed, this is good practice to provide a broad curriculum that enables learner outcomes to be good.

In addition to the three models above you also need to be aware that as a teacher you will also be considering the five main areas of curriculum in your design.

- Official: The full course content as published by the awarding body.
- Actual: The reality, the actual modules chosen from the official, based on staffing and resources.
- Formal: Areas outside the official curriculum – work experience, English and maths.
- Informal: Activities, sports, student union.
- Hidden: Areas such as personal safety (use of lanyards), recycling and conservation activities.

Activity ?

Locate the official curriculum for your discipline and subject specialism as published by your awarding body.

» How has this been transformed into the actual, formal, informal and hidden curriculum in your area?

» What theories of curriculum development can you see in the development of subject knowledge?

Embedding maths and English into your subject and curriculum

As previously discussed, it is a requirement that all learners continue English and maths post-16 if they have not achieved a grade 4 or above in their GCSE. In addition, as a subject specialist there is an ever-increasing focus on the embedding of, and supporting the development of, literacy and numeracy skills into the subject-specific curriculum. This section will explore some of the strategies that are available to you as a subject specialist.

Naturally occurring opportunities

All subjects will have naturally occurring opportunities for you to include maths and English in the curriculum. Some subjects lend themselves more easily to maths or English than others. For example, travel and tourism programmes have opportunities to look at temperature variations over the months (mean, median, mode), the creation of graphs and pie charts to illustrate the changes, the reading of train or bus timetables and presenting information on a destination in the form of a flyer. Hospitality has opportunities for measuring out ingredients, working out the ratio of one ingredient to another and the production of menus, to name but a few.

Activity ?

» Consider your subject. What naturally occurring opportunities might there be to embed maths or English?

Discussion

The following table provides a few suggestions for some subject areas.

Subject	English	Maths
Art and design	Articulate the types of shapes within a particular artist's painting.	Work out angles and dimensions for a portrait drawing.
Business	Present an idea for a new product (*Dragons' Den* style).	Create a simple costing plan for the product.
Childcare	Write up a care plan for a youngster in your charge.	Measure out food portions for babies.
Dance	Design a flyer for a production.	Work out the rhythm counts for a particular choreography.
Electrical	Complete test sheets.	Work out amps drop.

In summary, opportunities exist and we need to ensure that we are using them. As part of your training and development, we would suggest you make time to meet with your maths and English teams, as they will be able to help you identify naturally occurring opportunities that you may not have considered. Also go and observe other subject specialists within your area to get ideas for seamless integration. The Education and Training Foundation also has specific courses available that you can access as part of your CPD for embedding English and maths in post-16 education.

Summary

This chapter has considered how you can develop your subject-specialist knowledge and approaches, exploring threshold concepts and troublesome knowledge and how these may be embedded into curriculum design. It has also covered ways in which you can embed maths and English to provide an inclusive and coherent curriculum for your learners.

Check your understanding (level 5)

1. Why is subject-specialist knowledge important in the FES sector?
2. What do you understand by threshold concepts and troublesome knowledge?
3. What are the four stages of teacher development that can be aligned to subject knowledge?
4. What are the types of curriculum you need to consider when designing your subject-specialist curriculum?

Developmental questions L6+7

1. Critically annotate the curriculum that you are working with. What theories are there and what is missing?
2. Evaluate the curriculum models available to you. How can you best use them in your teaching?
3. Consider the Ofsted framework. How can you synthesise your subject knowledge into the intent, implementation and impact statements?

Further reading

- Button, L (2021) Curriculum Design, Development and Models: Planning for Student Learning. In *Curriculum Essentials: A Journey*. [online] Available at: https://oer.pressbooks.pub/curriculum essentials/chapter/curriculum-design-development-and-models-planning-for-student-learning-there-is-always-a-need-for-newly-formulated-curriculum-models-that-address-contemporary-circumstance-an (accessed 24 September 2024).
- Council for Subject Associations (CfSA) (2024) [online] Available at: www.subjectassociations.org.uk (accessed 24 September 2024).
- FutureLearn (nd) Instructional Design and Curriculum Development: Definitions and Differences. [online] Available at: www.futurelearn.com/info/blog/instructional-design-and-curriculum-development (accessed 24 September 2024).
- Gov.UK (2023) Effective Practice in Curriculum Planning. [online] Available at: www.gov.uk/government/publications/effective-practice-in-curriculum-planning (accessed 24 September 2024).

References

Bloom, B (1956) *Taxonomy of Educational Objectives: The Classification of Educational Goals*. New York: David McKay Company Inc.

Bruner, J (1960) The Process of Education. London: Vintage Education.

Council for Subject Associations (CfSA) (2024) [online] Available at: www.subjectassociations.org.uk (accessed 24 September 2024).

Department for Education (2022) Delivering World Class Teacher Development. [online] Available at: https://assets.publishing.service.gov.uk/government/uploads/system/uploads/attachment_data/file/1076587/Delivering_world_class_teacher_development_policy_paper.pdf (accessed 15 November 2024).

Department of Education (NI) (2024) Teachers' Professional Development. [online] Available at: www.education-ni.gov.uk/articles/teachers-professional-development (accessed 28 September 2024).

Education and Training Foundation (ETF) (2022) *Professional Standards for Teachers and Trainers*. [online] Available at: www.et-foundation.co.uk/professional-standards/teachers (accessed 29 September 2024).

Fuller, F (1969) Concerns of Teachers: A Developmental Conceptualization. *American Educational Research Journal*, 6: 207–26.

Institute for Apprenticeships and Technical Education (IfATE) (2024) *Learning and Skills Teacher*. [online] Available at: www.instituteforapprenticeships.org/apprenticeship-standards/learning-and-skills-teacher (accessed 28 September 2024).

McDonald, M, Kazemi, E and Kavanagh, S (2013) Core Practices and Pedagogies of Teacher Education: A Call for a Common Language and Collective Activity. *Journal of Teacher Education*, 64(5): 378–86.

Meyer, J and Land, R (2003) *Threshold Concepts and Troublesome Knowledge: Linkages to Ways of Thinking and Practising within the Disciplines.* ETL Project, Occasional Report 4.

Ofsted (2019) *Education Inspection Framework*. [online] Available at: www.gov.uk/government/publications/education-inspection-framework (accessed 28 September 2024).

Parker, M, Patton, K and O'Sullivan, M (2016) Signature Pedagogies in Support of Teachers' Professional Learning. *Irish Educational Studies*, 35(2): 137–53.

Perkins, D (1999) The Many Faces of Constructivism. *Educational Leadership*, 57(3): 6.

Pitt, E and Quinlan, K M (2021) Signature Assessment and Feedback Practices in the Disciplines. *Assessment in Education: Principles, Policy & Practice*, 28(2): 97–100.

Shulman, L S (2005) Signature Pedagogies in the Professions. *Daedalus*, 134(3): 52–9.

Stenhouse, L (1975) *An Introduction to Curriculum Research and Development.* London: Heinemann Educational Publishers.

Tyler, R (1949) *Basic Principles of Curriculum and Instruction.* Chicago, IL: University of Chicago Press.

12 Education for sustainable development

Professional links

This chapter contributes to the following professional links:

The Diploma in Teaching mandatory content (DfE, 2024)

- 1.7 Sustainability in your area.
- 2.6 Their wider expectations.
- 2.8 Role and currency of research and evidence.
- 3.1 The role of a teacher.
- 4.16 Professional responsibilities.

Learning and Skills Teacher Occupational Standards (IfATE, 2024)

- K4 Methods for creating and adapting inclusive learning resources.
- K5 Evidence-informed inclusive teaching, learning and assessment strategies.
- S1 Integrate subject and pedagogic research into teaching activity to enhance teaching and support changes of practice.
- S6 Promote understanding of equality and diversity and sustainable development.
- S9 Engage and inspire learners.
- S13 Encourage learners to develop: autonomy and resilience, personal and interpersonal effectiveness, social awareness and respect for others, essential employability skills, a solutions mindset, and the ability to create change.
- S16 Prepare learners for their transition through education, further training, and into employment.
- B5 Act in a manner that is ethical, fair, consistent and impartial, valuing equality, diversity and champion British values within professional boundaries.
- B6 Model sustainable practice and promote sustainable development principles, values and goals in relation to their subject specialism.

→

Professional Standards (ETF, 2022)

- 1 Critically reflect on and evaluate your practices, values, and beliefs to improve learner outcomes.
- 2 Promote and embed education for sustainable development (ESD) across learning and working practices.
- 5 Value and champion diversity, equality of opportunity, inclusion and social equity.
- 8 Develop and update knowledge of your subject specialism, taking account of new practices, research and/or industry requirements.
- 12 Understand your teaching role and responsibilities and how these are influenced by legal, regulatory, institutional and ethical contexts.
- 13 Promote and support positive learner behaviour, attitudes and well-being.

Chapter objectives

At the end of this chapter you will be able to:

- discuss the importance of education for sustainable development with your students;
- apply the core concepts of education for sustainable development in the planning and delivery of your sessions;
- critically evaluate the impact of education for sustainable development within the boundaries of your specific subject specialism;
- identify and inform learners of the importance for sustainable practices within your subject specialism for the purpose of employability within that field.

Introduction and definitions

This chapter covers an extremely important and topical theme within education at present, that of education for sustainable development. The chapter aims to provide you with an insight into this field of education from three perspectives: as a subject specialist, as a teacher and as a member of an educational organisation. The goal is to provide you with sufficient information so that you can feel comfortable with your awareness of this subject, develop your skills and habits to allow you to incorporate them into your teaching by modelling best practices, and enable you to follow the principles, values and goals of these areas in relation to your individual sessions.

It was reported in 2015 (McDonald, 2015) that all the world's population is currently using resources equivalent to 1.5 Earths as a whole. We in the United Kingdom, as a developed country, are also quite poor in this respect. If everyone in the world lived in the same manner as UK citizens, we would need 2.4 Earths to sustain us. In addition, these figures do not consider crop sustainability; indeed, a number of top scientists quoted in McDonald's (2015) article state that these figures are a massive underrepresentation of the true picture. In 2023, the statistics portal Statista revisited this topic and increased the UK's need for resources to 2.6 Earths, which is obviously unsustainable both as a nation and a planet. The overuse of natural resources worldwide has come to the fore in a number of national and international forums, with efforts being made to address it. At the forefront of these efforts, and intrinsically linked to the United Nations Educational, Scientific and Cultural Organization's (UNESCO) Sustainable Development Goals, is education (UNESCO, 2017). The UK is not alone in its current unsustainable approach to natural resources and Table 12.1 shows a pictorial representation of the number of Earth's resources required by country at their current rate of consumption.

Table 12.1 *The number of Earths/its resources needed if the population lived like the following countries*

USA	Denmark	Germany	UK	China	Brazil	Indonesia
5.0	4.3	2.9	2.6	2.3	1.8	1.1

Source: Adapted from Statista.com (2023)

What is education for sustainable development?

Education for sustainable development (ESD) is a crucial aspect of modern education, particularly for young people aged over 16 as they prepare to enter the modern workforce, as well as for their individual futures as members of their communities and beyond. Understanding sustainability and fostering practices that support it are essential in today's world and are highly sought after by employers. ESD empowers young people to make informed decisions, develop critical thinking skills and take action to protect the environment and promote social equity.

ESD helps young people understand the impact of human activities on the environment. The world faces significant environmental challenges, such as climate change, deforestation and pollution (UNESCO, 2017). By learning about these issues, young people can understand how their actions and the actions of others contribute to these problems and how they can help mitigate them. For instance, understanding the importance of reducing waste, conserving energy and protecting natural habitats can lead to more environmentally friendly behaviours. Human-induced climate change is causing dangerous and widespread disruption in nature, affecting the lives of billions of people around the world, despite efforts to reduce the risks (IPCC, 2022). As a modern educator in the United Kingdom, it is vital that you have a rounded understanding of this facet of education and model best practice for your students, enabling them to firmly understand and embed ESD into their everyday thought process.

Definitions

What is sustainability? There are many definitions on the internet but a very level and rounded one is from McGill University:

> *Sustainability means meeting our own needs without compromising the ability of future generations to meet their own needs. In addition to natural resources, we also need social and economic resources. Sustainability is not just environmentalism. Embedded in most definitions of sustainability we also find concerns for social equity and economic development.*
>
> (McGill University, 2022)

This leads on to the UNESCO definition of what sustainability education or ESD is:

> *Education for sustainable development (ESD) is UNESCO's education sector response to the urgent and dramatic challenges the planet faces. The collective activities of human beings have altered the earth's ecosystems so that our very survival seems in danger because of changes more difficult to reverse every day. To contain global warming before it reaches catastrophic levels means addressing environmental, social and economic issues in a holistic way.*
>
> (UNESCO, 2022)

Governmental and Ofsted policies

The UK government has implemented several policies and initiatives to support ESD, specifically targeting post-16 learners in the FES sector. These efforts aim to equip young people with the necessary skills, knowledge and attitudes to contribute to a sustainable future and to meet the demands of a green economy.

One of the primary initiatives is the integration of sustainability into vocational education and training as a golden thread throughout every programme. This is reflected by the integration into the newly updated Professional Standards from the Education and Training Foundation for our sector of a specific new standard, number 2: '*Promote and embed education for sustainable development (ESD) across learning and working practices*' (ETF, 2022).

The UK government also promotes the development of green skills through apprenticeship programmes and qualifications in key sectors such as renewable energy, sustainable construction and environmental management. These programmes are designed to ensure that young people entering the workforce are prepared to support the transition to a low-carbon/sustainable economy as most of the apprentice standards across the various disciplines have a knowledge, skill or behaviour intrinsically linked to ESD and sustainability (HM Government, 2022; IfATE, 2024).

The Department for Education's (DfE) Sustainability and Climate Change Strategy, launched in April 2022 and updated in December 2023, outlines the government's vision for sustainability education up to 2030, with a significant focus on the FES sector as shown in the strategy's vision to be a world-leading education sector in sustainability and climate change by 2030.

> *The strategy's vision is for the United Kingdom to be the world-leading education sector in sustainability and climate change by 2030. In England, we will achieve this through 4 strategic aims:*
>
> 1. *Excellence in education and skills for a changing world: preparing all young people for a world impacted by climate change through learning and practical experience.*
> 2. *Net zero: reducing direct and indirect emissions from education and care buildings, driving innovation to meet legislative targets and providing opportunities for children and young people to engage practically in the transition to net zero.*
> 3. *Resilient to climate change: adapting our education and care buildings and system to prepare for the effects of climate change.*
> 4. *A better environment for future generations: enhancing biodiversity, improving air quality and increasing access to, and connection with, nature in and around education and care settings.*
>
> (Extract of a policy paper from the Department for Education, 2023)

This strategy includes commitments to improve teaching and learning about climate change and sustainability within FES colleges. It also aims to create pathways for students to gain practical experience in sustainability through work placements and industry partnerships, which are an integral part of the new T level provisions with 20 per cent of the course hours being a compulsory placement (Gov.UK, 2023).

In support of this strategy, the Department for Education has developed resources and guidelines for FES institutions to integrate sustainability into their curricula and operations. This includes the promotion of environmentally friendly practices within colleges, such as energy efficiency measures, waste reduction and sustainable transport options (Department for Education, 2023). By implementing these practices, FES institutions can serve as models of sustainability for their students and generations of the future.

Research and development play a crucial role in advancing ESD in the FES sector. The UK government funds research into effective ESD practices and the development of educational resources that promote sustainability. This includes collaborations with universities, FES colleges and industry stakeholders to ensure that the curriculum and training programmes are aligned with the latest sustainability standards and industry needs (HEFCE, 2014).

Teacher training and professional development are also essential components of the government's ESD strategy. The Department for Education provides professional development opportunities for FES educators to enhance their understanding of sustainability issues and to integrate these topics into their teaching (DfE, 2023). This training helps ensure that educators are well equipped to inspire and engage students in sustainability initiatives.

Furthermore, the government supports initiatives like the Green Skills Taskforce, which works to identify and address skills gaps in the green economy. This taskforce aims to ensure that the FES sector can meet the demand for green jobs by developing appropriate training programmes and qualifications (HM Government, 2022).

Higher education institutions also play a role in ESD for post-16 learners. Universities and colleges are encouraged to integrate sustainability into their curricula and research activities. The Higher Education Funding Council for England (HEFCE) has supported projects that promote sustainable development within higher education institutions, which often collaborate with FES colleges to provide pathways for students to advance their sustainability education (HEFCE, 2014).

In summary, the UK government's policies and initiatives for ESD in the FES sector focus on integrating sustainability into vocational training, enhancing teacher professional development, supporting research and development, and promoting sustainable practices within educational institutions. These efforts aim to prepare post-16 learners to address environmental challenges and contribute to a sustainable economy.

Critical question ?

» Consider your classroom practice. From what you have just read/learnt, what are you already doing in your subject specialist area to promote and model ESD?

Discussion

While not exhaustive, you may have come up with some of the following examples.

- Integrating sustainability topics: Including lessons on sustainability, environmental impact and ethical practices related to your subject.

- Resource management: Demonstrating efficient use of resources in the classroom, such as reducing paper use or recycling materials.
- Collaborative learning: Promoting teamwork and collaboration on sustainability projects, fostering a sense of community and shared responsibility.
- Critical thinking: Encouraging students to think critically about sustainability issues and their impact on society and the environment.
- Project-based learning: Encouraging students to undertake projects that address real-world sustainability challenges.

Education for sustainable development as a subject

From an FES teacher's/lecturer's perspective, ESD has a much wider impact on a range of skills beyond purely sustainability and resource management. It encourages critical thinking skills and promotes social equity and active citizenship as it prepares learners for future careers. As FES educators, we can integrate and model sustainability in education to empower the next generation to make the correct choices and create a more sustainable and equitable world. Education is a major step forwards in ensuring a better future for our students and generations to come. Next, we look at some examples of how embedding ESD into our practice can help our learners' development.

Developing critical thinking and problem-solving skills

ESD develops critical thinking and problem-solving skills. It has long been recognised that sustainable development is complex. As Sterling (2001) notes, it requires individuals to think critically about how to balance economic growth, environmental protection and social well-being. By engaging with these topics and your subject specialist knowledge, your students learn to analyse problems from multiple perspectives and develop creative solutions. This was supported by UNESCO (2014), who also identified that these skills are not only essential for addressing sustainability issues but are also highly valuable in many areas of life and work.

Promoting social equity

Sustainable development is about more than just the environment; it's also about social equity. ESD teaches young people about the interconnectedness of social, economic and environmental issues (United Nations, 2015). They learn about the importance of social justice, gender equality and human rights. This holistic understanding encourages them to consider how their actions affect others and to strive for a more equitable society. For example, learning about fair trade can lead to more ethical consumer choices, and understanding global inequalities can inspire actions to support disadvantaged communities (Leicht et al, 2018).

Encouraging active citizenship

ESD encourages active citizenship. Young people learn that they can make a difference and are empowered to take action (Jensen and Schnack, 2006). This could be through participating in local environmental projects, advocating for policy changes or simply making more sustainable choices in their daily lives. Active citizenship fosters a sense of responsibility and community engagement, which is essential for driving collective efforts towards a sustainable future (Huckle and Wals, 2015).

Preparing for future careers

Furthermore, ESD prepares young people for future careers. As sustainability becomes increasingly important across all UK employment sectors, there is a growing demand for professionals with awareness, knowledge and skills in this area (Hopkins and McKeown, 2005). By incorporating sustainability into FES, young people can gain a competitive edge in the job market. They might pursue careers in renewable energy, sustainable agriculture, environmental science or corporate social responsibility, among many others. These careers not only offer personal fulfilment but also contribute to the broader goal of sustainable development (Tilbury, 2011).

Fostering innovation

Sustainability, as we mentioned earlier, requires critical thinking skills; however, the challenges it presents also require innovative solutions. ESD fosters a mindset of innovation by encouraging young people to think creatively about how to solve complex problems (Sterling, 2001). They learn about new technologies and practices that can help reduce environmental impact and improve quality of life. For example, understanding how renewable energy sources like solar and wind power work can inspire young people to explore careers in developing these existing technologies and create a mindset to address future technologies. This is best summed up by UNESCO (2017, p 1), who stated: '*Global issues – such as climate change – urgently require a shift in our lifestyles and a transformation of the way we think and act. To achieve this change, we need new skills, values and attitudes that lead to more sustainable societies*'.

Building resilience

Finally, ESD builds resilience. Young people learn about the importance of being adaptable and prepared for change. This is particularly important as the world faces increasing environmental uncertainties and economic challenges (Leicht et al, 2018). By understanding these issues and developing the skills to address them, young people can better cope with and respond to future challenges. This resilience is crucial for their personal development and for the sustainability of their communities and the world (Jensen and Schnack, 2006). Resilience and confidence are vital in a modern teenager as they exit the post-Covid pandemic era and embrace the modern world. Resilience gives them the ability to manage the stress, challenges, trauma or adversity in life and bounce back from them, while still providing them with the confidence to be curious and adaptable to the world around them (Family Lives, 2024).

As a teacher or trainee teacher in the FES sector, you need to consider four key viewpoints when addressing ESD within your subject specialism, as detailed in Table 12.2.

Table 12.2 *ESD viewpoints and associated examples*

Viewpoint	Examples
Subject specificity	Reusable nappies (early years), heat source pumps (construction), cloud servers (ICT), waste reduction (catering), etc.
Educational	More electronic resources to save on handouts, online learning material and submissions etc.
Institutional	Campus-wide 'green' initiatives, reducing carbon footprint, updating energy conservation methods, electric vehicle chargers, movement-controlled lighting, internal operations/processes and supply chains. In addition, offering green skills and careers.
National	Having an educational policy aligned to the UNESCO Sustainable Development Goals, most of which contain an aspect of education/training.

As a teacher or trainee teacher, you can address and influence the first three, but the fourth, national viewpoints, needs to be worked towards collectively as an FES sector because FES colleges are major socio-economic contributors to the local economy (Senior and Barnes, 2023).

How to think about education for sustainable development as a subject specialist

Firstly, consider your own practices and how you work, as all the little things add up to big changes. Consider the following about your general practices:

- working online/collaboratively;
- reducing photocopying;
- more electronic resources/e-books;
- class discussions;
- smarter practices;
- hot desking/home working.

Then move on to area of specialism and what can you do as a teacher/lecturer to increase awareness of sustainability around your subject. Reflect on your area of subject specialism and consider what you and your colleagues are already doing and what can be altered, adapted and improved. Here is a short but not exhaustive list that looks at some ideas around the subject of construction.

- What eco-friendly materials are there or emerging technologies that reduce the impact on the environment (ie lime mortar in training, prefab buildings, recycled insulation)?
- Heat source pumps and renewable energies will be used more as we move as a nation from reliance on fossil fuels. Also economically, there are normally grants, either locally or nationally, to support this type of venture as we all strive to hit emissions targets regionally and nationally.
- Alternative construction methods; some construction methods are much worse for the environment than others.
- Sustainable sourcing of materials, the ethical stance of companies, wood from sustainable forests, etc.
- Carbon offsetting – if a certain practice is vital, can it be offset to reduce the impact?
- Thinking of own practices and altering them accordingly. Green vehicles/smaller commutes, hybrid working reduces commuting emissions, online/virtual meetings (not only reduces carbon emissions from commuting but also can increase productivity by not losing time on the commute).

Critical question ?

» Think about your subject and your practice. Take a recent session you have delivered or one that you are planning and take extra time to consider ESD. Consider it from two viewpoints: first what you are already doing. Then secondly, what could you additionally put in from the ideas and inspiration you have just read?

Education for sustainable development as an institution: leading the way and modelling best practices

It is not all about the teaching; it is also about setting a positive example: the development of sustainable infrastructure in FES colleges can drive community engagement and partnerships as well as provide best use of public funds. Colleges can collaborate with local governments, businesses and non-profits to develop and implement sustainable projects, fostering a sense of community and shared responsibility for sustainable development. These partnerships can provide students with practical experience and networking opportunities, enhancing their employability and preparing them for careers in the growing green economy (Scott and Gough, 2003).

As major employers in our community (Senior and Barnes, 2023), we are all part of a wider community and supply chains that feed our everyday operations. Most organisations within our sector have some form of green working group or committee which you can become involved in to try to effect more change within your own organisation, so find out about yours and how you get involved.

Sustainable infrastructure in FES sector buildings aligns with and models the principles of social equity and inclusivity, core components of sustainable development. By creating accessible, inclusive and environmentally friendly campuses, our sector can ensure that all students, regardless of their background, have the opportunity to learn in and contribute to a sustainable environment. This approach promotes a culture of inclusivity and responsibility, essential for fostering positive citizens and sustainable development (Tilbury, 2011). Some organisations have embraced the sustainable philosophy, while some are a little slower to do so.

Some possible suggestions to identify around your campuses/buildings are:

- electric car charging bays;
- green days/volunteer days in the local community on green initiatives;
- cycle to work scheme;
- declaring a climate emergency;
- replacing and updating infrastructure to more modern versions, ie triple glazing instead of double glazing;
- recycling centres/renewable energies;
- online working practices instead of paper;
- flexible working policies;
- reusable cups in catering facilities/water bottle refilling stations instead of bottled water.

Again, this list is not exhaustive and as technologies improve and awareness grows so will support and opportunities for green initiatives and employability. In fact, ONS data shows that the green sector grew four times faster than the rest of the UK economy between 2020 and 2021, but the UK government is still behind its pledge to deliver two million jobs by 2030 in the green sector (Green Intelligence, 2023).

CASE STUDY

Micha has just delivered a session on textiles to a level 3 design cohort in an FES setting. The session followed the supply chain from the far east through to a budget high street retailer. Micha looks at the production of cotton in India, the transportation and manufacturing in Thailand of a cotton T shirt, the transport chain from Thailand to the United Kingdom wholesaler, from the wholesaler to the high street store dispatch and from dispatch to the store and onto the store shelf.

Critical questions

Consider the following questions and consider creating mind maps to visually represent your ideas.

- » What natural resources do you think were used at the various stages of the production and supply chains?
- » What could be done to mitigate or reduce the impact of the resources?
- » Where was carbon dioxide used/produced and what could be done to limit this production of carbon dioxide?

Summary

In this chapter we have looked at what ESD is, how it can improve the 'soft skills' of your learners and turn them into better citizens with more career and future opportunities, as well as how you can support this movement by incorporating elements of best practice into your delivery sessions and everyday life.

ESD is contained at a teacher level within your subject and modelling of best practice, but it goes beyond that and will hopefully become a way of life for future generations as we try to reduce the impact of human civilisation on the planet. This must be a positive outcome for everyone on the planet and so is a vital cause. Reducing and recycling natural resources, as well as educating people about why it is important, is going to be a long process that requires 'buy-in' from a global perspective. To put it bluntly, we cannot continue as we have been and most developed countries, the United Kingdom included, are some of the worst offenders. However, together we can unite and drive the required change, starting with educating this generation and future generations.

Check your understanding (level 5)

1. What are the six areas of soft skills that can be developed for your students if you successfully embed ESD?
2. What are the four key viewpoints to consider within ESD?
3. How many planets' worth of resources would the world consume if everyone lived like residents of the United Kingdom?

Developmental questions L6+7

1. Research the UNESCO Sustainable Development Goals (UNESCO, 2022) and consider how you would explain ESD to a colleague within your subject specialist area.
2. Consider a peer observation of an experienced practitioner – they do not have to be from the same specialism – and watch to see how ESD is embedded within their session. Then critically review your planning and/or delivery of a recent session to identify ideas in the six generic skills listed above in which you could have expanded ESD more effectively.
3. How can you embed ESD in your subject teaching?
4. Locate your organisation's sustainability plan. What could you do to enhance or develop this in your area?
5. Consider the government manifesto on sustainability in education. What are the key elements that you could apply directly to your teaching?

Further reading

- Unesco (2015) Unesco and Sustainable Development Goals: The 2030 Agenda for Sustainable Development. [online] Available at: www.unesco.org/en/sdgs (accessed 24 October 2024).
- Department for Education (DfE) (2023) *Sustainability and Climate Change Strategy*. [online] Available at: www.gov.uk/government/publications/sustainability-and-climate-change-strategy (accessed 29 September 2024).

References

Department for Education (DfE) (2023) *Sustainability and Climate Change Strategy*. [online] Available at: www.gov.uk/government/publications/sustainability-and-climate-change-strategy (accessed 29 September 2024).

Department for Education (DfE) (2024) Diploma in Teaching (Further Education and Skills) qualification framework. [online] Available at: www.gov.uk/government/publications/further-education-initial-teacher-education/diploma-in-teaching-further-education-and-skills-qualification-framework (accessed 8 October 2024).

Education and Training Foundation (ETF) (2022) *Professional Standards for Teachers and Trainers.* [online] Available at: www.et-foundation.co.uk/professionalstandards (accessed 29 September 2024).

Family Lives (2024) Building Resilience in Children and Teens. [online] Available at: www.familylives.org.uk/advice/your-family/wellbeing/building-resilience-in-children-and-teens (accessed 29 September 2024).

Gov.UK (2023) *Introduction of T Levels*. Policy paper. [online] Available at: www.gov.uk/government/publications/introduction-of-the-T-levels/introduction-of-the-t-levels (accessed 29 September 2024).

Green Intelligence (2023) *Green Industries Growing Four Times Faster Than the Rest of the UK Economy*. [online] Available at: www.greenintelligence.org.uk/news/green-industries-growing-four-times-faster-than-the-rest-of-uk-economy (accessed 29 September 2024).

Higher Education Funding Council for England (HEFCE) (2014) Sustainable Development in Higher Education. [online] Available at: https://dera.ioe.ac.uk/id/eprint/21777/1/HEFCE2014_30.pdf (accessed 9 October 2024).

HM Government (2022) *Green Skills and Jobs*. [online] Available at: www.gov.uk/government/publications/green-jobs-taskforce-report (accessed 29 September 2024).

Hopkins, C and McKeown, R (2005) *Guidelines and Recommendations for Re-orientating Teacher Education to Address Sustainability*. [online] Available at: https://unesdoc.unesco.org/ark:/48223/pf0000143370 (accessed 9 October 2024).

Huckle, J, and Wals, A E J (2015) The UN Decade of Education for Sustainable Development: Business as Usual in the End. *Environmental Education Research*, 21(3): 491–505.

Institute for Apprenticeships and Technical Education (IfATE) (2024) *Learning and Skills Teacher*. [online] Available at: www.instituteforapprenticeships.org/apprenticeship-standards/learning-and-skills-teacher (accessed 29 September 2024).

Institute for Apprenticeships and Technical Education (IfATE) (2024) *Occupational Standards*. [online] Available at: www.instituteforapprenticeships.org/occupational-standards (accessed 29 September 2024).

Intergovernmental Panel on Climate Change (IPCC) (2022) *Climate Change: A Threat to Human Wellbeing and the Health of the Planet. Taking Action Now Can Secure Our Future*. [online] Available at: www.ipcc.ch/2022/02/28/pr-wgii-ar/6 (accessed 29 September 2024).

Jensen, B and Schnack, K (2006) The Action Competence Approach in Environmental Education. *Environmental Education Research*, 12(3–4): 471–86.

Leicht, A, Heiss, J and Byun, W J (eds) (2018) *Issues and Trends in Education for Sustainable Development*. Paris: UNESCO.

McDonald, C (2015) How Many Earths Do We Need? [online] Available at: www.bbc.co.uk/news/magazine-33133712 (accessed 29 September 2024).

McGill University (2022) *What Does Sustainability Mean?* [online] Available at: www.mcgill.ca/sustainability/files/sustainability/what-is-sustainability.pdf (accessed 29 September 2024).

Scott, W and Gough, S (2003) *Sustainable Development and Learning: Framing the Issues*. London: Routledge.

Senior, L and Barnes, N (2023) Are Our Further Education Colleges Still an Anchor in Our Society? *London Review of Education*, 21(1): 8.

Statista.com (2023) The World Is Not Enough. [online] Available at: www.statista.com/chart/10569/number-of-earths-needed-if-the-worlds-population-lived-like-following-countries (accessed 29 September 2024).

Sterling, S (2001) *Sustainable Education: Re-visioning Learning and Change*. Totnes: Green Books.

Tilbury, D (2011) *Education for Sustainable Development: An Expert Review of Processes and Learning*. Paris: UNESCO.

UNESCO (2014) *Shaping the Future We Want: UN Decade of Education for Sustainable Development (2005–2014). Final Report*. Paris: UNESCO.

UNESCO (2017) *Education for Sustainable Development Goals: Learning Objectives*. Paris: UNESCO.

UNESCO (2022) Definition of ESD. [online] Available at: www.unesco.org/en/education/sustainable-development (accessed 29 September 2024).

United Nations (2015) *Transforming Our World: The 2030 Agenda for Sustainable Development*. New York: United Nations.

13 Research and scholarship

Professional links

This chapter contributes to the following professional links:

The Diploma in Teaching mandatory content (DfE, 2024)

- 4.10 Application of evidence-based methods.
- 4.15 Updating and CPD.
- 4.18 Professional status.

Learning and Skills Teacher Occupational Standards (IfATE, 2024)

- K19 Ways to access personal and professional development, and to maintain sector and/or subject specific currency.
- S16 Prepare learners for their transition through education, further training, and into employment.
- S21 Continually update and maintain their own knowledge and skills as a teaching professional and a subject specialist as part of managing their own continual professional development (CPD).
- B2 Underpin their practice by reference to professional standards and evidence-based teaching and learning.
- B3 Committed to continuous professional development.

Professional Standards (ETF, 2022)

- 7 Engage with and promote a culture of continuous learning and quality improvement.
- 9 Critically review and apply your knowledge of educational research, pedagogy, and assessment to develop evidence-informed practice.
- 10 Share and update knowledge of effective practice with colleagues, networks and/or research communities to support improvement.

Chapter objectives

At the end of this chapter you will be able to:

- define evidence-based practice and explain where the concept originated;
- discuss the promises and limitations of an evidence-based approach to teaching practice;
- explore the role of postgraduate study in supporting teachers to become evidence-informed practitioners;
- define and articulate the role of the Society for Education and Training and Qualified Teacher Learning and Skills (QTLS) status.

Introduction

Many authors (eg Goldacre, 2013) share the view that '*education is too important to be determined by unfounded opinion, whether of politicians, teachers, researchers or anyone else*' (Coe, 1999), and for Slavin (2002, p 21) that sparked a culture '*in which evidence is valued over opinion*'. This transition was particularly pertinent to education because traditionally '*few professionals have been more steeped in mythology and less open to empirical findings than teachers*' (Maggs and White, 1982, p 131). Smith et al (2007, p 121) discuss how teachers' practice has been instead guided by '*anecdotal evidence and a collective sense of expert opinion*', neither of which they argue '*provide educators with precise or enough information to determine which educational practices are truly effective, for whom, and under what circumstances*'. Consequently, increasing attention is being paid internationally to developing ways in which evidence can be used to shape educational policy and practice, and ultimately improve student achievement (Cain, 2016). This perspective is commonly labelled as a drive towards evidence-based education.

What is evidence-based education?

Tripney et al (2014) describe evidence-based education as an approach to improving outcomes for learners by using the 'best evidence' available to shape education policy and teaching practice. Proponents of evidence-based approaches to practice (eg Whitty, 2013; Tripney et al, 2014) attribute improved outcomes within other fields (eg medicine, social work, agriculture) to the adoption of this approach. A key principle of evidence-based practice is that practitioners (eg teachers) will make better decisions if they are aware of the available evidence supporting and contradicting 'what works' and use it to guide their practice.

A fundamental issue in developing evidence-based education is uncertainty about what constitutes evidence. The Oxford Dictionary (2014) defines evidence as '*the available body of facts or information indicating whether a belief or proposition is true or valid*'. Therefore, information (eg student achievement or evaluation data) can only be considered 'evidence' in light of a belief or proposition (eg good- or poor-quality teaching).

Broadly speaking, there are two perspectives on the extent to which teachers' practice can and should be influenced by evidence. The first perspective is commonly referred to as evidence-based education and proposes that teaching practice should be *based* on or 'directed by' (Everton et al, 2002) evidence. Using evidence created through research as an example, an idealistic example of this perspective in action would be for teachers to indiscriminately implement research-based pedagogical interventions in their practice in a bid to raise student achievement. Van Schaik et al (2018) highlight several flaws in this perspective: firstly, it inaccurately implies that the available body of research provides sufficient detail of practices being examined to enable teachers to accurately replicate them. Secondly, over-emphasising the role of 'evidence' can diminish the influence of experience and the 'tacit knowledge' that teachers possess. Teachers and researchers share concern that research-based knowledge is a '*poor substitute for actual experience*' (Beycioglu et al, 2010, p 1088) and may undermine knowledge acquired through teachers' professional experience (eg tacit knowledge, vicarious experience) (Brown and Zhang, 2016). Finally, this perspective also implies that research findings are unambiguous, whereas the complex nature of research means that research findings must be considered with an understanding of the subjective decisions and interpretations which take place throughout the research process.

The second, and more broadly accepted, perspective is commonly labelled as evidence-informed education and proposes that teaching practice should be *informed* by evidence. The Department for Education (DfE) is a central driver in the ambition for teachers' increased use of evidence to guide practice and wants: '*All teaching practice to reflect both individual teaching expertise and the best and most up-to-date external evidence from systematic research*' (DfE, 2017). Essentially, they are endorsing an approach whereby teachers guide their practice using an interplay of different types of evidence in conjunction with their 'practitioner expertise'. 'External evidence from systematic research' predominantly relates to the role of evidence created through different forms of academic (ie peer-reviewed) research. Practitioner expertise is an ambiguous concept which authors use a range of terms to describe (eg virtuosity (Biesta, 2012), practical wisdom (Goodfellow, 2003) and professional knowledge (Shalem and Slonimsky, 2013)). See the related discussion in Chapter 11.

Both of the above perspectives endeavour to increase the regularity with which research findings are incorporated into teaching practice under the hypotheses that it will enable better decision making, more effective practice and, ultimately, improved student achievement. Advocates of an evidence-informed approach to education (eg McMillan and Schumacher, 2014; Tripney et al, 2014) argue that while research can direct teachers towards a range of potential interventions or resolutions, it often cannot be prescriptive. This perspective is shared by most academics (eg Brown and Zhang, 2016) and is echoed in the Department for Education's (2017) directive as a consensus seems to be developing that: a) teachers' practice cannot be based solely on research evidence, and b) teachers should use educational research in conjunction with other forms of information and knowledge (eg 'practitioner expertise').

How can teachers develop evidence-informed practice?

As illustrated in the Department for Education's (2017) directive, the role of evidence sourced from research plays a significant role in the development of evidence-informed practice. Various definitions of 'research' exist, and a more all-encompassing example is offered by the Higher Education Funding Council for England (HEFCE) (2011): '*a process of investigation leading to new insights, effectively shared*' (p 6). This definition is somewhat vague, but it provides a starting point for considering the different ways that teachers can engage *with* or *in* research (Nelson et al, 2017).

CASE STUDY

Jermaine is a highly experienced teacher of science, having taught at a range of sixth form colleges for several years. He has recently began teaching at a general FES college and is experiencing disruptive student behaviours that are more regular and having a more adverse impact on student learning than he has experienced previously. Jermaine quickly identifies the detrimental impact that the disruptive behaviours are having on student learning and begins to consider how he can promote behaviours more conducive to a positive learning environment. The first step that Jermaine takes is to speak with his new colleagues and they offer some suggestions as to how he can alter his practice. However, after implementing the suggested strategies for some time, Jermaine sees no improvement in the regularity and severity of the disruptive behaviours posed by some students and begins to look to other sources for support. Another colleague suggests that Jermaine should read some research about classroom management strategies.

Critical questions

» How might research support Jermaine in this aspect of his practice in a way that is more beneficial than his colleagues' suggested strategies?

» What problems might Jermaine have in finding, reading and using research?

» What steps could Jermaine take to overcome those challenges?

Engaging with research

This usually involves teachers accessing academic research, that is, research which is produced externally (often through higher education institutions [HEIs]), peer reviewed and published most commonly in academic journals or textbooks. Academic research is conducted with the intention of achieving the following HEFCE (2011) objectives: significance, originality and rigour. Significance is determined by the extent to which it addresses 'important' issues.

Originality is achieved when research generates new knowledge, and rigour is ascertained by conducting research in a way that is systematic and complies with established scientific protocols. Achieving those objectives might support the assertion that academic research most adequately meets the Department for Education's (2017) drive for teachers to use the '*best ... external evidence from systematic research*' (p 781).

Academic research can take different forms but broadly falls into the categories of a research synthesis (eg meta-analyses) or an individual study (eg experiment, case study). A research synthesis is a set of related methods that researchers use to bring together the findings of separate (usually empirical) studies. In their application to teaching practice, they can provide teachers with a more intellectually accessible summary of key outcomes from a body of literature related to a particular aspect of TLA. Summarising (or conflating) individual research studies brings its own limitations; for example, there is an argument that the complexities of individual pieces of research cannot be accurately captured and accounted for in a research synthesis.

The Education Endowment Foundation (EEF) is an independent charity that has created 'Toolkits' advertised as '*accessible summaries of the best available evidence on different topics for teaching and learning*' (EEF, 2018). The Toolkits provide a snapshot of the cost, impact and strength of the research evidence behind different teaching strategies and practices. To provide an example, they summarise the findings of 155 individual empirical (ie experimental) studies which have investigated the impact of feedback on student achievement and conclude '*based on extensive evidence*' that feedback has a '*very high impact*' on student achievement for '*very low cost*' to the setting. Notably, the Toolkits are currently predominantly aimed towards supporting teachers in early years, primary and secondary school settings but, in 2018, the EEF announced a £40million government grant '*to further build the evidence-base and support effective practice*' in FES. Issues relating to availability of research evidence sourced from FES will be elaborated upon later in this chapter.

A benefit of teachers engaging with individual studies is that they then have an opportunity to analyse and evaluate the research methodology, data collection methods, analytic strategy and the researcher's subsequent interpretation. Furthermore, by engaging with individual research investigations, teachers can tailor the research that they access to that which they believe more closely reflects their context (eg subject area, setting, student body). However, engagement with individual studies can be incredibly time consuming for teachers given their already high workloads, and that research can be difficult to access both physically and intellectually. It can be physically difficult to access because individual studies are generally published in academic journals situated behind subscription-based paywalls. Engaging with individual studies can also be intellectually challenging because of the specialist terminology and concepts that researchers use. Both previous assertions are supported by a wealth of research which has investigated the research literacy (ie ability to read and understand research) of teachers across primary and secondary school settings (eg Levin et al, 2011; Nelson et al, 2017). Although related research in the FES domain seems largely absent, there are a couple of reasons to believe that FES teachers' research literacy may be further diminished.

Firstly, Gov.UK (2023) report that in the previous academic year, 51 per cent of the FES teaching workforce's subject specialism was vocational. That is significant because teachers of vocational subjects are less likely to have undertaken any HE-level study (ie QCF level 4 or above) than teachers of academic subjects. To provide a comparison, the Education and Training Foundation (ETF) (2019) reported that '*over 90 per cent*' of humanities teachers are qualified in their subject area to level 6 (or above), whereas only 25 per cent of engineering/manufacturing teachers and 14 per cent of retail/commercial enterprise teachers have qualifications at that level. This data is important because development of research literacy is a universal feature of HE study. Therefore, engaging in HE study is likely to better equip teachers to find, select, read, understand and subsequently implement the findings of academic research in their practice.

Secondly, in 2012 Lord Lingfield afforded employers within the lifelong learning sector increased flexibility to recruit teachers without a teaching qualification. The ETF (2019) provides data that shows the number of teachers within the FES sector without any recognised teaching qualification doubled between 2016 and 2018. This is significant because, like that discussed in the previous paragraph, a core feature and requirement of level 5 (and above) teaching qualifications is research engagement which is supported and facilitated through that provision.

Engaging in research

The primary distinction between teachers engaging *with* vs. *in* research is that the former involves teachers using already published academic research and the latter involves teachers conducting inquiry (ie research), usually within their setting. Engagement *in* research (ie teacher research, action research) places teachers as active agents in the research process as they take a leading role (individually or collaboratively) in planning, conducting and analysing the impact of their research in their context, practice and student outcomes. For Cochran-Smith and Lytle (1999), teacher research is conducted to support teachers in gaining insights into teaching and learning, promote reflectivity and effect change in the classroom. Stremmel (2002, p 2) provides a similar rationale for teachers engaging in action research, and that is '*to seek practical solutions to issues and problems .... The ultimate goal is change or the improvement of the problematic situation*'.

Teacher research can sometimes be thought about as an extension of teacher reflection because both involve identifying challenges in your professional practice and considering/making changes to improve the efficacy of your practice and therefore student outcomes. Although a teacher research often stems from their reflection, it is a more elaborate process because it also necessitates teachers acting in a more systematic way as they: link theory to practice and gather and analyse data, which subsequently provides an opportunity for the knowledge created to be shared less formally (eg internal setting CPD days) or more formally (eg publication in practitioner journals).

Teacher research is undertaken with quite different objectives to those of scientific rigour, as previously discussed for academic research (see HEFCE objectives). In subscribing to the HEFCE objectives, academic research is better placed to generate theoretically valuable knowledge which can then be generalised beyond the sample and setting involved in that particular study. Usually, the objectives of action research have a practical, context-specific orientation and are focused on creating 'local knowledge' which can improve aspects of one's practice (Stremmel, 2002). Consequently, teacher research tends to fare unfavourably compared with academic research in terms of significance, originality and rigour, which might imply that academic research is better placed to meet the Department for Education's (2017) explicit desire for the '*best ... systematic research*' (p 781) to be used to guide teaching practice.

Postgraduate study (to be discussed in more detail later in this chapter) is a step that teachers can take for further support their engagement *with* and *in* research. For example, it supports teachers in overcoming the physical and intellectual barriers aforementioned because: a) it necessitates enrolment within an HEI, which typically have more comprehensive access to academic research than FES settings; b) development of research literacy is a broadly universal component of postgraduate study; and c) most postgraduate study culminates with a substantial independently planned and conducted research project under the supervision of an experienced researcher (commonly referred to as a dissertation or thesis).

Activity ⑦

» Consider the challenges that you are currently facing in the classroom and create a plan for an action research project which will support you in enhancing your practice and learner outcomes.

Discussion

You may have considered using SMART targets (specific, measurable, achievable, realistic and with a timescale attached) to help you create the plan. Regardless, creating a research plan for action research involves several key steps. Table 13.1 provides a structured approach to help you get started.

Table 13.1 *Structuring your action research project*

Identify the problem	Clearly define the issue or area you want to investigate. Ensure the problem is specific, measurable and relevant to your context.
Review literature	Conduct a thorough review of existing literature related to your topic. Identify gaps in the current research that your study aims to fill.
Formulate research questions	Develop clear and concise research questions or hypotheses. Ensure they are aligned with the problem you identified.

⟶

Table 13.1 (*Cont.*)

Design the study	Participants: Decide who will be involved in your study. Methods: Choose appropriate data collection methods (eg surveys, interviews, observations). Timeline: Create a timeline for each phase of your research.
Data collection	Collect data systematically according to your plan. Ensure ethical considerations are addressed, such as informed consent and confidentiality.
Data analysis	Analyse the data using appropriate techniques. Look for patterns, themes and insights that address your research questions.
Implement findings in your practice	Make changes to your practice based on the analysis
Evaluate	Has it worked? What difference has it made?

Limitations of evidence-informed practice

Cain (2018, p 10) highlights a common perception that using research-based evidence to inform teaching practice is '*better than its alternatives*', and this view is illustrated by Estelle Morris, former Secretary of State for Education and Chair of the Institute of Effective Education, as she argued that '*teaching needs less ideology and more evidence*' (Morris, 2014). Although '*the need for teachers to draw on evidence rather than ... custom and practice is not difficult to argue*' (Wrigley, 2018, p 359), perspectives such as those above carry several assumptions that remain without sufficient supporting evidence. Firstly, questions remain as to whether a consistent and robust body of knowledge constructed through research which is useful for guiding teachers' practice exists. Secondly, although there is some evidence of a relationship between teachers' awareness of research findings and their practice (eg Piasta et al, 2020), Cain (2018, p 21) and Coldwell et al (2017) describe the available evidence of a relationship between research-informed education and student achievement as 'thin' and based on little more than assumption.

Additionally, the extent to which research can (and should) be of practical relevance to teaching practice remains contested. In one camp are those (eg Slavin, 2002; Goldacre, 2013) arguing that the primary goal of educational research should be to provide teachers with strategies which they can import into their practice, and there is reason to believe that policy-makers concur (eg DfE, 2010). In the other camp are academics (eg Hammersley, 2005) who maintain that educational research cannot be at the forefront of guiding teaching practice and that the primary goal of educational research should be to develop knowledge of education as a discipline in its own right.

The thrust for teachers to better use research to enhance their practice is evident through mechanisms introduced by recent governments to: a) increase the production of research relevant for guiding teachers' practice (eg EEF Toolkit), b) distribute research more widely (eg 'open access' policy) and c) enhance teachers' ability to intellectually access educational research (eg ResearchED) (Tripney et al, 2014). Despite the substantial financial investment committed by recent governments to create those mechanisms and smoothen the transfer of knowledge between its point of conception in research and teachers' implementation in the classroom, research-informed education remains difficult to achieve. Hammersley (2005) goes some way to explaining this by categorising criticisms aimed at both research users (ie teachers) and more typically at educational researchers. Teachers are criticised for: a) resistance to research-based teaching strategies, b) failing to accurately interpret educational research findings and c) lacking motivation to engage with educational research as a means to improve their practice. Researchers have been accused by peers (eg Hargreaves, 1996) and teachers (eg Cain, 2016) alike of failing to: a) conduct research addressing concerns/challenges of teachers, b) develop a consistent and coherent evidence base from which teachers can draw, c) conduct methodologically robust research and d) disseminate research using accessible language through accessible platforms.

Teachers can engage with academic research through more direct (eg journal articles) or less direct (eg social media) means. As might be expected given the prevalence of social media, Coldwell et al (2017) report that an increasing number of teachers are drawing on social media for links to research evidence sources, and some are using social media as a means of sharing research-based evidence. This can be problematic because research is complex and the nuances inherent in the research process might be prone to dilution.

Critical question ?

» What steps can teachers take to best equip themselves to physically and intellectually access complex academic research?

Postgraduate study

Postgraduate study refers to bachelor's degree (eg BA, BSc; QCF level 6) graduates studying towards a higher-level degree (QCF level 7–8) typically within a HEI on a full-time (one-year) or part-time (two-year) basis. Teachers without a QCF level 6 qualification would need to complete a 'top-up' degree to become eligible for postgraduate study. Top-up degrees offer an opportunity to build upon your existing qualification (eg HND, foundation degree) to achieve a bachelor's degree with just one or two years' study.

The basic premise of postgraduate study is that students will enrol already equipped with foundational knowledge in their subject area acquired through their undergraduate degree (eg BA, BSc). Postgraduate study will then provide an opportunity to specialise in their learning and gain a deeper understanding in a more specific aspect of their chosen subject area. For teachers in the lifelong learning sector, postgraduate study could be undertaken to develop knowledge and expertise in an aspect of either their specialist subject (ie the subject(s) that they teach) or teaching practice. To provide an example of the latter, teachers might complete postgraduate study to develop an evidence-informed understanding of SEND and the most effective ways to support those with related barriers to learning.

Broadly speaking, there are two paths that postgraduate study can take: taught courses and research degrees. Taught courses (eg MSc, MA) involve learning in typical HEI learning environments (ie lectures, seminars, tutorials) on a modular basis with each module comprising independent assessments. Students typically have a choice of modules that they will complete and can therefore tailor their learning to meet their interests and/or professional development needs. Taught courses usually culminate in designing and conducting a research project under the supervision of an experienced researcher.

Research degrees (eg MRes, PhD) are more independent endeavours as they broadly involve working independently on a research project for the duration of the course under the supervision of an experienced researcher. The project culminates in a viva voce (ie oral examination) where the student presents their work to a panel of experts, justifying the design of their study and the original contribution to knowledge that their thesis has made.

Some of the generally advertised benefits of completing postgraduate study for teachers include:

- developing pedagogical expertise;
- expediting career development;
- increased networking and collaboration opportunities with peers from across the lifelong learning sector;
- studying under the supervision of experts in the selected subject area(s);
- having access to specialist university resources (eg research labs).

Before pursuing postgraduate study, there are some important considerations that you should make. Teachers completing or having recently completed postgraduate study consistently reported feeling '*moderate to high levels of stress*' (Fadare et al, 2023, p 241). Initially, participants were concerned about the financial commitments postgraduate study requires (eg tuition fees) but during their course other challenges, including '*balancing their time, effort, and resources*' (p 245) between their teaching and study, became more prominent leading to burnout and increased rates of absence from their employment. Perhaps more specifically applicable to research degrees, there is a significantly higher requirement to progress through your study independently, and therefore the ability to self-motivate is fundamental.

Activity ⑦

» Determine which postgraduate study pathway and subject area would be most beneficial in developing your pedagogical expertise and supporting your career development, and identify appropriate corresponding postgraduate opportunities.

The Society for Education and Training (SET)

SET is part of the Education and Training Foundation, and their primary role is to raise the status of the profession and champion quality teaching. They are our professional membership body, and they advocate three career stages following qualification;

- early career teacher (ECT);
- experienced teacher;
- advanced teacher.

With regards to moving through the career stages, SET offers a series of awards that can be achieved following on from initial teacher education.

Critical question ⑦

» What do you feel are the advantages and disadvantages of having a professional membership body for the sector?

Qualified Teacher Learning and Skills

Qualified Teacher Learning and Skills (QTLS) is a professional status obtained through the SET and is available to teachers in the lifelong learning sector who meet selected criteria (see the next activity). Some of the more notable criteria include: current employment of teaching post-14 learners; holding a level 5 (or above) FES teaching qualification; level 2 (eg GCSE) qualifications in English and maths. Teachers applying for QTLS must complete a six-month period of professional formation administered by the SET. The professional formation programme has been designed to provide applicants with an opportunity to demonstrate their progression and commitment to excellence within the lifelong learning sector.

Following the Wolf Report (2011), teachers with QTLS share legal parity with the more commonly known Qualified Teacher Status (QTS). Consequently, obtaining QTLS opens up additional employment opportunities in the schools sector (primary and secondary) on the same contractual terms and conditions as a teacher with QTS. More specifically, schools who recruit a teacher with QTLS '*must pay them as qualified teachers on the relevant pay scale and treat them as if they hold QTS for the purposes of performance management, pay progression etc*' (SET, 2023b). Although employing schools and local authorities have the autonomy to determine whether a candidate holding QTLS has the requisite knowledge, experience and skills for the role, the SET explicitly discourages primary schools from recruiting teachers with QTLS because their training will have been designed to teach in the lifelong learning sector (SET, 2023a).

Activity

» Go to the SET website (www.set.et-foundation.co.uk) and work through the interactive eligibility guide provided to better familiarise yourself with the eligibility criteria for QTLS.

Advanced Teacher Status

Advance Teacher Status (ATS) is the status that SET can confer on staff who have held their teaching qualification and QTLS for four years or more or who have held their qualification for five years. ATS is gained after successfully completing a 14-month period of professional development.

Those who achieve ATS will be conferred with the Chartered College of Teaching's Chartered Teacher designation.

Summary

This chapter has explored three approaches to developing your professional practice through research and scholarship: evidence-based teaching practice, postgraduate study and acquiring professional status through professional formation with the SET. Although discussed independently, the three approaches are linked in that they each require engagement with academia and research, albeit to different extents and through different channels.

The discussion began by explaining the broad concept of evidence-based practice, successes attributed to it in improving outcomes for service users within other fields (eg medicine, agriculture), along with an introduction to how it can be applied to education and teaching practice. That discussion created a basis for unpicking the term 'evidence' and the role of research in constructing evidence that teachers might use. Diverging perspectives about the extent to which teaching practice can be *based on* or *informed by* evidence were then explored, followed by a discussion about how teachers can engage *in* or *with* research.

Thereafter, the focus shifted to an exploration of the promises offered by a transition to evidence-informed education and the (largely unsuccessful) mechanisms that recent governments have taken to realising it by: a) enhancing the quality and robustness of the body of relevant research teachers can draw upon (eg EEF); b) better facilitating and encouraging teachers to access and engage with research (eg What Works Teach-Meets); and c) implementing 'mediating' mechanisms to smoothen the transition of knowledge created by researchers to teachers (eg open access).

The chapter progressed to considering how a teacher's pursuit of postgraduate study can enhance teaching practice by better equipping teachers to engage *in* and *with* the research process but also affording them opportunities to network and collaborate with peers. The focus shifted in the concluding discussion to the role of the SET and the benefits of a teacher acquiring a professional status.

Check your understanding (level 5)

1. What is the broad argument for education becoming an evidence-based practice?
2. What are the two perspectives which exist under the umbrella of evidence-based education and how do they differ?
3. Describe the difference between teachers engaging *with* research and teachers engaging *in* research.
4. How might postgraduate study support your practice and career development?
5. What is the primary role of the Society for Education and Training?
6. What is ATS an abbreviation for?

Developmental questions L6+7

1. To what extent does research-based evidence influence your teaching practice?
2. Consider reasons why teachers might object to using evidence-based research to inform their practice.
3 To what extent does the setting in which you teach promote and facilitate evidence-based practice?
4. What limitations might the setting face in supporting teachers to develop evidence-based practice?
5. Government-led initiatives to develop evidence-based education are largely considered to have been ineffective in bringing teachers and research closer together. What else can the government do to promote evidence-based education?
6. How might achieving ATS benefit you and the setting in which you teach?

Further reading

- Bennett, T (2013) *Teacher Proof: Why Research in Education Doesn't Always Mean What It Claims, and What You Can Do About It*. London: Routledge.
- British Educational Research Association (BERA) (nd) [online] Available at: www.bera.ac.uk (accessed 28 September 2024).
- Carter, A (2015) *Carter Review of Initial Teacher Training (ITT)*. London: DfE.
- Didau, D (2015) *What if Everything You Knew About Education Was Wrong?* Carmarthen- House Publishing.
- Education and Training Foundation (ETF) (nd) [online] Available at: www.et-foundation.co.uk (accessed 28 September 2024).
- FindAMasters (nd) [online] Available at: www.findamasters.com (accessed 28 September 2024).
- Hattie, J (2009) *Visible Learning: A Synthesis of Over 800 Meta-analyses Relating to Achievement*. Abingdon: Routledge.

References

Beycioglu, K, Ozer, N and Ugurlu, C (2010) Teachers' Views on Educational Research. *Teaching and Teacher Education*, 26(4): 1088–93.

Biesta, G (2012) The Future of Teacher Education: Evidence, Competence or Wisdom? *Research on Steiner Education*, 3: 8–21.

Brown, C and Zhang, D (2016) Is Engaging in Evidence-Informed Practice in Education Rational? What Accounts for Discrepancies in Teachers' Attitudes Towards Evidence Use and Actual Instances of Evidence Use in Schools? *Cambridge Journal of Education*, 47(2): 277–95.

Cain, T (2016) Denial, Opposition, Rejection or Dissent: Why Do Teachers Contest Research Evidence? *Research Papers in Education*, 32(5): 611–25.

Cain, T (2018) *Becoming a Research-Informed School: Why?* What? How? Abingdon: Routledge.

Cochran-Smith, M and Lytle, S (1999) The Teacher Research Movement: A Decade Later. *Educational Researcher*, 28(7): 15–25.

Coe, R (1999) Manifesto for Evidence-Based Education. [online] Available at: https://f.hubspotusercontent30.net/hubfs/5191137/attachments/ebe/manifesto-for-ebe.pdf (accessed 15 November 2024).

Coldwell, M, Greany, T, Higgins, S, Brown, C, Maxwell, B, Stiell, L, Willis, B and Burns, H (2017) Evidence-informed Teaching: An Evaluation of Progress in England. Research report. Department for Education.

Department for Education (DfE) (2010) *The Importance of Teaching*. London: DfE.

Department for Education (DfE) (2017) *Evidence-Informed Teaching: An Evaluation of Progress in England*. Research Report. [online] Available at: https://assets.publishing.service.gov.uk/media/5a749aca40f0b61938c7ece0/Evidence-informed_teaching_-_an_evaluation_of_progress_in_England.pdf (accessed 29 September 2024).

Department for Education (DfE) (2024) Diploma in Teaching (Further Education and Skills) qualification framework. [online] Available at: www.gov.uk/government/publications/further-education-initial-teacher-education/diploma-in-teaching-further-education-and-skills-qualification-framework (accessed 8 October 2024).

Education Endowment Foundation (EEF) (2018) *Sutton Trust–Education Endowment Foundation Teaching and Learning Toolkit*. London: Education Endowment Foundation.

Education and Training Foundation (ETF) (2019) *Further Education Workforce Data for England: Analysis of the 2018–2019 Staff Individualised Record (SIR) Data*. [online] Available at: www.et-foundation.co.uk/wp-content/uploads/2020/06/SIR27-REPORT-FOR-PUBLICATION.pdf (accessed 29 September 2024).

Education and Training Foundation (ETF) (2022) *Professional Standards for Teachers and Trainers*. [online] Available at: www.et-foundation.co.uk/professional-standards/teachers (accessed 29 September 2024).

Education and Training Foundation (ETF) (nd) What Works Teach-Meets. [online] Available at: www.et-foundation.co.uk/professional-development/what-works-teach-meets (accessed 29 September 2024).

Everton, T, Galton, M and Pell, T (2002) Educational Research and the Teacher. *Research Papers in Education*, 17(4): 373–401.

Fadare, S, Gumanoy, D, Cosain, H, Cayambae, D, Ansarie, A and Cassion, A (2023) Struggles and Coping Strategies of Teachers Pursuing Graduate Studies: A Basis for Intervention. *Kepes*, 56(11): 239–57.

Goldacre, B (2013) *Building Evidence into Education*. London: DfE. [online] Available at: https://assets.publishing.service.gov.uk/media/5a7a219140f0b66eab999f4f/Building_evidence_into_education.pdf (accessed 28 September 2024).

Goodfellow, J (2003) Practical Wisdom in Professional Practice: The Person in the Process. *Contemporary Issues in Early Childhood*, 4(1): 48–63.

Gov.UK (2023) Further Education Workforce. [online] Available at: https://explore-education-statistics.service.gov.uk/find-statistics/further-education-workforce (accessed 29 September 2024).

Hammersley, M (2005) The Myth of Research-Based Practice: The Critical Case of Educational Inquiry. *International Journal of Social Research Methodology*, 261(8): 317–30.

Hargreaves, D H (1996) Teaching as a Research-Based Profession: Possibilities and Prospects. Paper presented at the *Teacher Training Agency Annual Lecture*. [online] Available at: https://eppi.ioe.ac.uk/cms/Portals/0/PDF%20reviews%20and%20summaries/TTA%20Hargreaves%20lecture.pdf (accessed 29 September 2024).

Higher Education Funding Council (HEFCE) (2009) *Research Excellence Framework Second Consultation on the Assessment and Funding of Research*. Bristol: HEFCE.

Higher Education Funding Council (HEFCE) (2011) *Assessment Framework and Guidance on Submissions*. Bristol: HEFCE.

Institute for Apprenticeships and Technical Education (IfATE) (2024) *Learning and Skills Teacher*. [online] Available at: www.instituteforapprenticeships.org/apprenticeship-standards/learning-and-skills-teacher (accessed 29 September 2024).

Levin, B, Cooper, A, Arjomand, S and Thompson, K (2011) Can Simple Interventions Increase Research Use in Secondary Schools? *Canadian Journal of Educational Administration and Policy*, 126: 1–29.

Maggs, A and White, R (1982) The Educational Psychologist: Facing a New Era. *Psychology in the Schools*, 19: 129–34.

McMillan, J and Schumacher, S (2014) *Research in Education: Evidence-Based Inquiry.* 7th ed. Harlow: Pearson Education Limited

Morris, E (2014) Teaching Needs Less Ideology and More Evidence. *The Guardian*, 25 Nov. [online] Available at: www.theguardian.com/education/2014/nov/25/teaching-needs-less-ideology-more-evidence?utm_content=buffer54205&utm_medium=social&utm_source=twitter.com&utm_campaign=buffer (accessed 15 November 2024).

Nelson, J, Mehta, P, Sharples, J and Davey, C (2017) *Measuring Teachers' Research Engagement: Findings from a Pilot Study*. Education Endowment Foundation. [online] Available at: https://educationendowmentfoundation.org.uk/projects-and-evaluation/evaluation/eef-evaluation-reports-and-research-papers/methodological-research-and-innovations/measuring-teachers-research-engagement (accessed 29 September 2024).

Oxford English Dictionary (2024) [online] Available at: www.oed.com (accessed 15 November 2024).

Piasta, S B, Park, S, Farley, K S, Justice, L M and O'Connell, A A (2020) Early Childhood Educators' Knowledge about Language and Literacy: Associations with Practice and Children's Learning. *Dyslexia*, 26(2): 137–52.

Society for Education and Training (SET) (2023a) Updates to Qualified Teacher Learning and Skills (QTLS) Status Application Process Announced. [online] Available at: https://set.et-foundation.co.uk/set-news/updates-to-qualified-teacher-learning-and-skills-qtls-status-application-process-announced (accessed 29 September 2024).

Society for Education and Training (SET) (2023b) Is QTLS Equal to QTS? [online] Available at: https://set.et-foundation.co.uk/your-career/qtls/qtls-and-qts-parity (accessed 29 September 2024).

Shalem, Y and Slonimsky, L (2013) Practical Knowledge of Teaching Practice: What Counts. In Barrett, B and Rata, E (eds) *Knowledge and the Future of the Curriculum* (pp 198–212). London: Palgrave Macmillan.

Slavin, R E (2002) Evidence-Based Education Policies: Transforming Educational Practice and Research. *Educational Researcher*, 31(7): 15–21.

Smith, S W, Daunic, A and Taylor, G (2007) Treatment Fidelity in Applied Educational Research: Expanding the Adoption and Application of Measures to Ensure Evidence-Based Practice. *Education and Treatment of Children*, 30(4): 121–34.

Stremmel, A (2002) The Value of Teacher Research: Nurturing Professional and Personal Growth Through Inquiry. *Young Children*, 57(5): 62–70.

Tripney, J, Kenny, C and Gough, D (2014) Enabling the Use of Research Evidence within Educational Policymaking in Europe: Lessons from the EIPEE Project. *Journal of European Education*, 46(1): 55–74.

Van Schaik, P, Volman, M, Admiraal, W and Schenked, W (2018) Barriers and Conditions for Teachers' Utilisation of Academic Knowledge. *International Journal of Educational Research*, 90: 50–63.

Whitty, G (2013) Evidence-Informed Policy and Practice – We Should Welcome It, but Also Be Realistic! [online] Available at: https://cerp.aqa.org.uk (accessed 29 September 2024).

Wolf Report (2011) *Review of Vocational Education*. London: DfE.

Wrigley, T (2018) The Power of 'Evidence': Reliable Science or a Set of Blunt Tools? *British Educational Research Journal*, 44(3): 359–76.

Appendices

Appendix 1: The Diploma in Teaching mandatory content

Number	ETF suggested DiT unit name*	Essential content
1.0	Unit 1: Teaching my subject (15 credits)	**Chapters 6, 7, 10, 11 and 12**
1.1		Curriculum development
1.2		Pedagogic content knowledge
1.3		Threshold concepts and troublesome knowledge
1.4		Required wider or prerequisite knowledge
1.5		Embedding maths and English
1.6		Ensuring and maintaining subject expertise
1.7		Sustainability in your area
1.8		Progression advice
2.0	Unit 2: Learners and learning (15 credits) Part A: Learners	**Chapters 2, 3, 4, 5, 6, 7, 8, 9, 10, 11 and 12**
2.1		Getting to know your learners in FES
2.2		Their journeys to FES
2.3		Range of support needs
2.4		Safeguarding or EDI
2.5		English and maths abilities
2.6		Their wider expectations
2.7	Part B: Learning	Contemporary learning theory, neuroscience
2.8		Role and currency of research and evidence
2.9		Application of theory to practice

* These names are not compulsory and you may find different titles in your award.

→

(Cont.)

Number	ETF suggested DIT unit name*	Essential content
2.10		Encouraging learners to be independent and aim high
3.0	Unit 3: Teachers and teaching (15 credits) Part A: Teachers	**Chapters 3, 4, 6, 7, 10 and 12**
3.1		The role of a teacher
3.2		What makes a good teacher?
3.3		Working with and learning from other teachers
3.4		Other sources of support
3.5	Part B: Teaching	Rigorous curriculum thinking
3.6		Person centred approach
3.7		Planning and delivering sessions
3.8		Developing resources to meet learner needs
3.9		Individual support [incl. SEND, mental health]
3.10		Teacher expectations of learners including classroom management
3.11		Face to face and remote delivery
3.12		Assessment and feedback
3.13		Embedding English, maths and digital
4.0	Unit 4: Professional Practice (30 credits) Part A: Teaching practice	**Chapters 1, 3, 5, 7, 9, 10, 11, 12 and 13**
4.1		Micro teaches
4.2		Preparation for placement
4.3		Observation of other teachers
4.4		Team and solo teaching
4.5		Curriculum planning and review
4.6		Lesson planning and adaptations
4.7		Planning and conducting assessment

(*Cont.*)

Number	ETF suggested DiT unit name*	Essential content
4.8		Using assessment to inform planning
4.9		Assessment feedback and advice or guidance
4.10		Application of evidence-based methods
4.11		Managing and supporting learners, including behaviour
4.12		Placement log
4.13	Part B: Being a professional	The Occupational Standards
4.14		Developing expertise
4.15		Updating and CPD
4.16		Professional responsibilities
4.17		Working with colleagues
4.18		Professional status
4.19	Part C: The FE and Skills sector	Overview of FE and Skills sector
4.20		Types of programmes
4.21		Timetables
4.22		Contracts
4.23		Government policy
4.24		Regulations (legal and local)
4.25		Funding
4.26		Organisational and wider support
5.0	Unit 5: Effective digital and online pedagogies (15 credits)	**Chapter 9**
5.1		Personal digital skills
5.2		Range of educational technology
5.3		Artificial intelligence, augmented reality, virtual reality and similar technologies
5.4		Managing digital delivery

Source: www.gov.uk/government/publications/further-education-initial-teacher-education/diploma-in-teaching-further-education-and-skills-qualification-framework#the-qualification-framework

Appendix 2: Occupational Standards

Number (K = knowledge; S = skills; B = behaviour)	**Occupational Standard**
K1	The pedagogical theory and how to apply this theory to practice
K2	How to support contextualised opportunities to develop English and maths
K3	The principles of designing, planning, and organising curriculum
K4	Methods for creating and adapting inclusive learning resources
K5	Evidence-informed inclusive teaching, learning and assessment strategies
K6	Strategies to engage and challenge all learners
K7	How to implement ongoing initial and diagnostic assessment to inform planning and progression
K8	Techniques to involve learners in taking ownership of their own progress
K9	Principles and practices of assessment and feedback
K10	How to promote and foster a safe and supportive learning environment
K11	Barriers to learning, and ways to overcome them and adapt teaching, learning and assessment
K12	The range of support available for learners related to health, well-being and safeguarding
K13	Sources of current information, advice, and guidance to support progression opportunities for learners
K14	The requirements and implications of organisational policies and procedures, such as internal and external regulatory bodies and frameworks
K15	Techniques to develop collaborative relationships
K16	Communication techniques and how to adapt these for different audiences, including leading difficult conversations
K17	Coaching and mentoring principles and techniques
K18	Strategies for quality improvement

(Cont.)

Number (K = knowledge; S = skills; B = behaviour)	**Occupational Standard**
K19	Ways to access personal and professional development, and to maintain sector and/or subject specific currency
K20	Advances in digital, online, and emerging technologies and their application in the teaching environment and principles of digital and online safety
S1	Integrate subject and pedagogic research into teaching activity to enhance teaching and support changes of practice
S2	Identify, consider and take steps to minimise the impact of barriers to learning
S3	Contextualise English and mathematics in a way that promotes understanding of key topics
S4	Use a variety of teaching and assessment methods depending on the learning environment and learners' needs
S5	Encourage learners to set challenging goals
S6	Promote understanding of equality and diversity and sustainable development
S7	Demonstrate through their teaching the wider context (policy, economic, societal, technological, legal, cultural and environmental) of the subject, recognising the implications for professional practice
S8	Design and use resources that are inclusive and add value to learners' development
S9	Engage and inspire all learners
S10	Identify and set outcomes to enable each learner to achieve or exceed targets
S11	Provide ongoing learner feedback
S12	Use the results of initial and diagnostic assessment to plan learning and differentiated support at the start of and throughout the learners' journey
S13	Encourage learners to develop: autonomy and resilience, personal and interpersonal effectiveness, social awareness and respect for others, essential employability skills, a solutions mindset, and the ability to create change
S14	Use assessment data to regularly review and develop own and others' practice and to report emerging gaps in progression and achievement amongst groups of learners

→

(Cont.)

Number (K = knowledge; S = skills; B = behaviour)	Occupational Standard
S15	Support the implementation and execution of safeguarding procedures and promote the welfare of children, young people and/or adults in accordance with statutory provisions
S16	Prepare learners for their transition through education, further training, and into employment
S17	Comply with internal and external regulations, legislation and guidance, such as: teaching, learning and assessment, recording, storing and sharing information relating to learners
S18	Adapt communication style, method, and terminology to reflect the needs of the audience including individual learners, colleagues, stakeholders
S19	Engage learners to establish standards of behaviour, mutual respect and safe working
S20	Challenge learners to address inappropriate behaviour or viewpoints
S21	Continually update and maintain their own knowledge and skills as a teaching professional and a subject specialist as part of managing their own continual professional development (CPD)
S22	Be proactive in seeking and responding to feedback from varied sources including learner voice, peers, colleagues, employers and stakeholders to improve own practice
S23	Manage workload through preparation and prioritisation, time management, and responsiveness to change
S24	Act within, the statutory frameworks which set out their professional duties and responsibilities
S25	Use innovative and up to date digital and online technologies in a way that is safe to improve teaching, learning and assessment
B1	Be resilient and adaptable when dealing with challenge and change, maintaining focus and self-control
B2	Underpin their practice by reference to professional standards and evidence-based teaching and learning
B3	Committed to continuous professional development
B4	Act in a professional manner, and in a way that builds and maintains positive relationships with colleagues, students and stakeholders
B5	Act in a manner that is ethical, fair, consistent and impartial, valuing equality, diversity and champion British values within professional boundaries
B6	Model sustainable practices and promote sustainable development principles, values and goals in relation to their subject specialism

Appendix 3: Professional Standards

Professional Values and Attributes	
1.	Critically reflect on and evaluate your practices, values, and beliefs to improve learner outcomes.
2.	Promote and embed education for sustainable development (ESD) across learning and working practices.
3.	Inspire, motivate, and raise aspirations of learners by communicating high expectations and a passion for learning.
4.	Support and develop learners' confidence, autonomy and thinking skills, taking account of their needs and starting points.
5.	Value and champion diversity, equality of opportunity, inclusion and social equity.
6.	Develop collaborative and respectful relationships with learners, colleagues and external stakeholders.
7.	Engage with and promote a culture of continuous learning and quality improvement.
Professional Knowledge and Understanding	
8.	Develop and update knowledge of your subject specialism, taking account of new practices, research and/or industry requirements.
9.	Critically review and apply your knowledge of educational research, pedagogy, and assessment to develop evidence-informed practice.
10.	Share and update knowledge of effective practice with colleagues, networks and/or research communities to support improvement.
11.	Develop and apply your knowledge of special educational needs and disabilities to create inclusive learning experiences.
12.	Understand your teaching role and responsibilities and how these are influenced by legal, regulatory, institutional and ethical contexts.
Professional Skills	
13.	Promote and support positive learner behaviour, attitudes and well-being.
14.	Apply motivational, coaching and skill development strategies to help learners progress and achieve.

→

(Cont.)

15.	Plan and deliver learning programmes that are safe, inclusive, stretching and relevant to learners' needs.
16.	Select and use digital technologies safely and effectively to promote learning.
17.	Develop learners' mathematics, English, digital and wider employability skills.
18.	Provide access to up-to-date information, advice and guidance so that learners can take ownership of their learning and make informed progression choices.
19.	Apply appropriate and fair methods of assessment and provide constructive and timely feedback to support learning and achievement.
20.	Develop enrichment and progression opportunities for the learners through collaboration with employers, higher education and/or community groups.

Index

Page numbers in *italics* and **bold** denote figures and tables, respectively.